First published in Great Britain in 2017
by Aurum Press an imprint of The Quarto Group
The Old Brewery
6 Blundell Street London
N7 9BH

A catalogue record for this book is available from the British Library.
ISBN 978-1-78131-692-4
Ebook ISBN 978-1-78131-693-1

3 5 7 9 10 8 6 4 2
2017 2019 2021 2020 2018

Printed in China

Staff Credits

Paileen Currie, Jennifer Barr, Rachel Ng. With special thanks to Caroline Curtis, Joel Jessup and Philip Parker.

Design: Darren Jordan

Illustrations created by Matthew Coles, Peter Liddiard and Darren Jordan.

THE YEAR OF THE GEEK

MANGA · SUPERHEROES · ANIME · CULT TV · OPEN SPACE · ALTERNATE REALITY · STEAMPUNK · CYBERPUNK · VIRTUAL REALITY · GAMING · ROLE PLAYING · LITERATURE

365 ADVENTURES FROM THE SCI-FI AND FANTASY UNIVERSE

JAMES CLARKE

Aurum
Press

INTRODUCTION

'Escape with reality.' Steven Spielberg

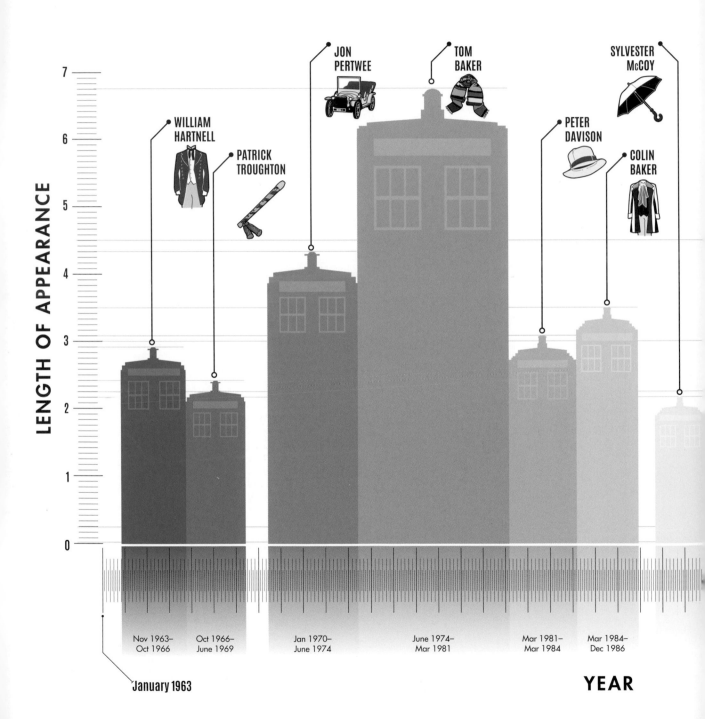

LENGTH OF APPEARANCE

7

6

5

4

3

2

1

0

WILLIAM HARTNELL

PATRICK TROUGHTON

JON PERTWEE

TOM BAKER

PETER DAVISON

COLIN BAKER

SYLVESTER McCOY

Nov 1963–
Oct 1966

Oct 1966–
June 1969

Jan 1970–
June 1974

June 1974–
Mar 1981

Mar 1981–
Mar 1984

Mar 1984–
Dec 1986

January 1963

YEAR

On 27 December 2016, as I was completing this book, Carrie Fisher's death was announced. The general outpouring of affection for her screen performances and her positive view on mental health brought together fans of both her movies and her books. A few weeks later countless participants at women's marches around the world carried signs and banners emblazoned with images of Carrie Fisher in her most famous role as Princess Leia, leader of the resistance in the Star Wars films. This geek stuff, we realized, really counts for something: it makes sense to people.

The news footage brought to mind a comment made by scholar Maria Tatar. Speaking of fairytales, and related kinds of stories, she said eloquently, 'The consolations of the imagination are not imaginary consolations.' Geek culture has proved a companion to many; certainly for me it filled a huge part of my life. There's just something glorious about the imaginative overdrive that sustains much of it. It's life-affirming in its vivid versions of reality and/or its transformations of reality. What can be better than settling down with a book, film, comic or computer game and being transported?

The book you're reading here, then, is an attempt to give the reader a set of entries that will guide you to a treasury of imaginative output. We can only skim the surface between these covers, but at least it's a start. My hope is that it leads you to countless fascinating new encounters across both science fiction and fantasy, genres in which the impossible is made believable.

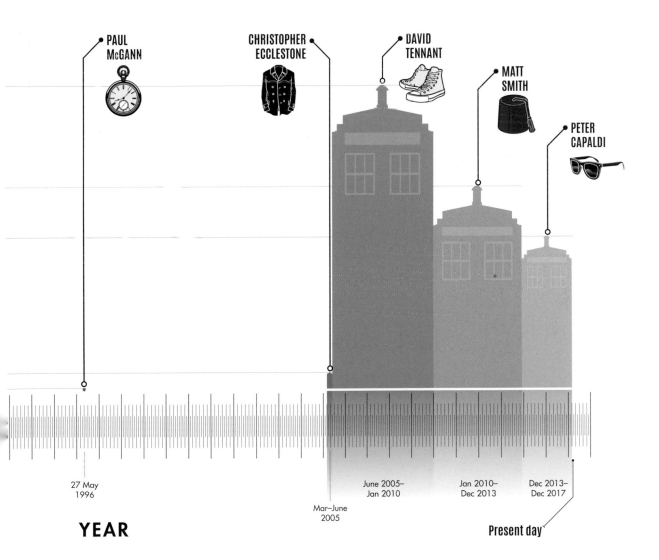

PAUL McGANN

CHRISTOPHER ECCLESTONE

DAVID TENNANT

MATT SMITH

PETER CAPALDI

27 May 1996

Mar–June 2005

June 2005– Jan 2010

Jan 2010– Dec 2013

Dec 2013– Dec 2017

YEAR

Present day

A WRINKLE IN TIME PUBLISHED IN 1962

Classic stories stay with us and have something new and arresting to say to successive generations.

The novel *A Wrinkle in Time* by Madeleine L'Engle is a now classic piece of American Young Adult (YA) science fiction, with strong feminist appeal. The novel is the first in the *Time Quintet* and tells the story of a brother and sister who voyage into space to find their scientist father.

In doing so, the siblings also discover an evil force that threatens the universe. This is a dazzling coming of age tale that throws our ordinary and most familiar relationships into a new light.

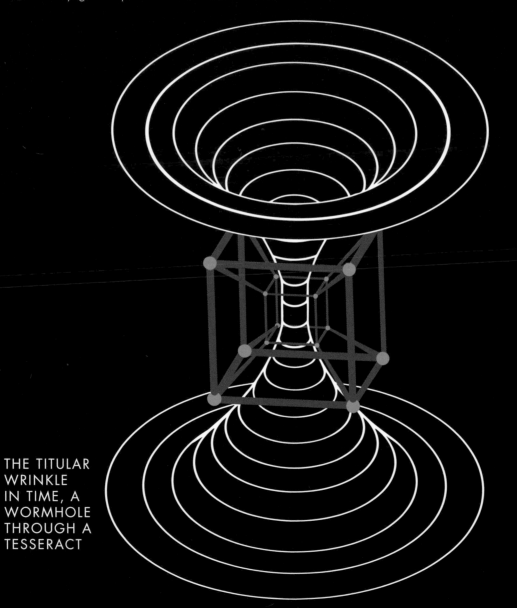

THE TITULAR
WRINKLE
IN TIME, A
WORMHOLE
THROUGH A
TESSERACT

NATIONAL SCIENCE FICTION DAY

Science Fiction Day began as an American-centred unofficial day of celebration and has increasingly found a home around the world. The date is considered the birthday of science fiction novelist Isaac Asimov who made a titanic contribution to twentieth century science fiction. Science Fiction Day is an opportunity for fans of the genre to indulge their love of sf in novels, comics, movies and TV.

J.R.R.TOLKIEN IS BORN IN 1892

Fantasy though it may be, *The Lord of the Rings* powerfully reflects Tolkien's experience of the First World War and his lifelong fascination with nature.

Tolkien had a deep love for the countryside – as did his friend and fellow author, C.S. Lewis – and his familiarity with English folklore and legend meant that he understood how those forms reimagined the real world.

An Oxford don for much of his life, Tolkien's imagination transformed the British landscape into the terrain of Middle Earth – and of other lands featuring in his lesser-known short stories and novellas.

While *The Lord of the Rings* and *The Hobbit* remain his most famous works, Tolkien's vivid imagination also created the charming short stories *Roverandom* and *Farmer Giles of Ham* and an essay entitled *On Fairy-Stories*, which should be essential reading for anyone who loves fantasy, in print or on screen.

MALCOLM WHEELER-NICHOLSON IS BORN IN 1890

Comic-book heroes are some of the most well known fictional characters of all time. Think of Batman, Wonder Woman, Superman. Almost unknown, though, is Malcolm Wheeler Nicholson, without whom they might not have come to light. Wheeler-Nicholson established *Fun Comics* and *New Fun Comics* in 1934 and, in due course, these evolved into DC Comics.

DC's heroes became lenses through which bigger issues could be explored. A DC comic tends to feature superheroes who hail from extraordinary circumstances or backgrounds. DC heroes are typically loners, not team players. In the 1960s and early '70s, DC's heroes inhabited pretty clear-cut moral worlds, but that's very much not the case now. The frontier was crossed in 1986 with the publication of *The Dark Knight Returns*, which disturbed the moral compass of superhero dynamics and introduced shades of grey.

5 JANUARY

IN 2016 *THE SHANNARA CHRONICLES* PREMIERES ON AMERICAN TV

Terry Brooks's expansive fantasy writing career sparked in 1977 with the publication of his debut novel *The Sword of Shannara* (1977). He has since written more *Shannara* epics and the comic-fantasy *Landover* series (from 1986).

6 JANUARY

AMERICAN ASTRONOMERS FIRST SIGHT THE BIRTH OF A GALAXY IN 1987

A team of astronomers from Berkeley University, the Harvard-Smithsonian Centre for Astrophysics and the University of Arizona in America collectively viewed and identify the birth of a galaxy on this day. Real world science such as this and the visual spectacle of science in action has long been exploited in TV, books and films, from *The Quatermass Experiment* (1953) to *Ex Machina* (2015). Even the birth of galaxies have been visualized on screen: just contemplate the Terrence Malick documentary *Voyage of Time* (2016). Indeed, the birth of celestial objects also results in one of the most memorable moments in a *Star Trek* movie when the planet of Genesis is shown being created in *Star Trek II: The Wrath of Khan* (1982).

FLASH GORDON FIRST PUBLISHED IN 1934

Flash's adventures were adapted for American serials starring Buster Crabbe in the 1930s, and in 1980 the now cult feature film version was released.

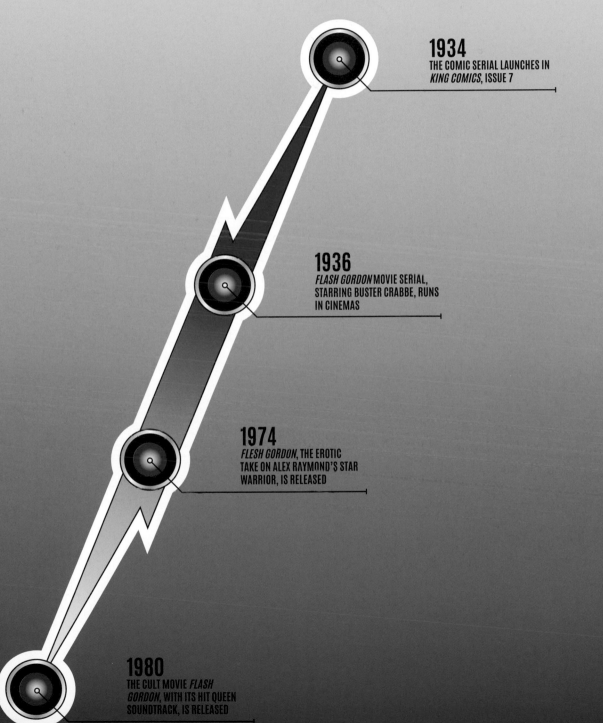

1934
THE COMIC SERIAL LAUNCHES IN
KING COMICS, ISSUE 7

1936
FLASH GORDON MOVIE SERIAL,
STARRING BUSTER CRABBE, RUNS
IN CINEMAS

1974
FLESH GORDON, THE EROTIC
TAKE ON ALEX RAYMOND'S STAR
WARRIOR, IS RELEASED

1980
THE CULT MOVIE *FLASH
GORDON*, WITH ITS HIT QUEEN
SOUNDTRACK, IS RELEASED

DAVID BOWIE WAS BORN IN 1947

It was, literally and metaphorically, a bleak January day in 2016,
when the news broke that David Bowie had died at the age of 69.

Bowie had long nurtured a creative connection to the cosmic and the fabulous. The song that made him a star was 'Space Oddity', while 'Loving the Alien' used a familiar image to write about understanding across cultures and time. For some, his film appearances made even more impact than his music. His background, not only in song but in mime and performance, gave him a particular gravity and effect as a screen actor, and he starred in three geek favourites.

In 1976, he portrayed Thomas Jerome Newton in *The Man Who Fell to Earth*. In 1983, he appeared in the horror film *The Hunger*, and in 1986, perhaps most famously, came his starring role as Jareth, the Goblin King in *Labyrinth*. This introduced him to a generation of people not born when he broke through. Much later, in 2006, Bowie portrayed Nikola Tesla in Christopher Nolan's film *The Prestige*.

As a screen presence, Bowie made good on his androgynous, otherworldly music persona and the video for his last single 'Blackstar' was suffused with Bowie's empathy for the cosmic, bringing him full circle to 'Space Oddity'.

THE MANY CHANGES OF DAVID BOWIE

1967   1969   1970   1972

1980   1983   1986   1987

AMERICAN SITCOM *THIRD ROCK FROM THE SUN* PREMIERED IN 1996

Comedy has a particular power to skewer and question what we so often take for granted. Gender relationships were one of the targets of American sci-fi sitcom *Third Rock From The Sun*. The series focused on several extra-terrestrials from an asexual civilization who come to Earth and disguise themselves as a typical American suburban family.

The series featured John Lithgow (who had starred in cult film *The Adventures of Buckaroo Banzai Across the 8th Dimension*) (1984) and young actor Joseph Gordon Levitt who has gone on to star in cult science fiction movie, *Looper* (2012). A notable entry in the sci fi sitcom subgenre, *Third Rock* follows in the very successful intergalactic footsteps of earlier sci-fi sitcoms like *Red Dwarf* (1988–1993, 1997–1999, 2009–2017), *ALF* (1986–1990), and of course *Mork & Mindy* (1978–82), which introduced the mass audience to the comic pairing of Pam Dawber and the late, great Robin Williams.

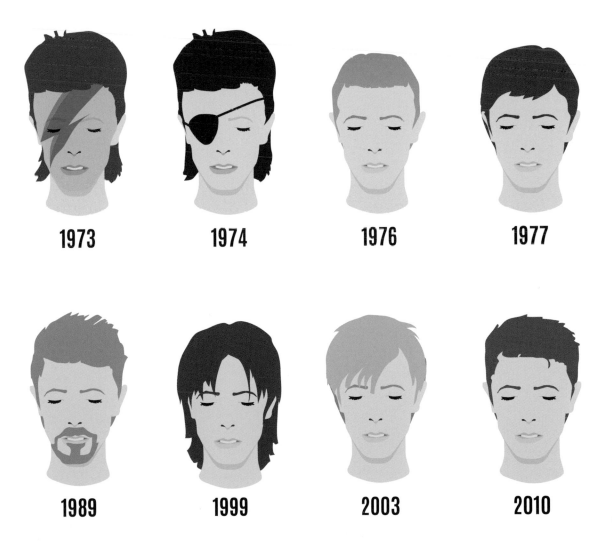

1973   1974   1976   1977

1989   1999   2003   2010

METROPOLIS RELEASED IN 1927

There are some films, and some images, that have to be acknowledged as essential frames of reference. *Metropolis*, directed by Fritz Lang, is such a case. During its production in 1926, the film generated a wave of publicity to build anticipation – so much for the brave new world of Internet hype.

Since then, Metropolis has become synonymous with the science-fiction genre, its images of the towering cityscape or of Maria in robot form often used as emblems of the entire science fiction genre.

Not only a meditation on the human relationship to technology and artificial intelligence, the film also satisfies as a demonstration of visual effects and spectacle. Its vision of a megacity has endured.

Blockbuster spectacle combines with philosophical drama to depict both utopia and dystopia in painfully close proximity.

Metropolis has gone on to influence a range of modern science-fiction films. Check out Ralph McQuarrie's early concept art for the character that became C-3PO in *Star Wars*, and you'll readily note Maria's influence. *Blade Runner* and Apple's first TV ad, directed by Ridley Scott, also owe a debt to Lang's massive film in all its glory.

Metropolis continues to be a powerful route to imagining the future as a place of both wonder and terror.

FILM LENGTH IN MINUTES

160 — 150 — 140 — 130 — 120 — 110 — 100

1927 · 2002 · 2010

YEAR OF RESTORATION AND RE-RELEASE

IN 2007 THE PILOT EPISODE
OF *ADVENTURE TIME* WAS BROADCAST

You know you've entered deep into pop culture when the Macy's Day Thanksgiving parade in New York city includes a balloon representing your show and when Doc Martens produce a pair of bright yellow boots based on the show's dog.

First broadcast in its full series in 2010, *Adventure Time*, created by Pendleton Ward, quickly became a tonic of sorts us audiences followed Finn and his dog Jake surviving happily in the aftermath of the tellingly named The Mushroom War. Both parody and pastiche, *Adventure Time* is classic geek stuff.

BATMAN THE TV SERIES
PREMIERED IN 1966

Camp and parody were never better rendered than in ABC's TV series *Batman* (1966–88), starring Adam West and Burt Ward. Far from the later dark and brooding atmosphere of the late 1980s reboot and subsequent Christopher Nolan entries, the TV series popped and fizzed with bright colour, great playfulness, comic font graphics, titled cameras and a theme song that was all too catchy. On 9 June On 9th June 2017 Adam West died and his passing prompted an outpouring of affection from fans.

A CLOCKWORK ORANGE PREMIERED IN 1972 IN THE UK

So incendiary was his adaptation of Anthony Burgess's novel, published in 1962, that Stanley Kubrick, the film's director, withdrew it from distribution in the UK.

Kubrick's film pushes the dystopian vision of Burgess's novel. Central to Kubrick's adaptation of the novel was finding a cinematic equivalent to Burgess's writing style, and it was the film's depiction of violence that caused controversy.

For Kubrick, the film represented an opportunity to dramatise the concept of free will and the relationship between our humanity and ideas of good and of evil. Significantly, the film's conclusion differs from that of the novel. Only in the wake of Kubrick's death in 1999 did the film make its way back into British cinemas.

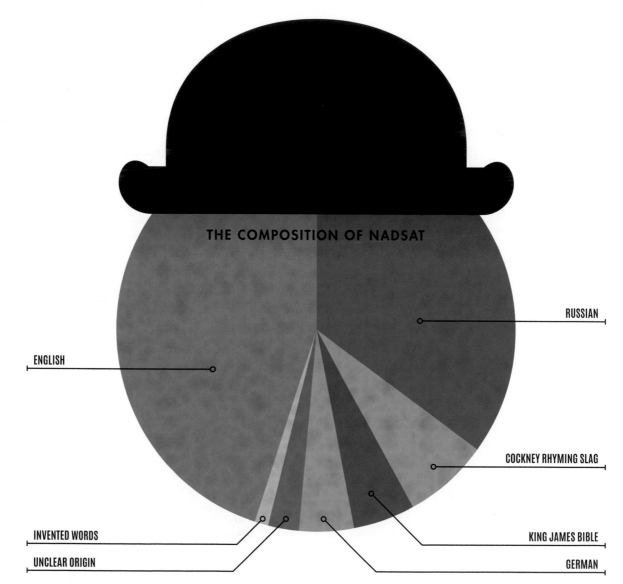

THE COMPOSITION OF NADSAT

RUSSIAN

ENGLISH

COCKNEY RHYMING SLAG

INVENTED WORDS

KING JAMES BIBLE

UNCLEAR ORIGIN

GERMAN

THE BIONIC WOMAN PREMIERED IN 1976 IN US

The Bionic Woman (1976–78) marked a moment for female science fiction protagonists who were strong, capable, confident. Ripley, Connor and Buffy all followed.

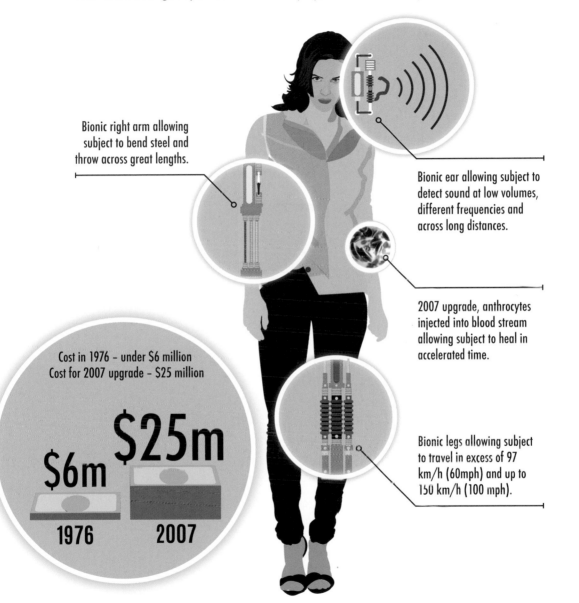

Bionic right arm allowing subject to bend steel and throw across great lengths.

Bionic ear allowing subject to detect sound at low volumes, different frequencies and across long distances.

2007 upgrade, anthrocytes injected into blood stream allowing subject to heal in accelerated time.

Cost in 1976 – under $6 million
Cost for 2007 upgrade – $25 million

$25m

$6m

1976   2007

Bionic legs allowing subject to travel in excess of 97 km/h (60mph) and up to 150 km/h (100 mph).

'THE TIME OF THE HAWK' EPISODE OF *BUCK ROGERS IN THE 25TH CENTURY* AIRED IN 1981

In 'Time of the Hawk', Buck's silent pal, Hawk, is a bird-man. The image of the human-animal mutant has had its share of attention in science fiction.

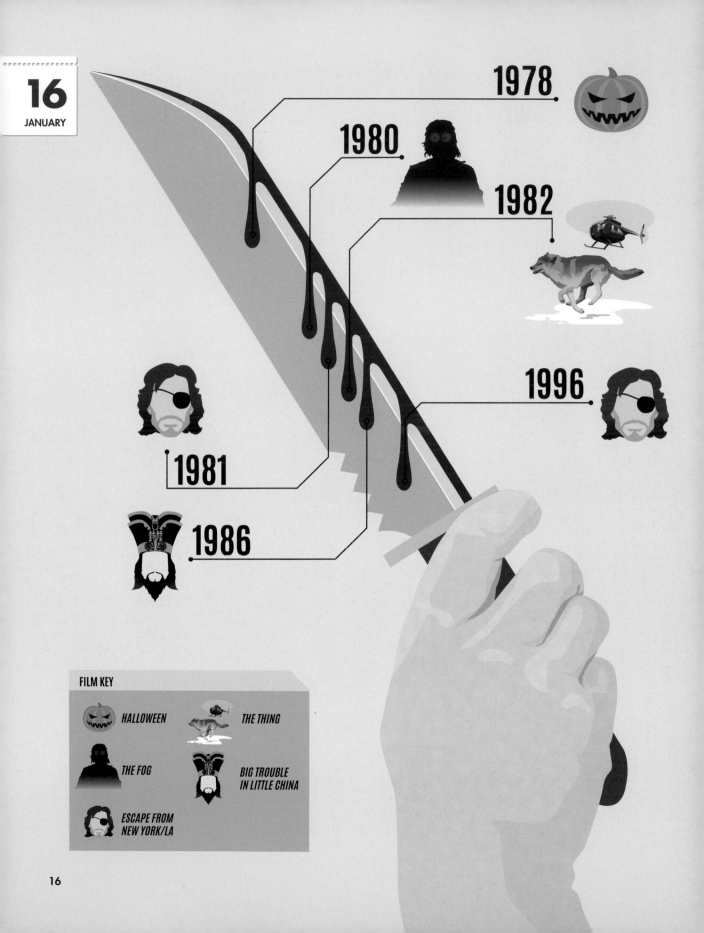

1978

1980

1982

1996

1981

1986

FILM KEY

HALLOWEEN

THE THING

THE FOG

BIG TROUBLE
IN LITTLE CHINA

ESCAPE FROM
NEW YORK/LA

FILMMAKER JOHN CARPENTER WAS BORN ON THIS DAY IN 1948

John Carpenter's often visceral and always intelligent contribution to horror, fantasy and science fiction during the 1970s and 80s mark his work as touchstones in the geek film landscape. Pessimism, cynicism and a sense of a world on the brink of threat and violence are central to Carpenter's vision.

In *Halloween* (1978), Carpenter reset what the horror film could be, and in *Big Trouble in Little China* (1986) he fused American all-action with pop mysticism. Carpenter is a king of cult films: *Dark Star* (1974), *Escape from New York* (1981) and the satirical and potent *They Live* (1988).

ACTOR JIM CARREY WAS BORN ON THIS DAY IN 1962

Jim Carrey's work in several geek classics is not to be overlooked. His broad physical comedy allied with his verbal dexterity and ability to capture something more melancholy lent itself very well to three modern classics: *The Mask* (1994) *The Truman Show* (1998) and *Eternal Sunshine of the Spotless Mind* (2004).

In *The Mask*, the titular character's anarchic spirit perfectly suited Carrey's physical energy, while *The Truman Show* sharpened the more muted side of his screen persona in a story about the media and a kind of virtual reality in which Truman lives. Working with Michel Gondry, Carrey's work in the film *Eternal Sunshine of the Spotless Mind* also explored the idea of reality, and the reality of memory. It became a must-see movie and favourite of film students everywhere.

WE HAVE REBUILT THEM

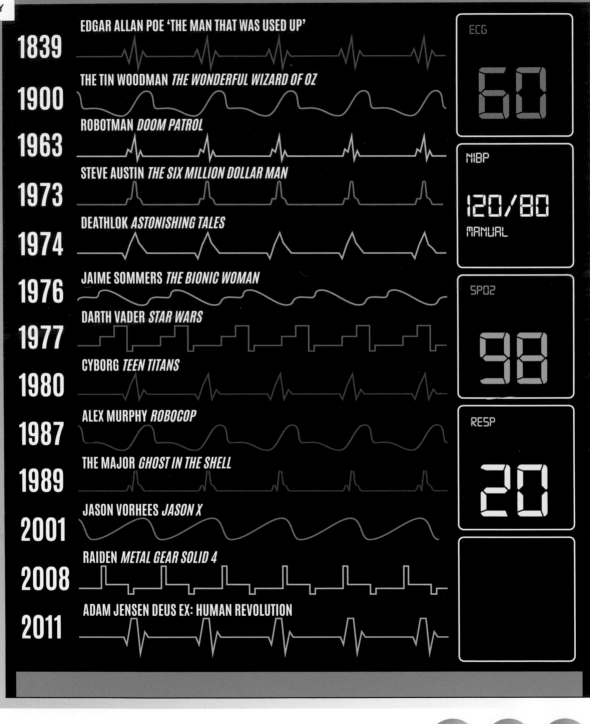

1839 EDGAR ALLAN POE 'THE MAN THAT WAS USED UP'

1900 THE TIN WOODMAN *THE WONDERFUL WIZARD OF OZ*

1963 ROBOTMAN *DOOM PATROL*

1973 STEVE AUSTIN *THE SIX MILLION DOLLAR MAN*

1974 DEATHLOK *ASTONISHING TALES*

1976 JAIME SOMMERS *THE BIONIC WOMAN*

1977 DARTH VADER *STAR WARS*

1980 CYBORG *TEEN TITANS*

1987 ALEX MURPHY *ROBOCOP*

1989 THE MAJOR *GHOST IN THE SHELL*

2001 JASON VORHEES *JASON X*

2008 RAIDEN *METAL GEAR SOLID 4*

2011 ADAM JENSEN *DEUS EX: HUMAN REVOLUTION*

ECG
60

NIBP
120/80
MANUAL

SPO2
98

RESP
20

THE SIX MILLION DOLLAR MAN IS FIRST BROADCAST ON AMERICAN TV IN 1974

The Six Million Dollar Man marked a flourishing of science fiction and fantasy during the 1970s on American TV. Steve Austin was a man literally fused with technology.

EDGAR ALLAN POE IS BORN IN 1809

19
JANUARY

Disturbances of mind and body, morbidity and melancholy all combine in Poe's 'The Fall of the House of Usher', 'The Tell-Tale Heart', and 'The Raven'.

DEFORREST KELLEY (DR MCCOY IN *STAR TREK*) WAS BORN IN 1920

20
JANUARY

Among the most iconic science-fiction doctors is Dr Leonard 'Bones' McCoy, medic aboard the USS *Enterprise* on its mission to 'explore strange new worlds'. Tricorder in hand, McCoy diagnosed a huge range of ailments throughout the show's run

Doctors are a fascinating subject in science fiction. The interest usually lies in how doctors deploy their talents. Will it be for good or for evil?

Dr Otto Octavius becomes Doctor Octopus, hell bent on destroying Spider-Man. Dr Hans Zarkov features in many of the adventures of Flash Gordon: aware that the planet of Mongo is on a collision course with Earth, he creates a rocket to save Earth from impending doom.

The inventor Rotwang of *Metropolis* (1927) has become iconic.

The idea of the mad, crazed, power-hungry doctor is an alluring one and the 1971 film *The Abominable Dr Phibes* is a vintage example.

Of all the doctors, though, perhaps its Doctors Who and Strange now looming most large.

21
JANUARY

THE FILM *EX MACHINA* WAS RELEASED IN 2015

AI (artificial intelligence) has made for a rich subject for treatment across a variety of media.

One of the great science fiction films of the early twenty-first century is *A.I. Artificial Intelligence* (2001), written and directed by science fiction icon Steven Spielberg: it's a spiritual odyssey through technology and humanity via the influence of *Pinocchio*. By contrast is *Robot & Frank* (2012), a comedy.

Consider too the 2016 TV series *Westworld*. Even music videos have given expression to artificial intelligence; just watch Björk's promo for her song 'All Is Full of Love' (1998).

Of course, there are other, more pessimistic takes on AI. None, perhaps, are more terrifying than the cyborgs that populate the franchise which developed from *The Terminator* (1984). The AI in that series are at odds with humanity.

British cinema has a rich science-fiction movie tradition, and *Ex Machina* presents a story of AI which heads towards tragedy rather than a climax based around wonder. It's a film that uses its technological subject to explore not only the relationship between people and robots but also ideas of masculinity and femininity.

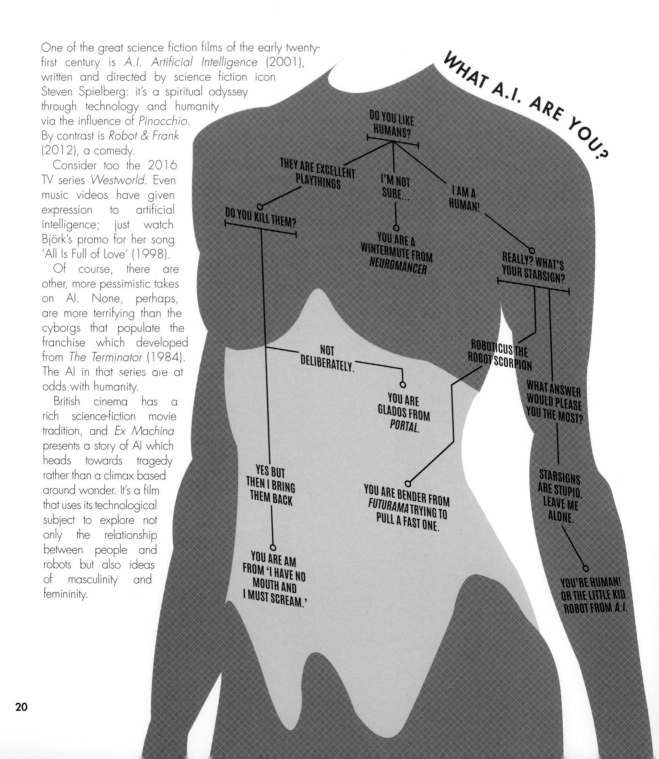

WHAT A.I. ARE YOU?

DO YOU LIKE HUMANS?

THEY ARE EXCELLENT PLAYTHINGS

I'M NOT SURE...

I AM A HUMAN!

DO YOU KILL THEM?

YOU ARE A WINTERMUTE FROM *NEUROMANCER*

REALLY? WHAT'S YOUR STARSIGN?

NOT DELIBERATELY.

ROBOTICUS THE ROBOT SCORPION

YOU ARE GLADOS FROM *PORTAL*.

WHAT ANSWER WOULD PLEASE YOU THE MOST?

YES BUT THEN I BRING THEM BACK

YOU ARE BENDER FROM *FUTURAMA* TRYING TO PULL A FAST ONE.

STARSIGNS ARE STUPID. LEAVE ME ALONE.

YOU ARE AM FROM 'I HAVE NO MOUTH AND I MUST SCREAM.'

YOU'RE HUMAN! OR THE LITTLE KID ROBOT FROM *A.I.*

ROBERT E. HOWARD WAS BORN IN 1906

Conan the Barbarian, the series of fantasy stories written by Howard, initally appeared in a American pulp magazine called *Weird Tales*, but the character has gone on to dominate books, film, television and gaming.

THE A-TEAM TV SERIES DEBUTS ON AMERICAN TV IN 1983

For the geek TV fan during the 1980s, *The A-Team* was required viewing. However, this cult series wouldn't have been possible without the the spy-focused series of the 1960s.

Coming most readily to mind are *The Man from U.N.C.L.E.* (1964–68) and *Mission: Impossible* (1966–1973) with its theme music, by Lalo Schifrin, offering such an enjoyable hit of energy and the promise of excitement. Coming out of some of the tensions around the Cold War, these series were inherently dramatic. Of course, in this same period, the first James Bond films were released.

24
JANUARY

ALFRED HITCHCOCK'S FILM *THE PLEASURE GARDEN* WAS FINALLY RELEASED IN 1927

The most famous films of British director Alfred Hitchcock were those he directed in Hollywood including his two horror films *The Birds* (1963) and *Psycho* (1960). The former was based on a novella (1952) by Daphne du Maurier, the latter on a novel (1959) by Robert Bloch.

Hitchcock was a total filmmaker, bringing together actors, music, genre and visual effects to create psychologically potent films. The scene at Mount Rushmore in *North by Northwest* (1959) is a clear influence on Spielberg's great science-fiction film *Close* *Encounters of the Third Kind* (1977).

Part of Hitchcock's geek legacy is that his films so influenced the generation of filmmakers whose movies have become geek gold dust: *Jaws* (1975), *Taxi Driver* (1976), *Carrie* (1976) and *The Fury* (1978).

25
JANUARY

IN 1947 A PATENT WAS REGISTERED THAT DESCRIBED ONE OF THE EARLIEST COMPUTER GAMES

Now, 70 years later, computer gaming has come of age. No longer a niche pastime, it's become a central force in pop culture and has fed powerfully into the lives of people globally; in doing so, it's impacted on the aesthetics of films and TV.

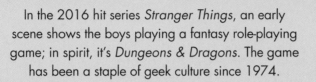

DUNGEONS & DRAGONS WAS FIRST RELEASED IN 1974

26
JANUARY

In the 2016 hit series *Stranger Things*, an early scene shows the boys playing a fantasy role-playing game; in spirit, it's *Dungeons & Dragons*. The game has been a staple of geek culture since 1974.

Conceived by Gary Gygax and Dave Arneson, it tapped into an interest in high fantasy when *Lord of the Rings* found a new audience.

The fantasy tabletop role-playing game (RPG) has been published by Wizards of the West Coast since 1997. It has been hailed as the originator of modern RPGs and the start of the RPG industry itself.

One player takes the role of Dungeon Master and oversees the storytelling and progress of the game. Characters solve problems, go into battle and seek to gather treasure and knowledge.

As players progress they earn experience points which allow them to become more and more powerful.

A rulebook, a character sheet for every player and a polyhedral dice are all that is needed to play.

A 1999 US survey conducted by the gaming industry, *D&D* is the most popular and bestselling RPG. It is estimated that over 20 million people have played the game.

Unsurprisingly, adaptions are common. An animated TV series ran throughout the early 1980s and the game gets a nod in the early part of the film *E.T. the Extra Terrestrial* (1982). The sitcom *The Big Bang Theory* (2007–present) has referenced the game to great comic effect and a film adaptation of the game was produced in 2000.

No stranger to negative publicity, *D&D* has been criticized by religious groups

for allegedly promoting devil worship, witchcraft, suicide and murder.

27
JANUARY

PATTON OSWALT WAS BORN IN 1969

Actor Patton Oswalt has, more than once, provided a useful barometer of what it means to live in a geek world. In an article for *Wired* magazine in 2010 he addressed the way that all things geek have become increasingly more mainstream since 1987: 'I wasn't seeing the hard line between "nerds" and "normals" anymore … Everyone considers themselves *otaku* about something.'

28
JANUARY

FRANK DARABONT WAS BORN IN 1959

One of the most popular TV series of recent years has been *The Walking Dead*, an adaptation of the comic book first published in 2003. The initial series was overseen by Frank Darabont.

Darabont was also involved in three of the best adaptations of Stephen King's writing: *The Shawshank Redemption* (1994), *The Green Mile* (1994) and *The Mist* (2007). With *The Mist*, Darabont delights in the horror/monster genre, showing us a community besieged by a monstrous force in a supermarket.

With *The Shawshank Redemption* and *The Green Mile*, Darabont excelled in bringing two prison set pieces to life. In both, Darabont – as screenwriter and director – teased out not only menace and monstrous human behaviour but also grace notes of compassion and the suggestion of greater benign powers at work.w

29
JANUARY

COMPUTER GAME COMPANY SQUARE HOSTS A MAJOR *FINAL FANTASY* EVENT IN 2000

The event that Square hosted centred around a reveal of the company's plan for the *Final Fantasy* game over the ensuing years – a key announcement was for *Final Fantasy IX* and *Final Fantasy X*.

Final Fantasy XV has been the most recent iteration and it testifies to the popularity of this fantasy world.
Final Fantasy's premise is based on a set of shared and recurring settings and character names that comprise stories in which heroes confront immense evil. The first iteration of *Final Fantasy* was released in autumn 1987. In 2001, a feature film, *Final Fantasy: The Spirits Within* was released.

THE LONE RANGER PREMIERED ON RADIO IN 1933

The Lone Ranger's popularity attests to the vibrancy and fascination of the Western genre. With its emphasis on violence and the possibility of peace and harmony, the genre has since then found a neat fit with science fiction.

The Wild Wild West had originally been a TV series (1965–69) and was rendered for the big screen in 1999 with a story about machines being made to rule America. In 2011, *Cowboys & Aliens* adapted the comic of the same name to tell of cowboys and Native Americans allying to fight invading aliens. The film owes a debt to the classic *The Searchers* (1956). In 2016, *Westworld* premiered on TV, offering a new version of the Michael Crichton film of the same name from 1973. Both versions pit robots against humans in a virtual Western landscape, and the TV series is as much about the power of storytelling as it is about the Western.

GRANT MORRISON WAS BORN IN 1960

Comics have long had their major authors and Grant Morrison is certainly one.

He began his career by writing *The Liberators* in 1985, and the year 1987 was key for Morrison, when he created Zenith with Steve Yeowell and took apart the idea of the superhero.

DC Comics invited him to work for them and in 1989 he wrote the Batman graphic novel *Arkham Asylum: A Serious House on Serious Earth*. His work for Batman has been extensive: for *Batman and Son* (2006), *Final Crisis* (2008–09), *Batman and Robin* (2010) and *Batman Incorporated* (2010–13), his work zeroed in on Batman's relentlessness.

Morrison's work has been crucial to DC Comics' ongoing evolution of its characters – not just Batman, but also Superman and Wonder Woman. In the graphic novel *Wonder Woman: Earth One* (2016), Morrison restored some of the weirdness that Wonder Woman's creator brought to the character.

With Neil Gaiman, Alan Moore and Jamie Delano, Morrison was part of a British invasion of the American comic book form. For some, Morrison's greatest work is *The Invisibles*, in which a diverse mix of characters come together to stop an impending apocalypse. Morrison has said that some of the concept for *The Invisibles* stemmed from a metaphysical experience, and his willingness to push for something clearly intellectual within the framework of pop culture is bold and powerful.

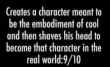

Writes himself into his comic to meet Animal Man and explain why he killed his family: 7/10

Writes a comic about a neurotic teenager planning to assassinate Margaret Thatcher that's based on his own diaries and ends up being discussed in the House of Commons: 6/10

Creates a character meant to be the embodiment of cool and then shaves his head to become that character in the real world:9/10

Creates another bald character based on himself who is a perverted shut-in having a possible nervous breakdown: 3/10

Writes a comic that is his version of *Watchmen* by his arch-rival Alan Moore but with 8 panels per page instead of 9 because of musical octaves: 8/10

THE SHRINKING AND EXPANDING EGO OF GRANT MORRISON

FILMMAKER GEORGE PAL WAS BORN IN 1908

George Pal was nominated for seven Oscars and was awarded an honorary Oscar in 1943. He gave fantasy filmmaking a much needed shot of legitimacy.

Pal's work in Europe saw him pursue his Puppetoons project: animated characters that used replacement animation for each facial expression. It was this work that brought him to Hollywood, where he went on to produce *When Worlds Collide* (1951), *The War of the Worlds* (1953) and *Destination Moon* (1950).

In 1975, Pal produced an adaptation of the character *Doc Savage*, but perhaps he was just a bit ahead of the geek curve with that action hero piece.

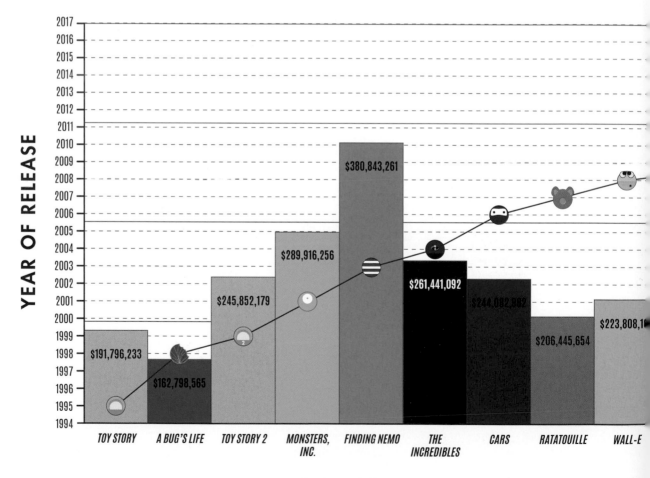

YEAR OF RELEASE

TOY STORY — $191,796,233
A BUG'S LIFE — $162,798,565
TOY STORY 2 — $245,852,179
MONSTERS, INC. — $289,916,256
FINDING NEMO — $380,843,261
THE INCREDIBLES — $261,441,092
CARS — $244,082,982
RATATOUILLE — $206,445,654
WALL-E — $223,808,1

FILM TITLE

GROUNDHOG DAY

A tradition has grown up around Punxsutawney Phil, a groundhog resident in this town. If he emerges on this day from his burrow and then sees his shadow and heads back underground, it is understood that winter will continue for another six weeks.

There's something metaphysical in all this, and the comedy fantasy *Groundhog Day* (1993) does a memorable job of comically extrapolating from this whimsical tradition. Bill Murray stars in one of his numerous fantasy film roles.

PIXAR WAS FOUNDED IN 1986

Pixar's animations have been part of a renaissance in American feature film animation, energising adventure, comedy, science fiction and fantasy with vividly designed characters.

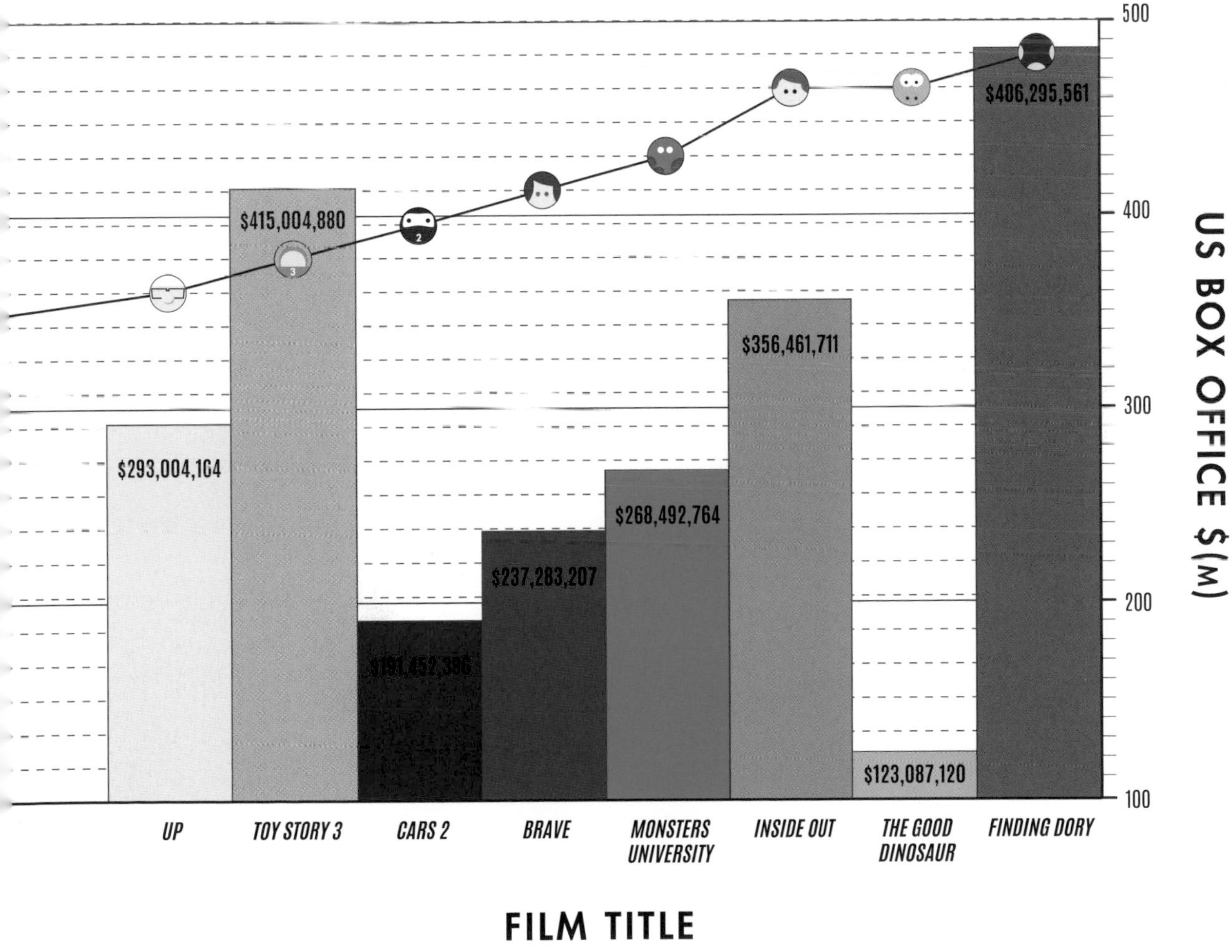

US BOX OFFICE $(m)

- $293,004,164 — UP
- $415,004,880 — TOY STORY 3
- $191,452,396 — CARS 2
- $237,283,207 — BRAVE
- $268,492,764 — MONSTERS UNIVERSITY
- $356,461,711 — INSIDE OUT
- $123,087,120 — THE GOOD DINOSAUR
- $406,295,561 — FINDING DORY

FILM TITLE

4 FEBRUARY

RUSSELL HOBAN WAS BORN IN 1925

Hoban's novel *Riddley Walker*, first published in 1980, is a key piece of post-apocalyptic literature. It is set in England after a nuclear holocaust.

5 FEBRUARY

NOLAN BUSHNELL WAS BORN IN 1943

For some, *Atari* is an almost enchanted word that transports them back to the 1970s and 1980s. Its logo is also globally recognised: designed by George Opperman, its silhouette looks like the letter A, created by three 'prongs' that allude to an early game, *Pong*, based on table tennis.

Established by Nolan Bushnell in 1972, Atari developed out of a creative rebellion: lots of newly minted computer programmers decided that instead of working for the defence industry, they'd do something more playful. In the process, Bushnell and his team (Ralph Baer and Al Alcorn) revolutionised entertainment. It was a new media startup.

Pong was released in 1972, *Space Invaders* by Taito in 1978, *Pac-Man* by Namco in 1980 and *Yar's Revenge* in 1982. In 1977, a quantum leap in home entertainment was made when Atari released the Atari 2600. So iconic have the Atari characters become that they even feature in two recent films, *Pixels* (2015) and *Wreck-It Ralph* (2013).

6 FEBRUARY

CHARLES WHEATSTONE, INVENTOR OF THE STEREOSCOPE, WAS BORN IN 1802

Things have come a long way since Victorian inventor Charles Wheatstone devised the stereoscope, a very early device for viewing 3D images. 2016 proved something of a watershed year in the evolution of virtual reality (VR) technology. Right now, the technology is being deployed to create a new kind of visual spectacle that moves beyond cinema.

7 FEBRUARY

THE FIRST UNTETHERED SPACE WALK FROM SPACE SHUTTLE *CHALLENGER* WAS MADE IN 1984

Space walks (EVA: extra-vehicular activity) have featured notably in movies.

Most famously and nerve-janglingly, it's a space walk that's the starting point for the film *Gravity* (2013), in which Sandra Bullock's struggles to get home to Earth. *2001: A Space Odyssey* (1968) offers equally memorable and perilous action.

JULES VERNE IS BORN ON THIS DAY IN 1828

Verne is a titan, the wellspring from which a great deal of pop and geek culture has flowed. Celebrating both science and nature, Jules Verne's books include *Journey to the Centre of the Earth* (1864) and *Around the World in Eighty Days* (1873).

His work is speculative, romantic and dosed with an understanding of science. What's more, as geek magazine publisher Hugo Gernsback noted, it's prophetic – which is also true of his near contemporary H.G. Wells.

The details of Nautilus, the submarine of *20,000 Leagues Under the Sea* (1870), have now nearly all been realised today. His novel *The Steam House* (1880) captures a sense of how the nineteenth century changed human experience so powerfully through science and engineering. His fantasy novel *The Child of the Cavern* (or *Strange Doings Underground*, 1877) mixes technology and anthrolopogy when a mine in Scotland is reopened, revealing a lost subterranean community.

As a child, Verne once ran away and, when recaptured by his father, apparently vowed, 'je ne voyagerai plus qu'en rêve' ('I will no longer travel except in my dreams'). As an adult he wrote, 'Reality provides us with facts so romantic that imagination itself could add nothing to them.'

HOW JULES VERNE LAUNCHED SCIENCE FICTION

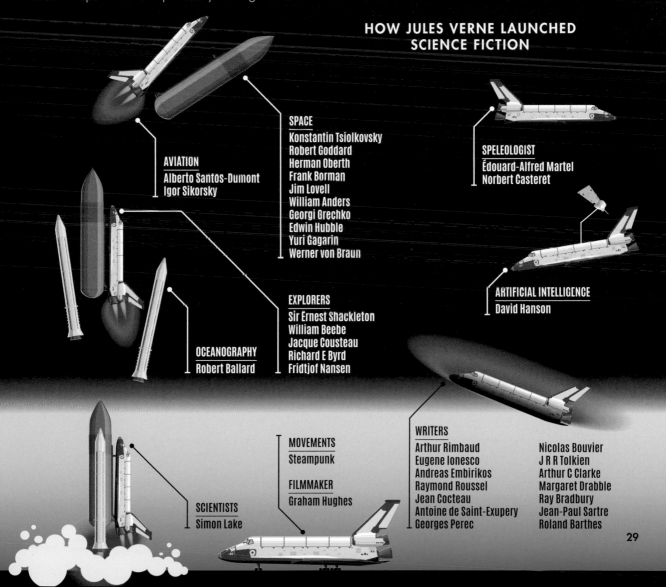

SPACE
Konstantin Tsiolkovsky
Robert Goddard
Herman Oberth
Frank Borman
Jim Lovell
William Anders
Georgi Grechko
Edwin Hubble
Yuri Gagarin
Werner von Braun

AVIATION
Alberto Santos-Dumont
Igor Sikorsky

SPELEOLOGIST
Édouard-Alfred Martel
Norbert Casteret

ARTIFICIAL INTELLIGENCE
David Hanson

EXPLORERS
Sir Ernest Shackleton
William Beebe
Jacque Cousteau
Richard E Byrd
Fridtjof Nansen

OCEANOGRAPHY
Robert Ballard

MOVEMENTS
Steampunk

FILMMAKER
Graham Hughes

SCIENTISTS
Simon Lake

WRITERS
Arthur Rimbaud
Eugene Ionesco
Andreas Embirikos
Raymond Roussel
Jean Cocteau
Antoine de Saint-Exupery
Georges Perec

Nicolas Bouvier
J R R Tolkien
Arthur C Clarke
Margaret Drabble
Ray Bradbury
Jean-Paul Sartre
Roland Barthes

9 FEBRUARY

FRANK FRAZETTA WAS BORN IN 1928

Frank Frazetta's fantasy art has brightened comics,
the covers of novels, and film posters.

He began as a comics illustrator and contributed to images of Buck Rogers for *Famous Funnies*.

Frazetta is perhaps best known for his images used in the 1960s for anthologies of *Conan* stories – created by Robert E. Howard and continued by L. Sprague de Camp. He also illustrated covers for Edgar Rice Burroughs's novels.

He collaborated with Ralph Bakshi on the animation film *Fire and Ice* (1983).

10 FEBRUARY

THE LEGO BATMAN MOVIE WAS RELEASED IN 2017 IN UK

The Lego toy company began life in Ole Kirk Christiansen's carpentry workshop in 1932. 'Lego' is a contraction of the Danish phrase *leg godt*, meaning play well. The plastic bricks now synonymous with the name were first created in 1947.

11 FEBRUARY

THE BBC BROADCASTS THE FIRST-EVER SCIENCE-FICTION TV PROGRAMME IN 1938

In 1921, the stage play *R.U.R.* (*Rossum's Universal Robots*), written by Karl Capek, introduced the word 'robot' to the mainstream world. *RUR* is the earliest example of British TV science fiction: it was a live broadcast and Capek's story is about robots leading a revolution against humans.

Many of the ideas that science-fiction TV continues to explore are all there in the BBC adaptation of *R.U.R.* In Capek's play these robots are more akin to clones than mechanical entities. To end on a sobering fact: the word 'robot' comes to us from the Czech word meaning 'forced labour'.

12 FEBRUARY

ALBERT EINSTEIN WAS INTERVIEWED BY ELEANOR ROOSEVELT IN 1950

Einstein has, at points, been reimagined and represented in science fiction movies.

He inspired Dr Know, the animated character (voiced by Robin Williams) in Steven Spielberg's film *A.I. Artificial Intelligence* (2001). The *Star Wars* sage Yoda is notable for his eyes, which were partly inspired by Einstein's, as, indeed, were those of E.T. In comic contrast, Doc Brown's dog in the *Back to the Future* series is called Einstein.

ARTIST ANUPAM SINHA WAS BORN IN 1962

Indian comic books in the superhero genre have a rich tradition.

Anupam Sinha has been credited with revolutionizing Indian comics thanks to his work as artists and writer at Raj Comics. It is partly thanks to Sinha and his colleagues that Indian comics are currently enjoying great popularity, having become an increasingly visible and vibrant part of the country's popular culture.

One of the notable comic publications of recent years is *18 Days*, which reimagined the *Mahabharata* and was based on an abandoned animated series scripted by Grant Morrison. In 2010, the project took on a new life as a comic project, illustrated with vivid detail and colour by Mukesh Singh, who captures a sense of immensity and of beauty.

Key to current Indian comic book culture is the work of Amruta Patil, whose graphic novel Kari was published in 2008. In her comic *Adi Parva* the women narrator of the story says '… you are not held captive by old narratives. Tales must be tilled like the land so they keep breathing.'

NAGRAJ
He can release snakes from his body, telepathy, immune to physical danger, venom.

DOGA
Can communicate with dogs, great endurance, martial arts, dodges bullets.

SUPER COMMANDO DHRUVA
Can communicate with birds, can breathe and talk within water, strong willpower.

PARMANU
Can fly at great speed, fires atom bolts from his chest.

BHOKAL
Can fly, wields a sword and shield of supernatural power.

SHAKTI
Can sense womens' pain and can travel at speed of light. One of the physically most strong Indian superheroes.

RAJ COMICS MOST FAMOUS SUPERHEROES

THE INCEPTION DATE OF THE REPLICANT PRIS IN 2016 IN *BLADE RUNNER*

One of the film's several physically menacing and utterly compelling replicants, Pris is a 'living doll', seemingly fragile and alone (thanks to Daryl Hannah's performance). However, as Rick Deckard, the detective charged with hunting her down, finds out, she's physically deadly.

In the years since 1982, the film has gathered a reputation as a major piece of American science fiction filmmaking. Harrison Ford's Deckard is a brooding and melancholy man, and the film's vivid production design presents us with a future that looks increasingly like the present.

HOW A VOIGT-KAMPFF MACHINE OPERATES

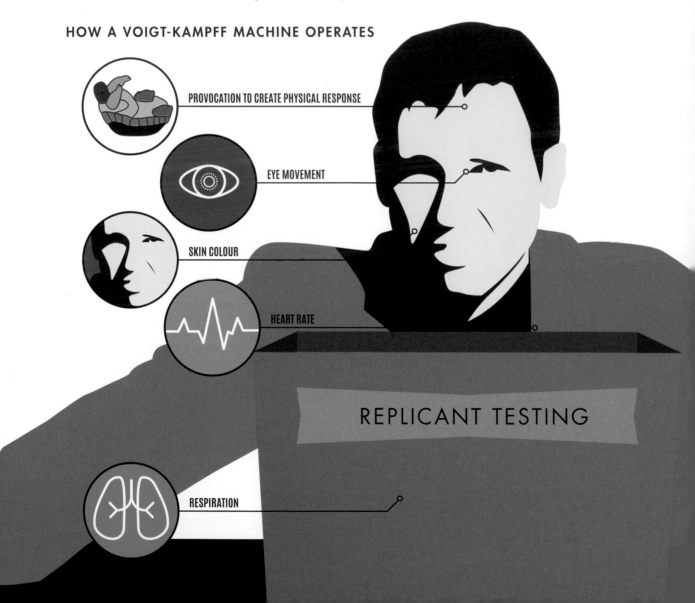

PROVOCATION TO CREATE PHYSICAL RESPONSE

EYE MOVEMENT

SKIN COLOUR

HEART RATE

REPLICANT TESTING

RESPIRATION

THE FIRST EPISODE OF *RED DWARF* WAS BROADCAST IN 1988

Doug Naylor and Rob Grant's landmark space sitcom was based on *Dave Hollins: Space Cadet*, a series of radio sketches broadcast in 1984. *Red Dwarf* centred its comedy around a technician and his non-human companions, comprising a hologram, a cat and a robot. Eleven series have been produced between 1988 and 2016, featuring lots of geek genre in-jokes. Both pastiche and parody, *Red Dwarf* is a sitcom that clearly loves all things geek.

IAIN M. BANKS WAS BORN IN 1954

Iain M. Banks created the *Culture* universe that he revisited across a series of novels. With *Consider Phlebas* (1987), the first of his *Culture* novels, he took classic space opera and rewired it. Though the series featured many space opera tropes, Banks used these stories to deliver serious messages about the state of our world. Banks's *Culture* novel *Look to Windward* (2000) is considered the strongest of the series.

BILL & TED'S EXCELLENT ADVENTURE WAS RELEASED IN 1989 IN THE US

Who wouldn't want to go back and correct a mistake or visit a lost world, or even a lost love? Who wouldn't want to rocket off into the future and see what fate has in store?

In his novel *The Time Machine* (1895), H.G. Wells pits the primal and the civilised against each other to suggest how things could be in a world with a refined, non-working class (the Eloi) and a labouring, subterranean class (the Morlocks). In *Bill & Ted's Excellent Adventure*, the eponymous high-school heroes time-travel to assemble a collection of historical figures, including Napoleon, whom they need to help answer questions in a history assignment.

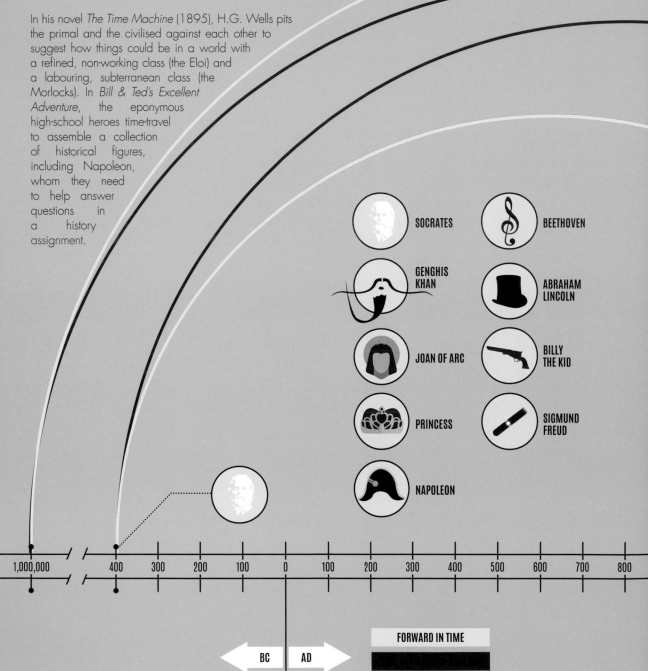

SOCRATES

BEETHOVEN

GENGHIS KHAN

ABRAHAM LINCOLN

JOAN OF ARC

BILLY THE KID

PRINCESS

SIGMUND FREUD

NAPOLEON

1,000,000   400   300   200   100   0   100   200   300   400   500   600   700   800

BC   AD

FORWARD IN TIME

MASAMI FUKUSHIMA WAS BORN IN 1929

Fukushima stands as a major figure in Japanese science-fiction literature. His work as editor of Japan's *SF Magazine* broadened the appeal of the genre in his home country by favouring material that was not just space opera. Fukushima also translated the work of Asimov, Clarke and Heinlein for Japanese readers.

NICOLAUS COPERNICUS WAS BORN IN 1473

Copernicus, Galileo Galilei and Nikola Tesla have each had their scientific inquiries made central to science fiction.

Copernicus proposed that the Sun and not the Earth was the centre of the universe. Fascinatingly, Copernicus's work informs the novel *Somnium*, first published in 1634 and very possibly the first science fiction novel, written by the astronaut Johannes Kepler.

Galileo is at the centre of Bertolt Brecht's play *Life of Galileo* (1943), which dramatises his efforts to prove the theories of Copernicus. Galileo refined the technology of the telescope and he wrote a book entitled *Dialogue Concerning the Two Chief World Systems* (1632).

Appropriately born during a lightning storm, Tesla was a futurist and inventor, who discovered alternating current machinery. For all of his technological focus, he was good friends with ecologist John Muir. He is imagined as a character in *The Prestige* (2006) and he also puts in a cameo of sorts in the film *Tomorrowland* (2015).

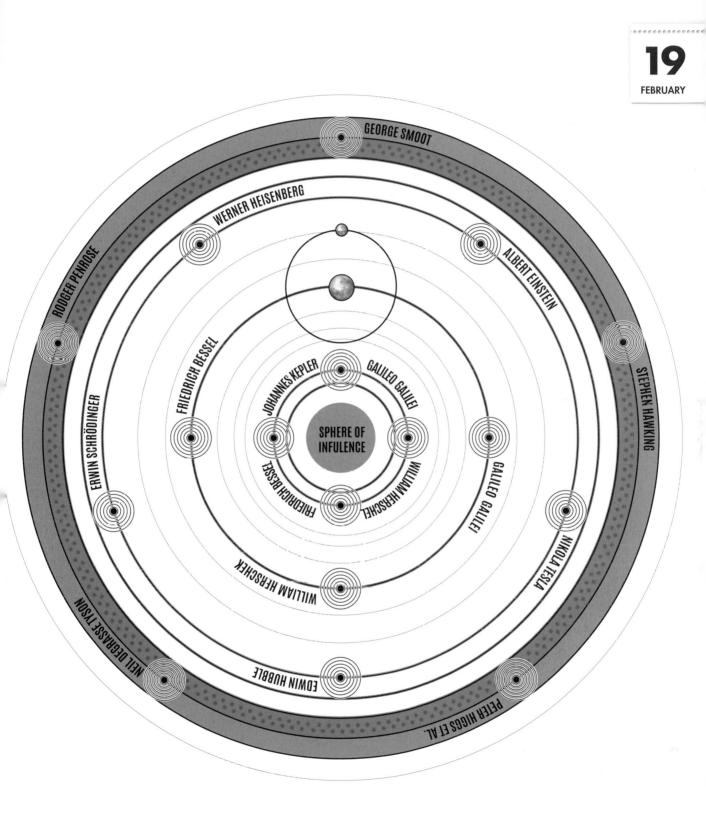

GEORGE SMOOT

WERNER HEISENBERG

RODGER PENROSE

ALBERT EINSTEIN

STEPHEN HAWKING

ERWIN SCHRÖDINGER

FRIEDRICH BESSEL

JOHANNES KEPLER

GALILEO GALILEI

SPHERE OF
INFULENCE

FRIEDRICH BESSEL

WILLIAM HERSCHEL

GALILEO GALILEI

NIKOLA TESLA

WILLIAM HERSCHEL

NEIL DEGRASSE TYSON

EDWIN HUBBLE

PETER HIGGS ET AL.

PIERRE BOULLE WAS BORN IN 1912

Boulle's novel *La Planète des Singes* (*Planet of the Apes*, 1963) has spawned an extensive range of feature films and a TV series. The striking premise of Boulle's novel functions as a potent allegory of race.

Boulle's novel centred on the discovery by human space travellers of an Earth-like planet that is dominated by apes, with humans as the underclass.

The novel became the basis for an American feature film that led to several sequels and an early 1970s TV series, cartoon series and line of toys.

In 2001, Tim Burton's film adaptation was released, but it was a later wave of *Apes* films that proved hugely successful: *Rise of the Planet of the Apes* (2011), *Dawn of the Planet of the Apes* (2014) and *War for the Planet of the Apes* (2017).

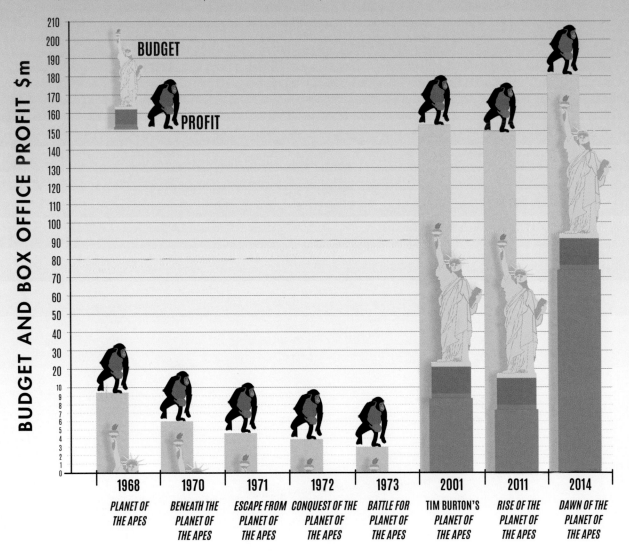

BUDGET AND BOX OFFICE PROFIT $m

BUDGET

PROFIT

1968	1970	1971	1972	1973	2001	2011	2014
PLANET OF THE APES	BENEATH THE PLANET OF THE APES	ESCAPE FROM PLANET OF THE APES	CONQUEST OF THE PLANET OF THE APES	BATTLE FOR PLANET OF THE APES	TIM BURTON'S PLANET OF THE APES	RISE OF THE PLANET OF THE APES	DAWN OF THE PLANET OF THE APES

FILM TITLE AND YEAR

THE LEGEND OF ZELDA WAS RELEASED IN 1986

Link is the young hero in the world of Hyrule and he embarks
on a quest for eight magical fragments.

There have been 21 Zelda computer games. In 2017,
a new Zelda iteration was released: *Breath of the Wild*.

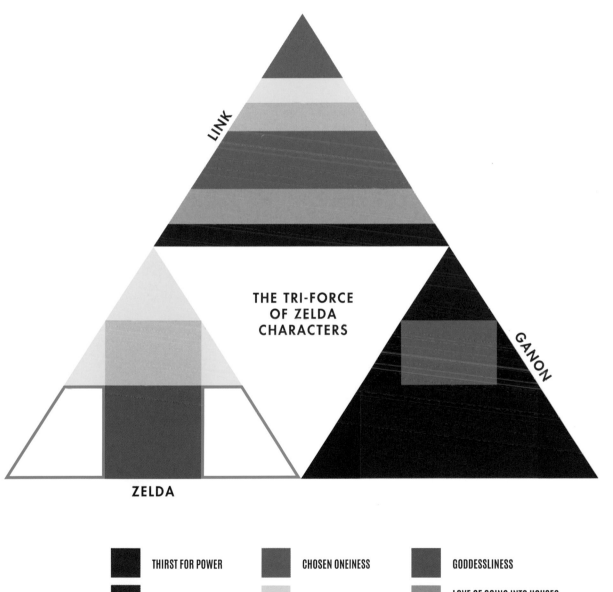

LINK

THE TRI-FORCE
OF ZELDA
CHARACTERS

GANON

ZELDA

THIRST FOR POWER

CHOSEN ONENESS

GODDESSLINESS

LOVE OF VIOLENCE

BEAUTIFUL HAIR

LOVE OF GOING INTO HOUSES
AND SMASHING ALL THEIR POTS

PIGHEADEDNESS

GOOD WITH A BOW

EPONYMOUSITY

THE INCREDIBLE SHRINKING MAN WAS RELEASED IN 1957

Richard Matheson looms large in American science fiction, fantasy and horror.

The work of this screenwriter and novelist includes *The Shrinking Man* (1956, filmed as *The Incredible Shrinking Man*), *I Am Legend* (1954) and *Steel* (1956), as well as episodes of *The Twilight Zone*. Matheson also wrote the novels *What Dreams May Come* (1978) and *Bid Time Return* (1975), each a story of memory and love. *Steel* was adapted into a film *Real Steel* (2011), executive produced by Steven Spielberg, bringing Matheson's work full circle in a way: Matheson wrote the short story 'Duel' (1971). That short story then became a TV movie directed by Steven Spielberg, and contained the essence of the films that would follow: an ordinary man ensnared and illuminated by an unsettling, extraordinary experience.

1966
FANTASTIC VOYAGE

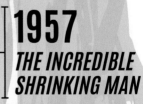

1957
THE INCREDIBLE SHRINKING MAN

NO SMALL PARTS, ONLY SMALL CHARACTERS

1987
INNERSPACE

2010
THE SECRET WORLD OF ARRIETY

1989
HONEY, I SHRUNK THE KIDS

ADAPTATION OF *WATCHMEN* PREMIERED IN 2009

In January 2010, *Time* magazine ran a list of 100 greatest novels. *Watchmen* was included on the list – the only graphic novel to make the cut. Its inclusion spoke to the seismic impact of the piece upon its original release in 1986.

Written by Alan Moore and illustrated by Dave Gibbons, it dared to depict the frailties of the superheroic.

Stylistically, the comic pushed the conventions of the medium: each page was based around nine panels, and often the text did not immediately correspond with what the images were showing.

WATCHMEN DOOMSDAY CLOCK

- 1953
- 2017
- 1949; 1984; 2015
- 1981
- 2007; 2012
- 1988; 2010
- 1947; 1960; 1968; 1980; 2002
- 1974; 1998
- 1969; 1990
- 1963; 1972
- 1995
- 1991

OCTAVIA BUTLER PASSED AWAY IN 2006

Butler's science fiction novels are powerful allegories that filter real-world issues and particularly the idea of oppression. Butler's career was productive and recognized with multiple awards. Her first published story 'Crossover' appeared in an anthology by the Clarion Science Fiction Writers Workshop in 1971 and her first novel *Patternmaster* was published in 1976.

Her work explores religious and non-religious ideas. Butler's work often fused science fiction in history, slave narratives and fantasy. Things aren't simple in Butler's work: her writing is cerebral and rooted in creative ways to explore ideas of oppression and feminism.

Her novel *Kindred* (1979) has recently been adapted into a graphic novel. The story uses time travel to explore the concept of slavery and identity.

Butler wrote several series of novels across her career. The *Xenogenesis* series (1984–89) was prompted by the nuclear arms race policies of President Ronald Reagan: in it, the human race has almost destroyed itself through humanicide (nuclear war). The war's survivors are taken by an alien species, and so begins a drama about genetic identity.

In the *Parable* series (1993–98), a young woman experiences hyperempathy and uses it as the basis for attempting to establish a new community in the wake of great violence in her home city. In the *Patternist* series (1971–84), psychic powers are the lens through which power relations are explored.

'There isn't any subject that you can't tackle by way of science fiction,' Butler explained and she is now a beacon for aspiring writers.

PHILIP JOSÉ FARMER DIED IN 2009

American author Philip José Farmer's fiction has been celebrated for the way in which it brought a smore adult sensibility to science fiction. Notable works includes the series *World of Tiers* (1965–93) and *Riverworld* (1971–83). One of his first titles, *The Lovers* (1952) featured a sexual relationship between a human and an alien. Farmer's work resonated so much that fans of his work established a fanzine entitled *Farmerphile* (2005–2009).

ISSUE 1 OF THE COMIC *2000 AD* WAS PUBLISHED FOR THE FIRST TIME IN 1977

British comic *2000 AD* was first published in 1977. Steeped in the spirit of the superhero comic tradition, *2000 AD* was distinctively British and its richly imagined characters have become globally recognised: Judge Dredd, Rogue Trooper, Slaine to name just three. *2000 AD* has been a constant on the geek culture landscape. Artists who started out on *2000 AD* include Dave Gibbons, Simon Bisley, Jamie Hewlett, John Higgins and John Wagner.

JEFF SMITH WAS BORN IN 1960

By the early 1990s American comics were in resurgence and a number of independent comic publishers made their mark. Standing out in a sea of action orientated superheroes was a squishy little guy named Bone. Created by Jeff Smith, the *Bone* comic series (1991–2004) became an epic adventure as Fone Bone and his cousins, Phoney and Smiley, find themselves far from home in a world of forests, mountains and mysterious encounters.

Smith's epic series was funny, sombre – and cute. Originally published in black and white, it has since been republished in colour and a series of spin-off novels have also been issued.

Combining the epic odyssey of Tolkien with the influence of cartoonist Carl Barks (best known for his work on Donald Duck stories), *Bone* was steeped in American humour.

JOHN CONNOR WAS BORN IN 1985

In the world of the *Terminator* films, John Connor was born on this day in 1985. Connor would go on to lead the human resistance against the robot uprising. Part action movie, part odyssey, the original *Terminator* film is also a reflection on technology, suggesting that our increasing reliance on technology makes it all the more necessary to connect with our human spirit.

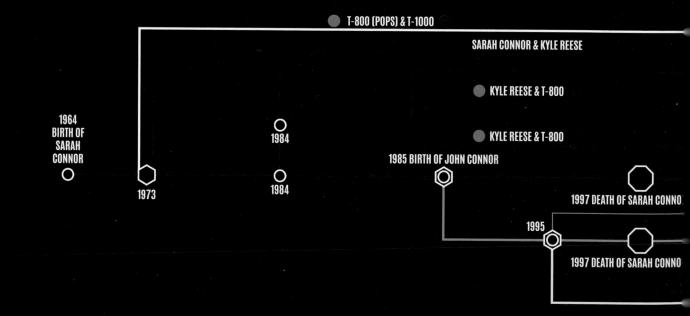

T-800 (POPS) & T-1000

SARAH CONNOR & KYLE REESE

KYLE REESE & T-800

KYLE REESE & T-800

1964
BIRTH OF
SARAH
CONNOR

1984

1985 BIRTH OF JOHN CONNOR

1973

1984

1997 DEATH OF SARAH CONNO

1995

1997 DEATH OF SARAH CONNO

GHOST IN THE SHELL WAS PUBLISHED IN ENGLISH IN 1995

Anime exerts a great power on the genre favourites of geekdom. Certainly, anime has the capacity to depict diverse imaginary worlds, and *Ghost in the Shell* stands as a touchstone in science-fiction anime, ranking alongside *Akira*.

Ghost in the Shell began as a manga, serialized every three months, in Young magazine, between 1989 and 1990. In America, the title was reprinted by Dark Horse comics, although certain scenes were censored. *Ghost in the Shell 2: Man–Machine* Interface was published as manga between 1991–1997

The manga and anime versions of *Ghost in the Shell* both explore the relationship between people and artificial intelligence and, by extension, what it means to be a human with a memory and identity. The film's great success hinged, partly, on its seriousness of tone. The film's core 'philosophical' scene is when Motoko and Batou talk on the boat about consciousness and memory.

Such is the popularity of the *Ghost in the Shell* story that a live action rendition of the tale was released in 2017. It stars Scarlett Johansson, who has made something of a niche for herself in science fiction movies: *Her* (2013), *Under the Skin* (2013) and *Lucy*.

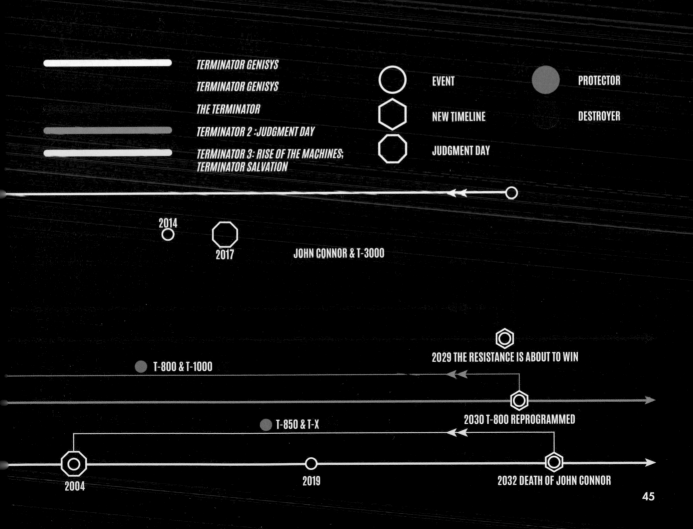

TERMINATOR GENISYS

TERMINATOR GENISYS

THE TERMINATOR

TERMINATOR 2 :JUDGMENT DAY

TERMINATOR 3: RISE OF THE MACHINES;
TERMINATOR SALVATION

EVENT

NEW TIMELINE

JUDGMENT DAY

PROTECTOR

DESTROYER

2014

2017

JOHN CONNOR & T-3000

2029 THE RESISTANCE IS ABOUT TO WIN

T-800 & T-1000

2030 T-800 REPROGRAMMED

T-850 & T-X

2004

2019

2032 DEATH OF JOHN CONNOR

KING KONG WAS RELEASED IN 1933

A landmark in the evolution of visual effects, courtesy of the film's effects man Willis O'Brien, *King Kong*'s stop-motion wonders inspired Ray Harryhausen, Phil Tippett (creator of the dinosaur effects in *Jurassic Park*, 1993) and director Peter Jackson.

KING KONG
APRIL 1933
$12 MILLION

KING KONG
LIVES 1986
$18 MILLION

KING KONG VS
GODZILLA 1962
$200,000

KING KONG 2005
$207 MILLION

KONG: SKULL ISLAND 2017
$190 MILLION

KING KONG 1976
$100 MILLION

SON OF KONG
DECEMBER 1933
$269,000

NEUROMANCER, THE OPERA, NEVER HAPPENED ON THIS DAY IN 1995

Sometimes, just sometimes, a book's title takes on a life far beyond the story that it immediately identifies and in the case of *Neuromancer*, by William Gibson, this is all too true … at least within geekdom.

Now synonymous with the subgenre of cyberpunk, *Neuromancer* (first published in 1984) set out a new fictional fabric and this novel, now more prescient than ever, explores the idea of cyberspace.

 Neuromancer developed from Gibson's own short story 'Burning Chrome'. Its premise is that computers are all interconnected and can be accessed by people. The novel also charts characters in Chiba City and in the Sprawl, a megacity on the American east coast.

The immense urban environment has become a classic science-fiction trope reaching back to *Metropolis*. Hugely well received, *Neuromancer* won the Hugo, Nebula and Philip K. Dick awards.

 Gibson has made the useful observation that 'Science fiction writers aren't fortune tellers. Fortune tellers are fakes.'

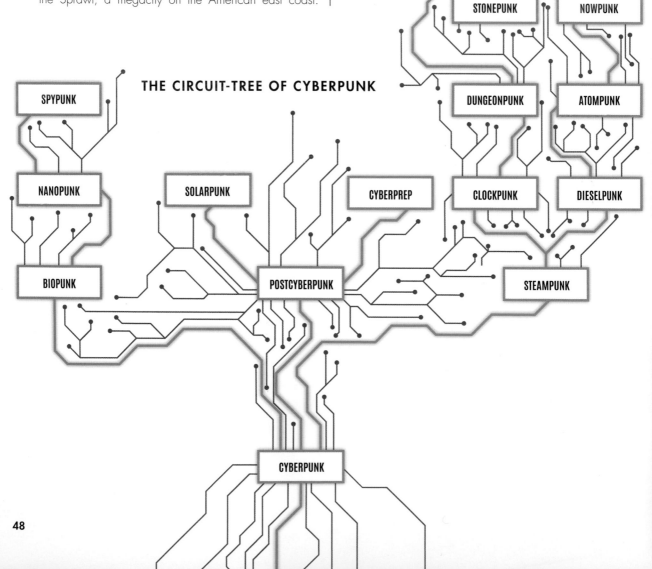

THE CIRCUIT-TREE OF CYBERPUNK

ABRAHAM LINCOLN WAS INAUGURATED IN 1861

In 1861, a noteable man from Illinois was inaugurated as the American president. Abraham Lincoln was his name, and he held the country together when it threatened to shatter following the American Civil War.

Lincoln has been much mythologised and, in more recent years, his image has been embraced by geek culture. *Abraham Lincoln: Vampire Hunter* (2012) is perhaps the most famous instance recently, but *Great Moments with Mr Lincoln* is a well-known attraction at Disneyland. He also turns up in *Bill & Ted's Excellent Adventure* (1989). He has even made a cameo appearance on *The Simpsons*, appeared in the *Star Trek* TV series and been described as America's first superhero.

In 2009, Lincoln starred in a Presidents' Day Special issue of Amazing Spider-Man. The cover shows him rolling up his sleeves as Spider-Man and Captain America hold his hat and coat, with Abe grimacing and saying, 'Thanks for holding my stuff, fellas.' Perhaps, though, Lincoln's call for 'malice towards none, charity for all' is his greatest superheroic moment.

JUDGE DREDD MADE HIS COMIC BOOK DEBUT IN 1977

2000AD's most recognised and emblematic character, Judge Dredd was created by John Wagner and Carlos Ezquerra. Dredd's appearance was inspired in part by the costume design in *Death Race 2000*, produced by Roger Corman.

Prog 7 Dredd removes his helmet, but it's covered by a censored sticker, implying he is hideously disfigured.

Prog 328 Dredd's helmet falls off, but he's a werewolf, so therefore not his usual self...

Prog 52 and **211** Dredd uses a face-changing machine to disguise himself as the member of a criminal gang to infiltrate them.

Prog 650–662 'The Dead Man' In a twist the horribly scarred lawman in this cursed earth set series was revealed to be Dredd with amnesia.

Judge Dredd, the movie, 1990- Dredd removes his helmet quite early in this flop, probably due to the star power of Sylvester Stallone. In the better-received 2012 film, Karl Urban's Dredd doesn't take it off once.

PROG 7

PROG 52, 211

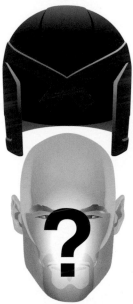

PROG 328

PROG 650–662

DREDD'S HELMETLESS MOMENTS

THE FINAL EPISODE OF *LOST IN SPACE* AIRED ON TV IN 1968

6

MARCH

With its jazzy fanfare, tinged with a sense of adventure and composed by Johnny Williams (before he became the John Williams of *Star Wars* fame), *Lost in Space* captured the 1960s' enthusiasm for space travel.

Lost In Space was American TV's first hour-long primetime series with weekly cliffhanger endings. Dr Zachary Smith was conceived as the series antagonist and he soon became the star of the series.

Irwin Allen's most popular series was originally entitled *Space Family Robinson*. *MAD* magazine said cuttingly that the show had 'about as much space equipment as is presently at the Houston Space Centre'.

COMPOSER MICHAEL GIACCHINO WINS THE OSCAR FOR THE FILM *UP* IN 2010

7

MARCH

Michael Giacchino has written music for films set deeply within geek territory, including *Rogue One* (2016), *Doctor Strange* (2016), *John Carter* (2012) and *The Incredibles* (2004).

In so doing he has picked up the mantle from composer John Williams, the man behind the music for *Star Wars* (1977), *Close Encounters of the Third Kind* (1977), *Superman: The Movie* (1978), *Raiders of the Lost Ark* (1981), *E.T. the Extra-Terrestrial* (1982), *Jurassic Park* (1993) and the *Harry Potter* series (2001–11).

James Horner composed scores steeped in a sense of wonder and tension, whimsy and expanse in films such as *Battle Beyond the Stars* (1980), *Cocoon* (1984), *Aliens* (1986), *The Land Before Time* (1988) and *Avatar* (2009).

And let's not overlook the work of Japanese composer Joe Hisaishi, who has drawn out the inner life of characters in the fantasies of Hayao Miyazaki. If we're lucky, then, a film score can sometimes break loose of the material for which it was originally created for and stand alone.

NEWTYPE POP CULTURE MAGAZINE LAUNCHED IN JAPAN IN 1985

8

MARCH

Newtype magazine is devoted to anime and manga and is named for the Newtypes who appear in the iconic anime series *Gundam* (1979–present). *Newtype USA* was published in English in America between 2002 and 2008. The magazine includes manga and prose fiction content and articles about Computer Generated art for video games.

BARBIE MADE HER DEBUT AT THE AMERICAN TOY FAIR IN 1959

Barbie hasn't just starred in her own films and appeared in *Toy Story*, she's also become part of the *Star Trek* universe on the occasion of the series' fiftieth anniversary in 2016. The *Barbie Star Trek* dolls that were made for the occasion faithfully depict Kirk, Spock and Uhura, as seen in the original series.

SILENT RUNNING WAS RELEASED IN 1972

For all of their tendencies towards technology and sprawling vistas, some science fiction films head in a slightly different direction, and the eco sci-fi story has a rich tradition.

Silent Running, a cult film if ever there was one, focuses on a spaceship that houses the last samples of Earth's plant life. In our eco-aware age, it's a film that has become all the more powerful.

Other films that warn against abusing nature are *Waterworld* (1995), *Avatar* (2009) and *Jurassic Park* (1993). In literature, John Wyndham's *The Day of the Triffids* (1951) and J.G.Ballard's *The Drowned World* (1962) are key pieces of eco sci-fi.

THX 1138 WAS RELEASED IN 1971

Science fiction films sometimes offer a strain of social comment.

Cult classic *THX 1138* which starred Robert Duvall and Donald Pleasence, charts the attempt of an individual to break free of a repressive society and its all-seeing, all-knowing surveillance superpower.

The Postman (1997), adapted from David Brin's novel (1985) into an underappreciated film directed by Kevin Costner, is about the value of community, while the *Star Trek* universe has often been recognised for its multicultural depictions and engagement with justice and moral choice.

Things to Come (1936) and the science-fiction films of the 1950s – made in America, the UK and Japan – register fears around 'the other' and the terrifying possibilities of technology when abused.

Children of Men (2006) adapts the P.D. James novel of the same name (1992) and is both war film and thriller, a piece of speculative fiction which resonates in our current moment when we face the reality refugees.

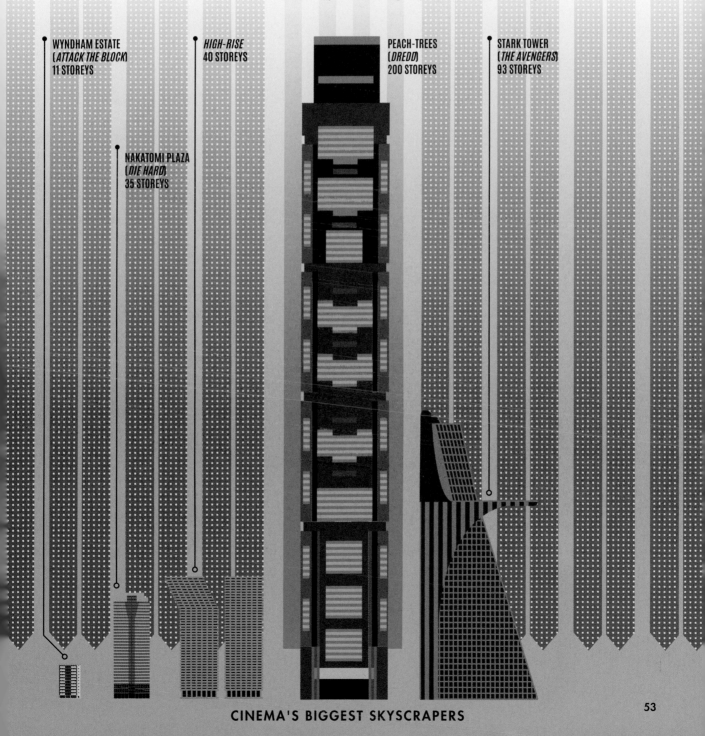

TYRELL PYRAMIDS
(*BLADE RUNNER*):
OVER 800
STOREYS HIGH

ATTACK THE BLOCK WAS RELEASED IN 2011

A south London tower block becomes the site of a close encounter
of the scary kind for a group of streetwise teenagers.

WYNDHAM ESTATE
(*ATTACK THE BLOCK*)
11 STOREYS

HIGH-RISE
40 STOREYS

PEACH-TREES
(*DREDD*)
200 STOREYS

STARK TOWER
(*THE AVENGERS*)
93 STOREYS

NAKATOMI PLAZA
(*DIE HARD*)
35 STOREYS

CINEMA'S BIGGEST SKYSCRAPERS

IN 2003 *NATURE* REPORTED THE DISCOVERY OF 350,000-YEAR-OLD HUMAN FOOTPRINTS

There are many books and films that relish the chance to imagine what that era might have been like. Jean M.Auel's *Earth's Children* series of novels (1980–2011), most famously *The Clan of the Cave Bear* (1980), is an epic imagining of prehistoric human life.

Another take on this era in the human story is *Neanderthal*, a 1996 thriller by John Darnton. Then, too, there's the British film *At The Earth's Core* (1976), based on Edgar Rice Burrough's story of the same name (1914) and, if you're really in the mood for the lesser known, see if you can track down *Iceman* (1984).

THE COMIC BOOK *SAGA* WAS FIRST PUBLISHED IN 2012

In a male-dominated geek culture there's a major female voice: artist Fiona Staples, co-author with Brian K. Vaughan of *Saga* (2012–present), an adventure story about two lovers, from opposing sides during wartime. Protecting their baby, Marko and Alana flee the authorities.

DAVID CRONENBERG WAS BORN IN 1943

David Cronenberg's films *Videodrome* (1983), *The Fly* (1986) and *Existenz* (1999) explore science, identity and our fleshy, fragile selves. He even directed a Nike TV commercial that was suitably visceral.

TODD MCFARLANE WAS BORN IN 1961

Spawn is to the renaissance of the American comic book in the early 1990s what *Batman* was to its genesis in the 1930s. Created by Todd McFarlane, *Spawn* became so popular that it was adapted as a feature film released in 1997. McFarlane subsequently went on to produce a very geek-friendly line of toys.

IN 1799 ETIENNE-GASPARD ROBERT SECURED A PATENT FOR A MAGIC LANTERN

Visual effects have been critical to bringing to life the kind of stories that have contributed to the delights of geek culture.

LUC BESSON WAS BORN IN 1959

American filmmakers aren't the only fabulists in town. Since his first feature film, *The Last Combat*, Frenchman Luc Besson has realised a handful of films that sit right in the heart of science fiction and fantasy.

The Last Combat (1983) is virtually a silent film, set in a post-apocalyptic landscape and photographed in black and white. We follow a loner as he goes about the business of surviving.

By contrast with such minimalism, *The Fifth Element* (1997) is a lavish intergalactic adventure starring Bruce Willis, Gary Oldman and Milla Jovovich. Willis portrays taxi driver Korben Dallas, who finds himself unexpectedly charged with the heroic mission to save the earth from destruction. The film's production design was handled by Jean 'Moebius' Giraud and Jean-Claude Mézières, who co-authored *Valérian and Laureline*.

With *Angel-A* (2005), Besson tells a Parisian-set fairy tale about salvation and true love.

In *Lucy* (2014), Besson cast Scarlett Johansson as the title character, whose psychokinetic powers intensify her perception of the world around her. It's arguably Besson's most overtly science-fiction movie yet.

In 2017, Besson returned to, and perhaps exceeded, the lavish scale of *The Fifth Element* with *Valerian and the City of a Thousand Planets*, his adaptation of the iconic French comic *Valérian and Laureline*.

Alongside his live-action science fiction, Besson has also directed a series of animated films, beginning with *Arthur and the Invisibles* (2006), in which a little boy shrinks to the tiniest of sizes and goes adventuring through the wilderness of a garden.

Of an overarching concept that appeals to him, Besson has observed: 'I'm always attracted by people who are lost in their time. I think it helps us.'

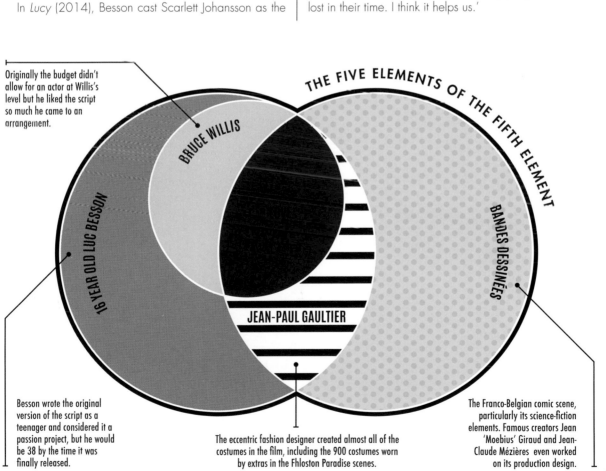

Originally the budget didn't allow for an actor at Willis's level but he liked the script so much he came to an arrangement.

THE FIVE ELEMENTS OF THE FIFTH ELEMENT

BRUCE WILLIS

16 YEAR OLD LUC BESSON

BANDES DESSINÉES

JEAN-PAUL GAULTIER

Besson wrote the original version of the script as a teenager and considered it a passion project, but he would be 38 by the time it was finally released.

The eccentric fashion designer created almost all of the costumes in the film, including the 900 costumes worn by extras in the Fhloston Paradise scenes.

The Franco-Belgian comic scene, particularly its science-fiction elements. Famous creators Jean 'Moebius' Giraud and Jean-Claude Mézières even worked on its production design.

SEAN CONNERY'S FIRST DAY OF FILMING
GOLDFINGER IN 1964

James Bond movies have variously touched on things geeky
and we might say that Q is the geek hero of the Bond world.

19 MARCH

SOLARIS WAS RELEASED ON THIS DAY IN 1972

Science fiction travels and it travels because, really, it's always about the one thing
that we all have in common: our humanity in all its strength and weakness.

20 MARCH

Solaris, by Polish writer Stanislaw Lem, is a novel that was published in 1961 and is essential to the science fiction genre. Such is the power of Lem's novel that, to date, it's been adapted twice into a major film: once in the Soviet Union by director Andrei Tarkovsky and once in America by Steven Soderbergh (2002).

Lem's novel centres on the following premise: a human encounter with alien life on the planet Solaris.

In writing the novel, Lem was seeking to reset expectations of what science fiction could be: a serious philosophical enquiry. After the death of Stalin in the mid 1950s, American science fiction made its way to communist Poland and Lem got himself up to speed with the genre. Recognising that the American take on the genre appeared to steer towards high adventure, he committed himself to showing how serious-minded science fiction could be.

Both film adaptations of the novel focus on psychologist Kris Kelvin, based on a space station circling Solaris. Kelvin is aboard to study the ocean on Solaris – but his dead wife then manifests.

Solaris, then, is rendered for films as a science-fiction love story. That's a combination also found in *Avatar* (2009) and *THX 1138* (1971) and *Passengers* (2016).

PANDORA
LEVEL 1 : GAIA STYLE ECO-SYSTEM HIVE MIND BUT UNABLE TO THINK.

SOLARIS
LEVEL 2: ABLE TO BRING BACK DEAD PEOPLE FROM SCANNING HUMAN MINDS BUT NOT NECESSARILY SENTIENT.

MOGO
LEVEL 3: POSSESSES SENTIENCE AND AN ABILITY TO CONTROL ITS OWN SURFACE, WHICH IS WHY THIS PLANET IS THE BIGGEST LONELIEST MEMBER OF THE GREEN LANTERN CORPS.

EGO THE LIVING PLANET
LEVEL 4: LIKE MOGO BUT WITH AN ACTUAL GIANT BEARDED FACE THAT CAN TALK. CAN ABSORB OTHER PLANETS FOR ENERGY.

UNICRON THE EVIL ROBOT PLANET
LEVEL 5: BASICALLY A ROBOTIC VERSION OF EGO, UNICRON IS DEDICATED TO CONSUMING ALL MATTER IN THE UNIVERSE AND CAN ALSO TRANSFORM INTO A GIANT PLANET-SIZED HUMANOID ROBOT.

FIRST EVER COMIC-CON
TAKES PLACE IN 1970

It was a friendship's shared enthusiasm for comics that spawned San Diego Comic-Con. Shel Dorf, Ken Krueger and Richard Alf, amongst others, launched the first Comic-Con on this day in 1970.

How could they have foreseen the geek behemoth it has become? Today it's a major entertainment destination, an oasis for geeks in a world that sometimes just doesn't understand what it's all about. The first Comic-Con was a one-day event attended by about 100 people. It's now an expansive four-day event, massively publicised and attended by around 13,000 fans each year.

21
MARCH

COMIC-CON ATTENDANCE

160'000
140'000
120'000
100'000
80'000
60'000
40'000
20'000
5'000
0

A B C D E F G

COMIC-CON YEAR

A
Mar 21	1970	145
Aug 1-3	1970	300
Aug 6-8	1971	800
Aug 18-21	1972	900+
Aug 16-19	1973	1,000+
July 31 - Aug 5	1974	2,500
July 30 - Aug 3	1975	2,500+
Nov 7-9	1975	1,100
July 21-25	1976	3,000+
July 20-24	1977	3,000+
July 26-30	1978	5,000+
Aug 1-5	1979	6,000
July 30 - Aug 3	1980	5,000
July 23-26	1981	5,000+
July 8-11	1982	5,000

B
Aug 4-7	1983	5,000
June 28-July 1	1984	5,500
Aug 1-4	1985	6,000
July 31-Aug 3	1986	6,500
Aug 6-9	1987	5,000
Aug 4-7	1988	8,000
Aug 3-6	1989	11'000

C
Aug 2-5	1990	13,000
July 4-7	1991	15,000+
Aug 13-16	1992	22,000
Aug 19-22	1993	28,000
Aug 4-7	1994	31,000

D
July 27-30	1995	34,000
July 4-7	1996	36,000
July 17-20	1997	40,000
Aug 13-16	1998	42,000
Aug 13-16	1999	42,000
July 20-23	2000	48,500

E
July 19-22	2001	53,000
Aug 1-4	2002	63,000
July 17-20	2003	70,000
July 22-25	2004	95,000

F
July 14-17	2005	103,000

G
July 20-23	2006	123,000
July 26-29	2007	125,000
July 24-27	2008	126,000
July 23-26	2009	126,000

H
July 22-25	2010	130,000+

I
July 21-24	2011	126,000+

J
July 12-15	2012	130,000+
July 18-21	2013	130,000+
July 24-27	2014	130,000+

K
July 9-12	2015	167,000
July 21-24	2016	167,000

COMIC-CON YEAR

ACTOR WILLIAM SHATNER WAS BORN IN 1931

22
MARCH

Most famous for his role as Captain James Tiberius Kirk in the original *Star Trek* TV series and subsequent feature films, Shatner also starred in one of the most well remembered episodes of *The Twilight Zone*: 'Nightmare at 20,000 Feet', as well as authoring a number of novels, beginning with *TekWar* set in Los Angeles in the 22nd century.

23
MARCH

KIM STANLEY ROBINSON WAS BORN IN 1952

Robinson's novels are major entries in the science-fiction literary canon. His *Mars* trilogy of novels – *Red Mars* (1993), *Green Mars* (1994) and *Blue Mars* (1996) – chart the experience of colonists to the red planet.

With a strong strain of ecological and philosophical thought running through them, Robinson's novels all offer a fresh take on reality.

In his novel *Galileo's Dream* (2009), he not only offers an account of Galileo's life and work, but also explores the ramifications of time travel.

Of life in the twenty-first century, Robinson has noted how much it is like living in a science-fiction novel.

FINAL EPISODE OF *ALF* IS BROADCAST IN 1990

ALF (or Alien Life Form, 1986–90) was the furry, conically nosed, kind-eyed alien companion of a suburban American family in the sitcom ALF, whose last episode aired on this date in 1990.

ALIEN DIETS IN POP CULTURE

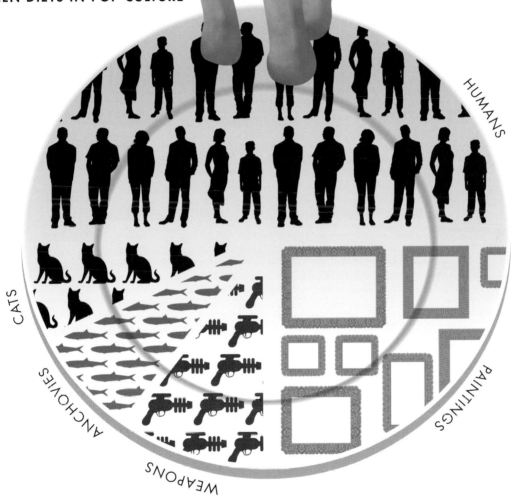

FINALE OF *THE POWERPUFF GIRLS* AIRED IN 2005

Geek girl culture is strong, and on this date in 2005 a geek girl classic aired its last TV episode: Powerpuff Girls.

Blossom, Bubbles and Buttercup were the crime-fighting toddlers collectively known as the Powerpuff Girls – the creation of Craig McCracken. Their manga-inspired design brought a freshness to American TV animation and in 2016 the series was rebooted.After *The Powerpuff Girls*, McCracken moved on to the TV series *Foster's Home for Imaginary Friends* (2004–09) and *Wander Over Yonder* (2013–16).

JAMES CAMERON REACHED THE BOTTOM OF THE MARIANA TRENCH IN 2012

The films of James Cameron have become so well known, and so much a part of geek film reference, that we might overlook their storytelling achievement: actors, visual effects and arresting sound and images in vivid combination.

Cameron's films not only offer believable and vividly imagined futures and other worlds, but they also carve out a space for the human interest amidst the intensely rendered artifice needed to bring the stories to life on screen. For all its technological marvel, *Avatar* (2009) zooms right in on a romantic love story, just as *The Terminator* (1984) and *The Abyss* (1989) do, too.

A Cameron film hero is marked by courage, resilience and an emphasis on action rather than words, responding with intelligence and determination to a crisis.

TITANIC: THE FINAL WORD WITH ...

THE LAST MYSTERIES OF THE TITANIC (2005), PRODUCER

VOLCANOES OF THE DEEP SEA (2003), EXECUTIVE PRODUCER

EXPEDITION: BISMARCK (2002), PRODUCER AND DIRECTOR

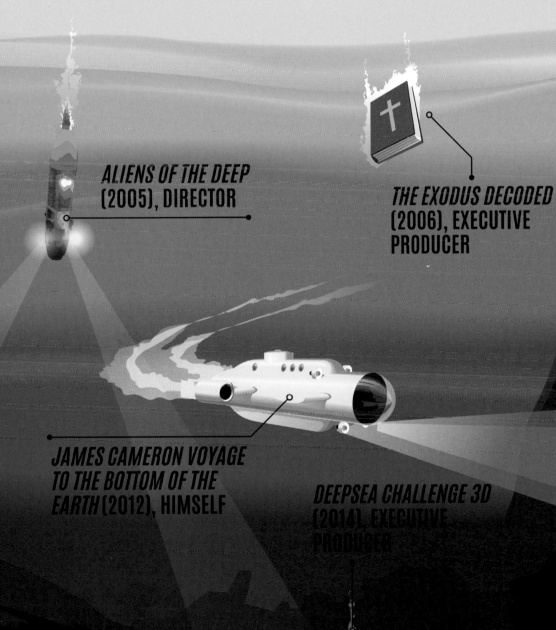

YEARS OF LIVING DANGEROUSLY (2014), EXECUTIVE PRODUCER

THE LOST TOMB OF JESUS (2007), EXECUTIVE PRODUCER

ALIENS OF THE DEEP (2005), DIRECTOR

THE EXODUS DECODED (2006), EXECUTIVE PRODUCER

JAMES CAMERON VOYAGE TO THE BOTTOM OF THE EARTH (2012), HIMSELF

DEEPSEA CHALLENGE 3D (2014), EXECUTIVE PRODUCER

ELIZABETH HOLLOWAY MARSTON DIES IN 1993

First published in 1941, in issue number 8 of *All Star Comics*, Wonder Woman challenged Fascism (like most American comic book heroes of the time) and fought for equal rights for women. Wonder Woman was the co-creation of a psychologist and his wife.

Marston's wife, Elizabeth Holloway, contributed significantly to *Wonder Woman*, a character who has channelled wider ideas about femininity, womanhood and the naturally superior quality of women over men.

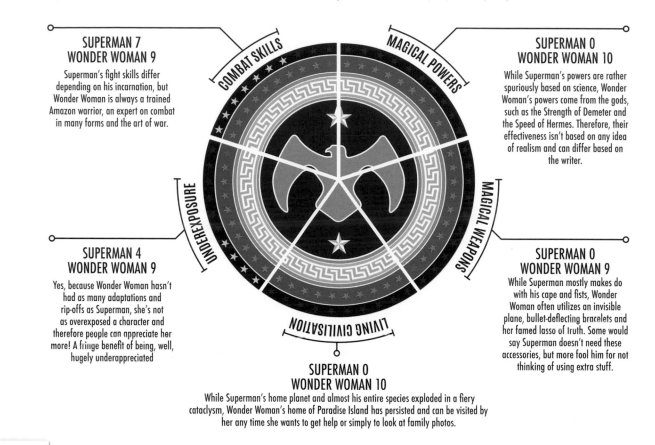

COMBAT SKILLS

SUPERMAN 7
WONDER WOMAN 9

Superman's fight skills differ depending on his incarnation, but Wonder Woman is always a trained Amazon warrior, an expert on combat in many forms and the art of war.

MAGICAL POWERS

SUPERMAN 0
WONDER WOMAN 10

While Superman's powers are rather spuriously based on science, Wonder Woman's powers come from the gods, such as the Strength of Demeter and the Speed of Hermes. Therefore, their effectiveness isn't based on any idea of realism and can differ based on the writer.

UNDEREXPOSURE

SUPERMAN 4
WONDER WOMAN 9

Yes, because Wonder Woman hasn't had as many adaptations and rip-offs as Superman, she's not as overexposed a character and therefore people can appreciate her more! A fringe benefit of being, well, hugely underappreciated

MAGICAL WEAPONS

SUPERMAN 0
WONDER WOMAN 9

While Superman mostly makes do with his cape and fists, Wonder Woman often utilizes an invisible plane, bullet-deflecting bracelets and her famed lasso of truth. Some would say Superman doesn't need these accessories, but more fool him for not thinking of using extra stuff.

LIVING CIVILISATION

SUPERMAN 0
WONDER WOMAN 10

While Superman's home planet and almost his entire species exploded in a fiery cataclysm, Wonder Woman's home of Paradise Island has persisted and can be visited by her any time she wants to get help or simply to look at family photos.

THE COMPUTER GAME *KINGDOM HEARTS* DEBUTS IN 2002

A hugely popular fusion of Japanese and American pop culture, *Kingdom Hearts* is a computer game series combining the worlds of *Final Fantasy* and *The World Ends With You* with the world of Disney animated characters, notably Mickey Mouse, Goofy and Donald Duck.

Sentimental, epic and whimsical, *Kingdom Hearts* is founded on a beat 'em up aesthetic, but is visually distinct thanks to its Disney-themed settings and 'guest' characters. A manga and novel series have extended the computer game experience.

SHAUN OF THE DEAD IS RELEASED IN 2004

Shaun of the Dead is a very British pastiche of the zombie movie. It combines the expected zombie elements with a romantic comedy.

75%
MACHINE GUNS

10%
CRICKET BAT

5%
MOLOTOV COCKTAIL

4%
CAR

2%
WINCHESTER RIFLE

1.5%
SHOVEL

1%
LAUNDRY POLE

0.7%
DARTS

0.5%
POOL CUES

0.2%
GARDEN FURNITURE

0.1%
THROWN RECORDS

WEAPON EFFECTIVENESS

BATMAN DEBUTS IN 1939 IN DETECTIVE COMICS NO.27 (COVER DATE MAY 1939)

Bob Kane's fabulously durable creation Batman is a sombre, Gothic, brooding symbol of the American city in the twentieth century.

VILLAIN EFFECTIVENESS, COMICS VS MODERN MOVIES

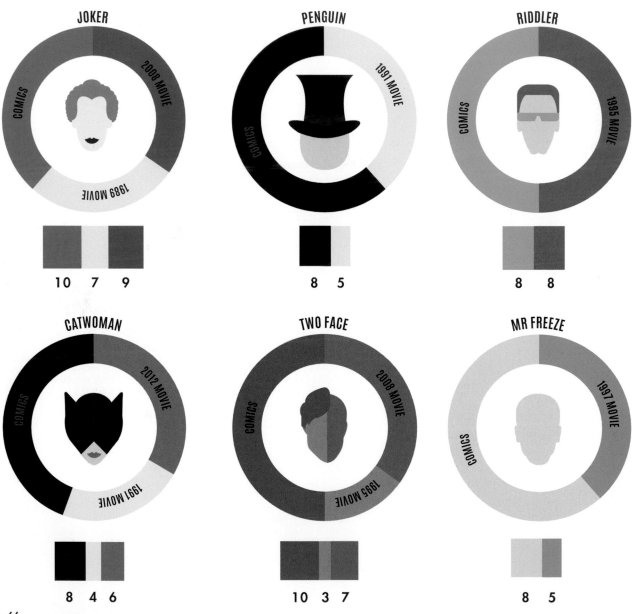

JOKER

COMICS · 2008 MOVIE · 1989 MOVIE

10 7 9

PENGUIN

COMICS · 1991 MOVIE

8 5

RIDDLER

COMICS · 1995 MOVIE

8 8

CATWOMAN

COMICS · 2012 MOVIE · 1991 MOVIE

8 4 6

TWO FACE

COMICS · 2008 MOVIE · 1995 MOVIE

10 3 7

MR FREEZE

COMICS · 1997 MOVIE

8 5

Violent, melancholy, compelled by anger and loss, Batman is the temperamental opposite to Superman. He is tortured, guilt-ridden, violent and civilized, brooding and hidden.

Kane and writer Bill Finger, created a comic-book hero who functioned in the tradition of characters such as Lee Falk's *The Phantom* (created in 1936) and Walter B. Gibson's *The Shadow* (1931).

Storylines that have defined Batman's comic-book heritage include *The Dark Knight Returns* (1986), *Batman: The Killing Joke* (1988) and *Arkham Asylum: A*

Serious House on Serious Earth (1999).

For many, Batman may be more well-known on account of the feature films produced since 1989.

Pop culture scholar Will Brooker has said of Batman that the character's appeal lies in how the 'the Batman image is open to … a multiplicity of readings.' Certainly, this goes some way to explaining the longstanding popularity of Batman in comics, films, TV programmes, animated series and computer games.

It seems that in the twenty-first century, we respond to his capacity for moral ambiguity.

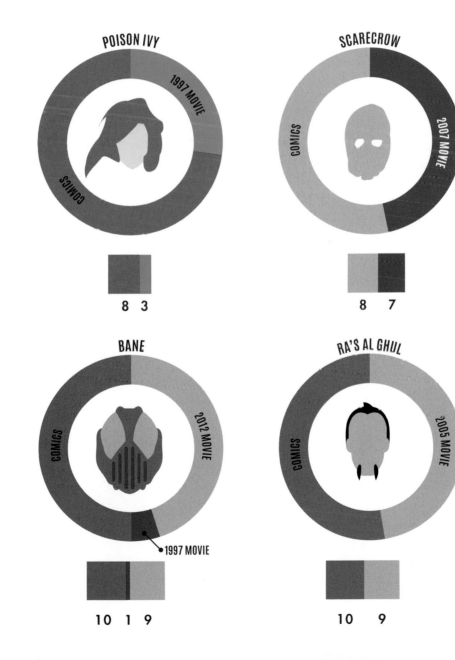

THE MATRIX WAS FIRST RELEASED IN 1999

The Matrix reset the science fiction film on the brink of the twenty-first century. A fable, action movie, and visual spectacle, it captured the zeitgeist around virtual realities and the information age. *The Matrix* was hugely successful and led to sequels: *The Matrix Reloaded* (2003) and *The Matrix Revolutions* (2003).

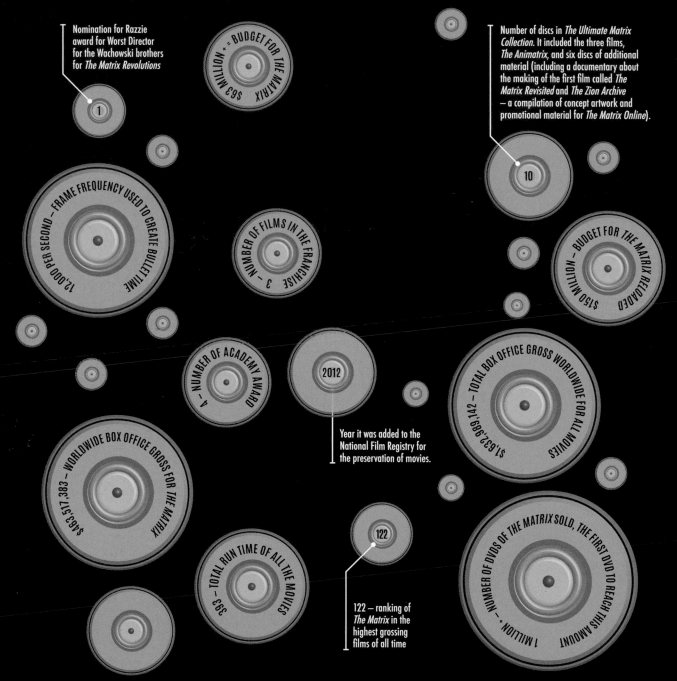

Nomination for Razzie award for Worst Director for the Wachowski brothers for *The Matrix Revolutions*

1

$63 MILLION + = BUDGET FOR THE MATRIX

Number of discs in *The Ultimate Matrix Collection*. It included the three films, *The Animatrix*, and six discs of additional material (including a documentary about the making of the first film called *The Matrix Revisited* and *The Zion Archive* — a compilation of concept artwork and promotional material for *The Matrix Online*).

10

12,000 PER SECOND – FRAME FREQUENCY USED TO CREATE BULLET TIME

3 – NUMBER OF FILMS IN THE FRANCHISE

$150 MILLION – BUDGET FOR THE MATRIX RELOADED

4 – NUMBER OF ACADEMY AWARD

2012

Year it was added to the National Film Registry for the preservation of movies.

$1,632,989,142 – TOTAL BOX OFFICE GROSS WORLDWIDE FOR ALL MOVIES

$463,517,383 – WORLDWIDE BOX OFFICE GROSS FOR THE MATRIX

393 – TOTAL RUN TIME OF ALL THE MOVIES

122

122 – ranking of *The Matrix* in the highest grossing films of all time

1 MILLION + – NUMBER OF DVDS OF THE MATRIX SOLD, THE FIRST DVD TO REACH THIS AMOUNT

PREMIERE OF THE COMIC *SIN CITY* IN 1991 BY DARK HORSE COMICS

With its stark blocks of black and white, and occasional bursts of colour, Frank Miller's *Sin City* brought a visceral, violent explosion of action to the comic book. *Sin City* refreshed the idea of comics for the older reader. Inflected by film noir, *Sin City* distilled the elements of the genre that had been part of Miller's earlier work *The Dark Knight Returns* (1986). Here was a version of chivalry in a rotten, corrupted world.

SPEED RACER ANIME TV SERIES BEGAN IN 1967

Created by Tatsuo Yoshida, *Speed Racer* was first a manga and then became a TV anime series. It was adapted into a Hollywood film in 2008. Written and directed by the Wachowski Brothers, it became a cult exercise in highly kinetic pure filmmaking: sound and colour in high-velocity combination.

COWBOY BEBOP PREMIERED IN 1998

Cowboy Bebop was an animated TV series that aired between 1998 and 1999 – and has been broadcast globally.

As the title suggests, it takes its cue from two staples of American pop culture: the Wild West and bebop jazz.

Set in the year 2071, a time when interplanetary travel is easy, the show wrapped up its heady content in vivid visuals and character designs as it charted the adventures of the bounty-hunter crew of the Bebop spaceship.

If proof were needed that animation – and, indeed, many things geek – is capable of substance, this TV series did the job. Each of the characters tie in with a specific philosophical viewpoint.

Spike Spiegel is the embodiment of a sustained existential angst. Faye Valentine seems defined by a sense of loneliness. Edward Wrong expresses an affinity for nature and Jet Black muses on karma.

Cowboy Bebop's enemies are various, but none is more notable than the character of Vicious. With his grey mop of hair and a hunger for power, he's something of a shadow form of Spike.

Perhaps the only character to be truly at peace is Ein, the Welsh Corgi who displays quite stunning levels of intelligence.

THE AMERICAN ROCKET SOCIETY IS FORMED IN 1930

Rockets have blasted their way across movies, comics, computer games and novels.

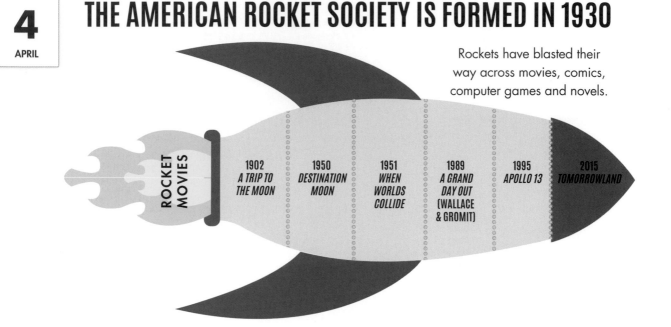

ROCKET MOVIES

1902
A TRIP TO THE MOON

1950
DESTINATION MOON

1951
WHEN WORLDS COLLIDE

1989
A GRAND DAY OUT (WALLACE & GROMIT)

1995
APOLLO 13

2015
TOMORROWLAND

IN *STAR TREK*, EARTH'S FIRST CONTACT WITH VULCAN SPECIES HAPPENED IN 2063

It's one of the great dramatic moments that sci-fi and fantasy genres have relished depicting: the moment of 'culture contact' between human and alien life. It's been a constant of literature, films and comics – from George Méliès' *A Trip to the Moon* (1902) and James Cameron's *Avatar* (2009) through to Ray Bradbury's *The Martian Chronicles* (1950) and Arthur C. Clarke's *Rendezvous with Rama* (1973).

Jack Kirby, the legendary American comic-book artist, worried that human efforts to contact aliens might result in unwanted extraterrestrial attention. It's this premise that makes the films *War of the Worlds* (2005) and *Independence Day* (1996) tick while the TV series *Falling Skies* (2011–15), charts human loyalties and tensions in the face of alien invasion. In the classic *The Day the Earth Stood Still*, (1951), an alien visitor to Earth advocates peace for humankind, warning that otherwise we face destruction for being a threat to other planets.

In Carl Sagan's novel *Contact* (1985), otherworldly encounters take us back to our essential humanity.

IN 648BCE, GREEKS RECORD FIRST KNOWN SOLAR ECLIPSE

Mark Twain Natural celestial phenomena as useful plot devices feature in the novel *Nightfall* (1990), written by Robert Silverberg and based on a short story by Isaac Asimov, and in the films *Fantasia* (1940) and *Ladyhawke*

GEEK GIRL COMIC *LUMBERJANES* HAD ITS FIRST COLLECTED VOLUME PUBLISHED IN 2015

Geek girl culture has come into its own in recent years. Characters that have fired up geek girl culture include Ramona Flowers from the *Scott Pilgrim* comics and Madame Vastra in *Doctor Who*. Other icons include Mystique, associated with the X-Men, and the sword and sorcery heroine of 1990s TV, *Xena: Warrior Princess*.

A key voice in geek girl culture has been the Australian writer Rosie X (Rosie Cross), and other notable geek girls include Felicia Day, Amy Ratcliffe and Bonnie Burton.

Returning to *Lumberjanes*: it's become a breakout comic sensation with its story about a group of girls who have gone to a wilderness camp. During their time at the camp the girls have all kinds of otherworldly encounters.

IN 1990 THE DAVID LYNCH AND MARK FROST SERIES *TWIN PEAKS* WAS FIRST BROADCAST

Without it, we might not have enjoyed the renaissance of American TV in recent years. Created by Mark Frost and David Lynch, *Twin Peaks* proved that TV drama could get weird and wonderful. It ran for two seasons, and Lynch then wrapped up the story with the feature film *Twin Peaks: Fire Walk With Me* (1992).

With its melancholy musical theme by Angelo Badalamenti, *Twin Peaks* followed FBI Agent Dale Cooper (Kyle Maclachlan) as he investigated the murder of Laura Palmer in Twin Peaks, a backwoods town populated by a spectrum of offbeat characters such as the Log Lady, Leland Palmer and Nadine Hurley.

Twin Peaks stands as a classic of American TV, taking an 'all-American' setting and giving it a suitable Lynchian twist. In May 2017, a new series launched, Lynch and producer Mark Frost collaborating once more.

IN 1959, THE SEVEN PILOTS WHO WILL BE THE PROTOTYPE AMERICAN ASTRONAUTS ON THE MERCURY PROJECT ARE REVEALED

What does a geek aspire to be? And what is the inspiration? Tim Peake, the British astronaut, explained in 2016 that seeing the film *E.T. the Extra-Terrestrial* captured his imagination so intensely that he knew what work he wanted to do. *Per ardua ad astra!*

HOUSE OF WAX WAS RELEASED IN 1953

3D was first deployed in the 1950s by the Hollywood studios, and *House of Wax* was the first to be shot in colour. In the 1980s, the format enjoyed a brief resurgence with *Metalstorm: The Destruction of Jared Syn* (1983), *Starchaser: The Legend of Orin* (1985) and *Jaws 3-D* (1983). In 1986, Disney produced the Michael Jackson 3D music short, *Captain EO*.

In the mid-2000s, the format resurfaced, the emphasis less on things apparently flying out of the screen and much more about the illusion of depth, pulling the audience into an environment. *Avatar* (2009), *Coraline* (2009), *A Christmas Carol* (2009) and *Alice in Wonderland* (2010) were memorable uses of the format.

FILM-MAKER JOHN MILIUS WAS BORN IN 1944

Milius co-wrote the screenplay for the film *Conan the Barbarian* (1982) and directed it, too. He has contributed a number of well-recognised lines of dialogue to films such as *Apocalypse Now* (1979), *Jaws* (1975) and *Dirty Harry* (1971). Most famous, in science-fiction terms, is the phrase 'Beam me up, Scotty.' This was never spoken in *Star Trek*. What was said was 'Beam us up, Mr Scott,' which was uttered in the 'Gamesters of Triskelion' episode of the series in 1968. Similarly, the following line in 'The Devil in the Dark' episode of *Star Trek*, was never spoken by Mr Spock: 'It's life , Jim, but not as we know it.'

MAD MAX PREMIERED IN 1979 IN AUSTRALIA

Loner and inadvertent adventurer, Max Rockatansky follows a classic hero's journey as he becomes a post-apocalyptic saviour. The franchise depicts a world in which Max helps the downtrodden rise to defeat the tyrants of the world.

MAX'S ALLIES AND ENEMIES

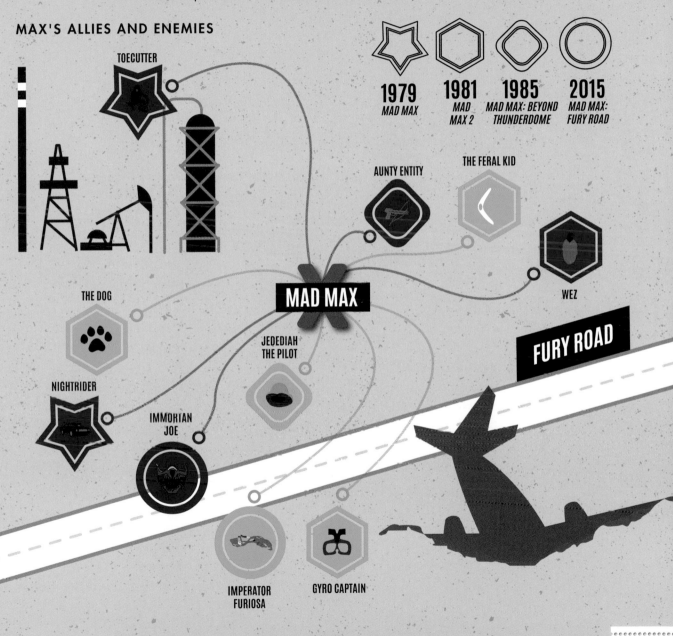

1979
MAD MAX

1981
MAD MAX 2

1985
MAD MAX: BEYOND THUNDERDOME

2015
MAD MAX: FURY ROAD

TOECUTTER

AUNTY ENTITY

THE FERAL KID

WEZ

MAD MAX

THE DOG

JEDEDIAH THE PILOT

FURY ROAD

NIGHTRIDER

IMMORIAN JOE

IMPERATOR FURIOSA

GYRO CAPTAIN

THE WORD MICROSCOPE IS COINED IN 1625

The Incredible Shrinking Man (1957), *Innerspace* (1987) and *Honey, I Shrunk The Kids* (1989) – all movies with humans made miniature, allowing them the chance to see the world afresh.

DAN DARE MADE FIRST APPEARED IN 1950

14 APRIL

Introduced to readers of the newly published *Eagle* comic in 1950, Dare was thoroughly British with his sense of honour and fair play. Of his challenges none was bigger than the Mekon.

Created by Frank Hampson – aided by a young writer named Arthur C. Clarke – *Dan Dare: Pilot of the Future,* was massively popular. He is to British geek comic culture what Flash Gordon is to American.

LEONARDO DA VINCI WAS BORN IN 1452

15 APRIL

Mikey, Raph, Donnie, Leo are the subterranean dwelling Teenage Mutant Ninja Turtles, each named for a Renaissance artist. The Turtles are major geek culture figures.

TEENAGE MUTANT NINJA TURTLES: OUT OF THE SHADOWS (2016) $244,451,601

TEENAGE MUTANT NINJA TURTLES (2014) $485,004,754

TMNT (2007) $96,096,018

TEENAGE MUTANT NINJA TURTLES II: THE SECRET OF THE OOZE (1991) $78,656,813

TEENAGE MUTANT NINJA TURTLES (1990) $202,000,000

TEENAGE MUTANT NINJA TURTLES III (1993) $42,273,609

TURTLES BOX OFFICE PIZZA PIE CHART

THE FILM *KILL BILL VOL. 2* WAS RELEASED IN 2004

In *Kill Bill Volumes 1 and 2*, Uma Thurman stars as the Bride, a distillation of the action movie heroine. The Bride is one of an ever-expanding sisterhood: Sigourney Weaver as Ellen Ripley, Linda Hamilton as Sarah Connor, Angela Bassett as Mace, Daisy Ridley as Rey, Milla Jovovich as Alice, Saoirse Ronan as Hanna, Jennifer Lawrence as Katniss Everdeen, Angelina Jolie as Lara Croft and Carrie Fisher as Princess Leia.

FLORENCE CARPENTER DIEUDONNÉ DIED IN 1927

Whilst her name is little known to most, American writer Florence Carpenter Dieudonné wrote a novel entitled *Rondah* (aka *Thirty-Three Years in a Star*) in which a mountain becomes a spaceship transporting the novel's characters to an asteroid and an encounter with the alien race who reside there. Dieudonné's novel is recognized as anticipating the very popular space opera mode of science fiction in the 20th century.

GAME OF THRONES PREMIERED ON UK TV IN 2011

For as long as visual effects have made lavish, high-fantasy landscapes and creatures more affordable to create, there have been increasingly spectacular realisations of high-fantasy novels reaching the movie and TV screens.

On TV, no series is more high profile than *Game of Thrones*, the vividly realized adaptation of George R.R.Martin's series of novels, bracketed under the title of *A Song of Ice and Fire*. The series is set in the fantasy realm of Westeros and focuses on seven dynastic houses as they view to maintain their lineage and power position in the hierarchy of Westeros.

THE SIMPSONS FIRST AIRED IN 1987

The Simpsons, a perennial geek favourite first appeared in a series of shorts on *The Tracey Ullman Show*. Matt Groening, creator of *The Simpsons*, would go on to create the animated sci-fi series *Futurama* with David X Cohen.

MAGGIE

Singer ('Holidays of Future Passed', 'Lisa's Wedding') 40%
Pregnant ('Holidays of Future Passed') 10%
Married to Gerald aka The Unibrow Baby ('Bart to the Future', 'Holidays of Future Passed') 40%
Living in Alaska ('Future-Drama') 10%

HOMER

Dead ('Days of Future Future') 20%
Cloned then on a flash drive ('Days of Future Future') 20%
Sober ('Holidays of Future Passed') 20%
Divorced ('Future-Drama') 20%
With plunger on his head ('The Front') 20%

BART

Deadbeat ('Days of Future Future, Holidays of Future Passed', 'Bart to the Future', 'Lisa's Wedding') 33.3%
Working at the Kwik-E-Mart ('Future-Drama') 8.4%
Supreme Court Justice ('Itchy & Scratch: The Movie') 8.4%
Artist/Musician ('Barthood', 'Bart to the Future') 16.6%
Divorced ('Days of Future Future', 'Holidays of Future Passed', 'Lisa's Wedding') 24.9%
Taste tester ('Whacking Day') 8.4%

SIMPSONS IN THE FUTURE

LISA

President ('Bart to the Future') 9%
Married to/Dating Milhouse Van Houten ('Holidays of Future Passed', 'Future-Drama', 'Days of Future Future', 'Future-Drama') 37%
Married to Ralph Wiggum ('Lisa the Simpson') 9%
Engaged to Hugh Parkfield ('Lisa's Wedding') 9%
Dating Nelson Muntz ('Barthood', 'Holidays of Future Passed') 18%
Business Woman ('Holidays of Future Passed') 9%
Going to Yale ('Future-Drama') 9%

MARGE

Trapped in a TV screen ('Days of Future Future') 33.33%
Divorced ('Future-Drama') 33.33%
Dating Krusty the Clown ('Future-Drama') 33.33%

'THE MURDERS IN THE RUE MORGUE' BY EDGAR ALLAN POE WAS PUBLISHED IN 1841

Edgar Allan Poe didn't only give us the melancholy and sometimes gruesome American Gothic of stories such as 'The Tell Tale Heart' and 'The Raven', he also contributed to launching the detective genre with his story 'The Murders on the Rue Morgue'.

THE *DAILY MAIL* PUBLISHED THE MOST NOTORIOUS PHOTO OF THE LOCH NESS MONSTER IN 1934

The Loch Ness Monster has fed our fascination with the idea of unidentified beasts in our midst. The Loch Ness Monster, or Nessie, as it is affectionately dubbed, has featured in the film *Loch Ness* (1996), Disney's short animated piece *The Ballad of Nessie* (2011) and *The Water Horse: Legend of the Deep* (2008).

MANGA TITLE, *THE WONDERFUL WORLD OF SAZAE-SAN*, WAS PUBLISHED IN 1946

The Wonderful World of Sazae-San was one of the earliest manga titles. Manga has established itself as vital part of Japanese otaku culture, and since the late 1970s and early 1980s, has found increasing readership in the West.

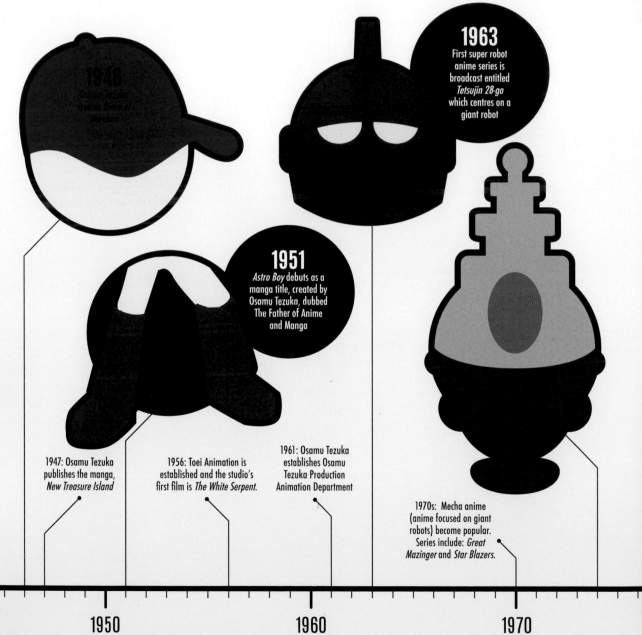

1946
Osamu Tezuka creates *Diary of Ma-chan*

1963
First super robot anime series is broadcast entitled *Tetsujin 28-go* which centres on a giant robot

1951
Astro Boy debuts as a manga title, created by Osamu Tezuka, dubbed The Father of Anime and Manga

1947: Osamu Tezuka publishes the manga, *New Treasure Island*

1956: Toei Animation is established and the studio's first film is *The White Serpent*.

1961: Osamu Tezuka establishes Osamu Tezuka Production Animation Department

1970s: Mecha anime (anime focused on giant robots) become popular. Series include: *Great Mazinger* and *Star Blazers*.

1950

1960

1970

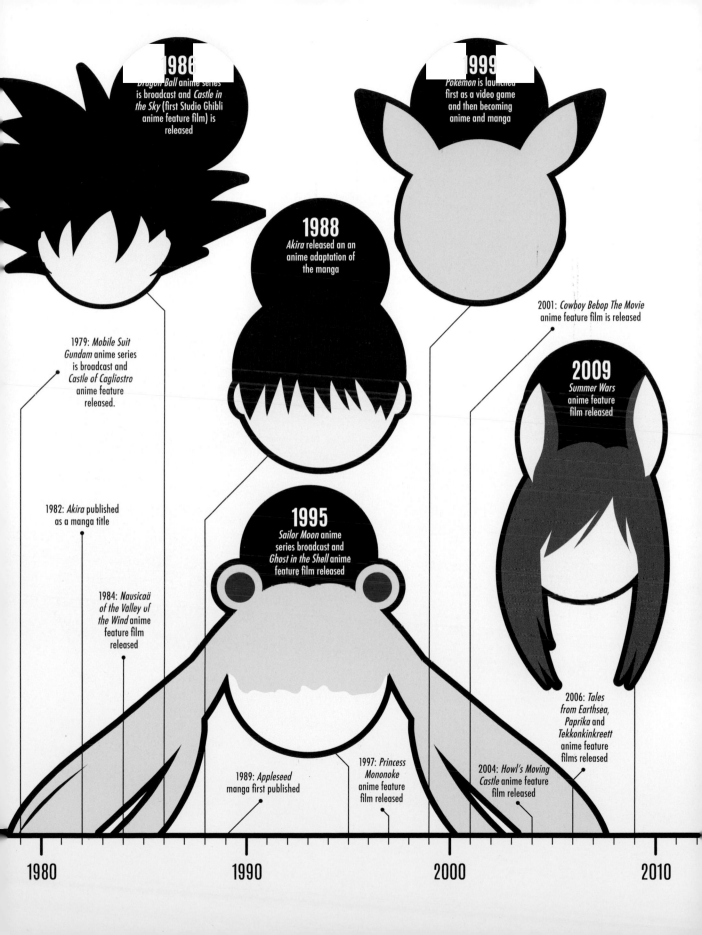

1986
Dragon Ball anime series is broadcast and *Castle in the Sky* (first Studio Ghibli anime feature film) is released

1999
Pokemon is launched first as a video game and then becoming anime and manga

1988
Akira released an an anime adaptation of the manga

2001: *Cowboy Bebop The Movie* anime feature film is released

1979: *Mobile Suit Gundam* anime series is broadcast and *Castle of Cagliostro* anime feature released.

2009
Summer Wars anime feature film released

1982: *Akira* published as a manga title

1995
Sailor Moon anime series broadcast and *Ghost in the Shell* anime feature film released

1984: *Nausicaä of the Valley of the Wind* anime feature film released

2006: *Tales from Earthsea*, *Paprika* and *Tekkonkinkreett* anime feature films released

1989: *Appleseed* manga first published

1997: *Princess Mononoke* anime feature film released

2004: *Howl's Moving Castle* anime feature film released

1980   1990   2000   2010

WILLIAM SHAKESPEARE DIES IN 1616

Shakespeare's play *The Tempest* (1611), possibly the last that he wrote, tells the story of a magician shipwrecked with his daughter on a magical island. It became the basis for science fiction film *Forbidden Planet* (1956) with Robby, the Robot the hi-tech embodiment of Shakespeare's character Ariel.

More recently, George Lucas went into all-out fantasy and fairy tale mode with the story that became the animated musical *Strange Magic* (2015). It was significantly influenced by Shakespeare's *A Midsummer Night's Dream* (1595/96) and combined with Lucas's familiar enthusiasm for depicting the hero's journey.

Writer Neil Gaiman also took the premise of *A Midsummer Night's Dream* and reimagined it in the story *Dream Country* (1991, part of the comic book series *The Sandman*). In Gaiman's take, the core of Shakespeare's play, allows him to explore the enchanted relationship between storyteller and audience.

SHAKESPEARE'S FORBIDDEN PLANET

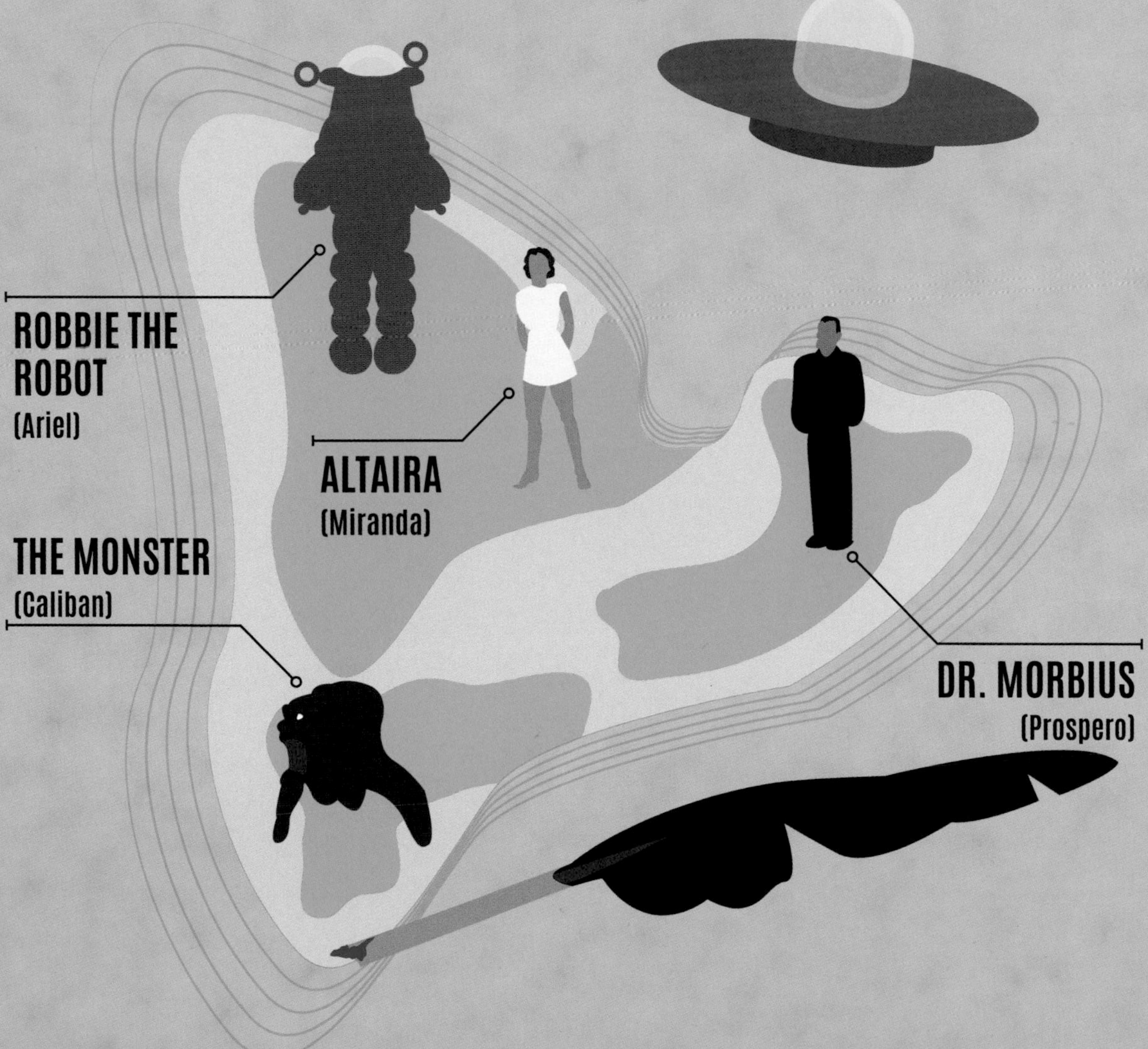

ROBBIE THE ROBOT
(Ariel)

ALTAIRA
(Miranda)

THE MONSTER
(Caliban)

DR. MORBIUS
(Prospero)

ANTHONY TROLLOPE WAS BORN IN 1815

Best-known for his *Chronicles of Barsetshire* (1855–1867) series which focused on English society, British novelist Trollope did write one science fiction novel. First published in instalments in *Blackwood's Magazine* in 1881–82 and as a novel in 1882, *The Fixed Period* is set in a dystopian 1980 on a fictional island called the Republic of Britannula and centres around questions of mortality and euthanasia.

ALBERT UDERZO WAS BORN IN 1927

Goscinny and Uderzo are legends of European comic culture. Their creations, Asterix the Gaul and his friend Obelix, are major European comic-book heroes. The series's amusing tales of intrepid Gauls resisting the might of the Roman Empire has been a staple of European readers for decades.

Settling down with an Asterix adventure has always promised a good time. Stories include *Asterix the Gaul* (1959), *Asterix and the Golden Sickle* (1960), *Asterix in Britain* (1965) and *Asterix and the Big Fight* (1964). Word play, humour for children and for older readers, along with and plenty of visual humour and whimsy characterize the Asterix adventures. Visual jokes and word play, as well as a humour that works for both children and older readers, characterise the Asterix adventures.

IN 1912 CANADIAN A.E. VAN VOGT WAS BORN

Van Vogt was to become a major player on the North American science-fiction scene and the magazine *Astounding Science Fiction* was his first major showcase.

Like F.E. 'Doc' Smith and Alex Raymond, van Vogt was a space opera specialist. Van Vogt's first novel was *Slan* (1946) and other novels went on to explore time travel, human contact with alien life and the fascinations of human psychology all brought a richness to van Vogt's fiction. In his novel *The Weapon Shops of Isher* (1951), van Vogt's affinity for the space opera mode was on full display. In his 1948 novel *The World of Null-A*, van Vogt explored ideas about memory and personal identity. The book was so popular in France that it somewhat rekindled the country's fascination with the science fiction genre.

THE FILM ADAPTATION OF *THE DAY OF THE TRIFFIDS* WAS RELEASED IN THE US IN 1963

This feature film version of John Wyndham's novel was a
British adaptation that is held in high regard to this day.

VILLAGE OF THE DAMNED WAS RELEASED IN 1995

John Carpenter's film adaptation (1995) of John Wyndham's novel starred Christopher
Reeve, who had become famous for his portrayal of Superman. When Reeve was
injured in a horse-jumping accident in spring that same year, this film heroism was
soon eclipsed by his real-life heroism as he dealt with the injuries sustained.

Reeve's angular face framed blue eyes that shone with an integrity just right for his landmark portrayal of the last son of Krypton in *Superman: The Movie* (1978). Perhaps even more affecting was his portrayal of Clark Kent: the scene in which he is introduced to Lois Lane hit just the right rom-com note in a superhero extravaganza.

It was the frailty of Superman that Reeve got so right: in *Superman II* (1980), Reeve powerfully communicates Superman's newfound frailty when he surrenders his natural-born powers for the love of Lois.

Reeve appeared in other films, but it was as Big Blue that he is best remembered. When Lois asks who Superman is, he replies: 'A friend', before then arcing high into the night sky, his smile capturing Superman's kindness for the ages.

THE LAST EPISODE OF *BATTLESTAR GALACTICA* AIRED ON AMERICAN TV IN 1979

Battlestar Galactica was the first major series to be produced
for American TV after the success of *Star Wars*.

Lasting just one season, between 1978 and 1979, it told the story of the crew of the Battlestar *Galactica* attempting to return home to Earth. The crew of the ship is endlessly engaged by the enemy forces of the Cylons. The series was briefly revived in 1980 and then rebooted in 2004, running for four series.

For some very observant and well-informed viewers, the 2004 reboot of *Battlestar Galactica* works as a parallel, space adventure spin on the Roman epic poem *The Aeneid* by Virgil.

MR POTATO HEAD WAS THE FIRST TOY ADVERTISED ON TV IN 1952

With *Toy Story*, Pixar Animation Studio launched into the feature film business, and Mr. Potato Head offers the voice of experience and a true romantic.

Since that release in 1995, Pixar has produced films that have made important contributions to the evolution of animation. Humorous and sentimental, with evident creative debts to Hayao Miyazaki, Walt Disney, Chuck Jones and Jim Henson, Pixar's films have become a brand that's globally recognised.

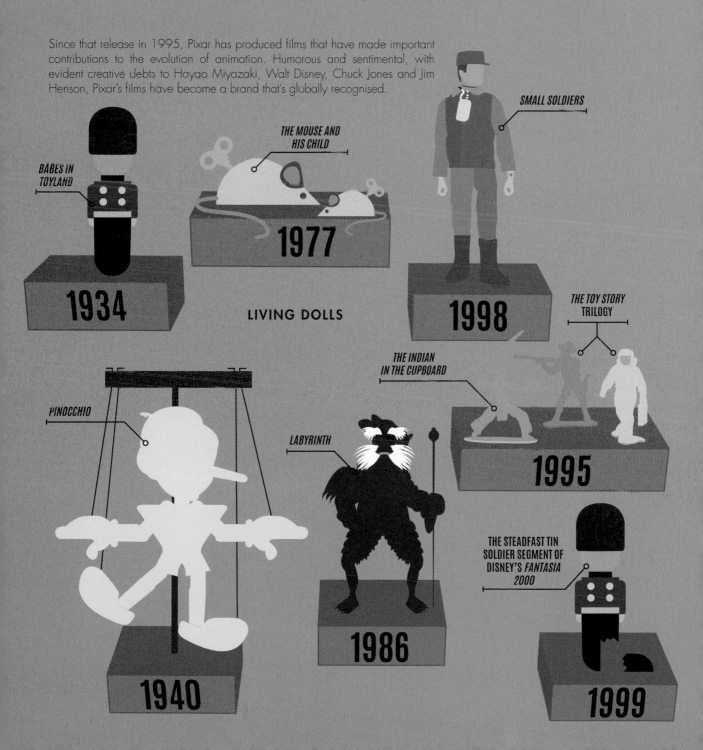

BABES IN TOYLAND

THE MOUSE AND HIS CHILD

SMALL SOLDIERS

1934

1977

LIVING DOLLS

1998

THE TOY STORY TRILOGY

THE INDIAN IN THE CUPBOARD

1995

PINOCCHIO

LABYRINTH

THE STEADFAST TIN SOLDIER SEGMENT OF DISNEY'S *FANTASIA 2000*

1940

1986

1999

J. ALLEN HYNEK WAS BORN IN 1910

J. Allen Hynek's definition of what constitutes a close encounter is now almost a household term, thank to Spielberg's film *Close Encounters of the Third Kind* (1977).

The film is also responsible for a galaxy of Spielberg-specific aliens. There's the beneficent Puck, a visitor who anticipates E.T. in Spielberg's later film. In his adaptation of *War of the Worlds* (2005), the aliens are very much less kind-hearted and in *Indiana Jones and the Kingdom of the Crystal Skull* (2008), the briefly seen aliens are a hive mind that punishes those who abuse knowledge for their own gain.

Intriguingly, Spielberg contemplated a sequel to *Close Encounters of the Third Kind* in which the aliens would have been much more menacing: the concept was for them to besiege a farm house. The project was provisionally entitled *Night Skies*, and in 2015, makeup artist and creature designer Rick Baker unveiled a number of designs that he had developed for the project.

HARKER'S JOURNEY TO TRANSYLVANIA

MUNICH TRAIN STATION
MÜNCHEN HBF

VIENNA TRAIN STATION
WESTBAHNHOF

GERMANY

AUSTRIA

THE SERIES *V* FINISHES IN 1983

Aliens in disguise as humans is an idea with a powerful appeal. It compels us to look and taps into how easily unsettled we can be by difference. V was massively popular. Created by Kenneth Johnson, *V* was his second major science fiction TV success after *The Bionic Woman* (1976–78).

JONATHAN HARKER HEADS TO TRANSYLVANIA

Bram Stoker's novel *Dracula* (1897) has been a mother lode of inspiration for vampire stories on screen, in novels, in comics and on TV.

True Blood, the American Gothic TV series (2008–14), traded on the longstanding connection between sexuality and vampires, as did Francis Coppola's feature film adaptation in 1992.

The vampire mythology fuses romance, violence and death into a brooding mass. Even Batman has confronted Dracula, in a three-part series published in 1991.

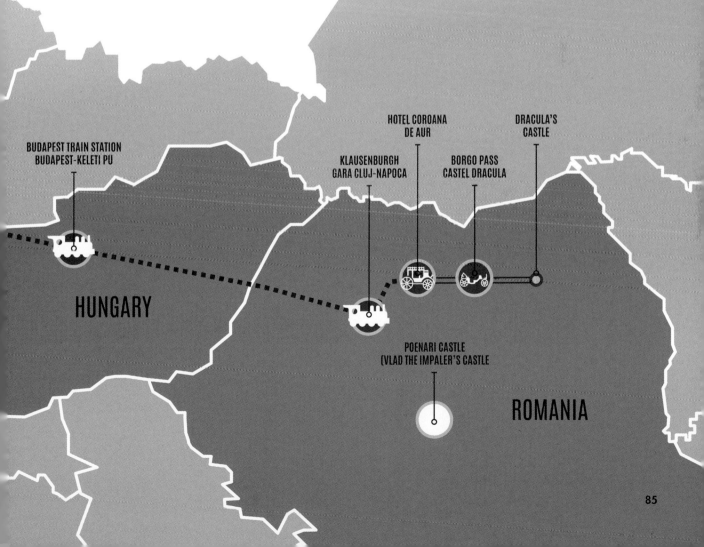

THE HOUND OF THE BASKERVILLES, PRODUCED BY HAMMER FILMS, WAS RELEASED IN 1959

Hammer Films are essential to the film landscape of British geekdom.

Founded in 1934, Hammer became synonymous with horror and fantasy genre movies. The breakthrough for Hammer was its production of the feature film *The Quatermass Xperiment* (1955), directed by horror specialist Val Guest.

The studio would go on to steady commercial success, producing a number of now classic films: *The*

Curse of Frankenstein (1957), *Dracula* (1958), *The Mummy* (1959), *The Curse of the Werewolf* (1961) and *Dracula: Prince of Darkness* (1966).

The studio stopped producing horror films in 1976 but it has now been rebooted for the twenty-first century. *The Woman In Black* (2012), starring Daniel Radcliffe, was a surefire hit.

1955
THE QUATERMASS XPERIMENT

MODE OF DEATH
Electrocution of Caroon

1957
THE CURSE OF FRANKENSTEIN

MODE OF DEATH
Death by flaming
oil lantern

1972
DRACULA AD

MODE OF DEATH
A pit of stakes

1960
THE BRIDES OF DRACULA

MODE OF DEATH
Windmill sails in the form of a cross with this to vanquish Baroness Meinster the vampire

1959
THE MUMMY

MODE OF DEATH
Gunfire and quagmire

1968
THE DEVIL RIDES OUT

MODE OF DEATH
Divine judgement

IN 2011 THE SMITHSONIAN ANNOUNCED THE LINE UP FOR THE ART OF VIDEO GAMES

Created by Swedish game designer Markus 'Notch' Persson, Minecraft is based on the concept of players building environments within which characters can be played. Simple but successful!

5
NUMBER OF MODES

121
MILLION - NUMBER OF COPIES
SOLD AS OF FEBRUARY 2017

7,500
NUMBER OF
ATTENDEES AT
MINECON 2013

53,000
COPIES SOLD PER DAY (JUNE 2016)

10,502
NUMBER OF BLOCKS IN LONGEST
TUNNEL EVER CREATED

$10m+
NUMBER OF REGISTERED
USERS BEFORE GAME WAS
OFFICIALLY RELEASED

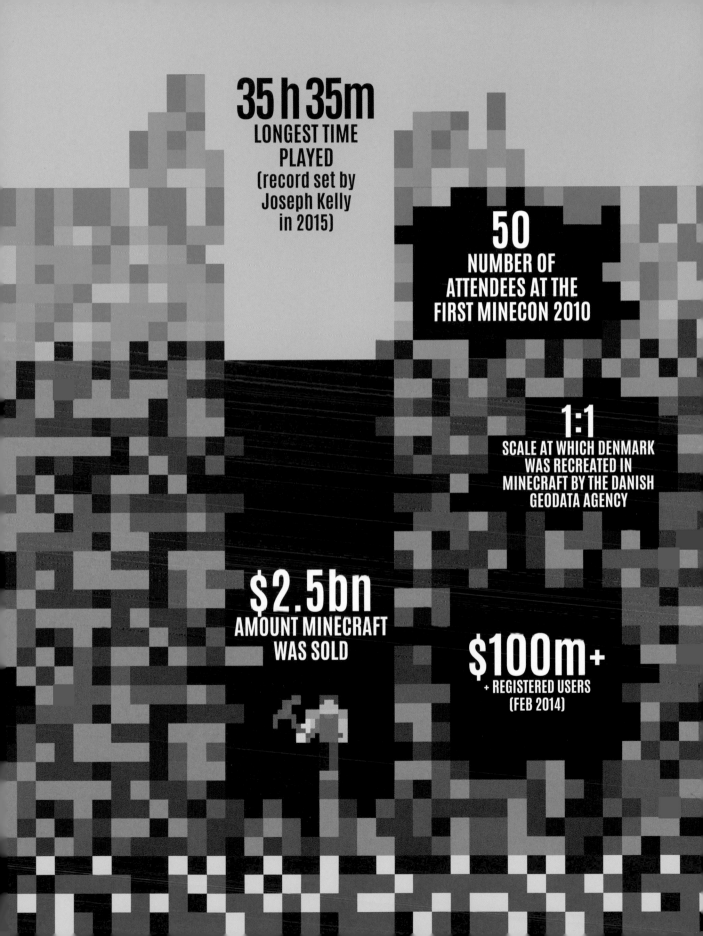

35 h 35m
LONGEST TIME
PLAYED
(record set by
Joseph Kelly
in 2015)

50
NUMBER OF
ATTENDEES AT THE
FIRST MINECON 2010

1:1
SCALE AT WHICH DENMARK
WAS RECREATED IN
MINECRAFT BY THE DANISH
GEODATA AGENCY

$2.5bn
AMOUNT MINECRAFT
WAS SOLD

$100m+
+ REGISTERED USERS
(FEB 2014)

ACTOR GEORGE CLOONEY WAS BORN IN 1961

George Clooney's suave screen persona has been playfully subverted in his collaborations with Joel and Ethan Coen and never more so than in *O Brother Where Art Thou?* (2000). In this movie, Clooney portrays Ulysses Everett McGill (Everett McGill is, in fact, the name of an actor who appeared in David Lynch's movie *Dune*) attempting to get back to his estranged wife and daughters, having escaped from a chain gang.

Clooney has also appeared in several genre-savvy films. In *From Dusk till Dawn* (1996), he and screen sibling Quentin Tarantino battle vampires in a Mexican bar. In *Solaris* (2002), Clooney portrays haunted Chris Kelvin, emotionally wrought and alone aboard a spaceship.

Most recently, in *Tomorrowland* (2015), Clooney portrays a jaded inventor who returns to a place where he had once excelled. Clooney's facility for both straight drama and comedy (both subtle and broad) brings warmth to the fanciful situations.

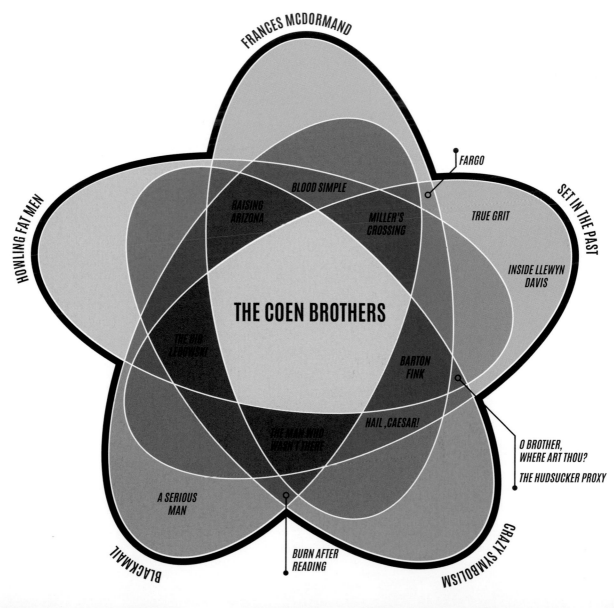

THE TIME MACHINE WAS PUBLISHED IN 1895

H.G.Wells once commented that 'Human history becomes more and more a race between education and catastrophe.' *The Time Machine* was Wells' first major novel, partially set in the year 802, 701. In the final years of the nineteenth century he published a run of science fiction novels: *The Island of Dr Moreau* (1896), *The Invisible Man* (1897) and *The War of the Worlds* (1898). His science fiction novels each use the genre to comment on reality.

JEAN 'MOEBIUS' GIRAUD IS BORN

If you like your comic books with a strong strain of the metaphysical coursing through them, look no further than the work of French comic book titan, Jean Giraud. Or, as you might more typically see him named: Moebius. Of his pen-name, Giraud pretty much encapsulated the spirit of his work when he explained that: 'Going from Giraud to Moebius, I twisted the strip; changed dimension. I was the same and yet someone else.'

At age 22, Moebius broke through with the innovative form of the adult graphic novel and allied visual dynamism with a metaphysical interest. Combining an often striking azure colour palette with intricate and elegant lines, Moebius's visual style became immediately identifiable. His work appeared in *Metal Hurlant* (the magazine that he co-launched), with the American underground comic movement of the 1970s fuelling international recognition of his art.

Paradoxically, Moebius's esoteric, off-the-beaten track take on comics led him into the mainstream moviemaking world during the late 1970s and 1980s; he was commissioned to develop film concept art for *Alien*, *Tron*, *Masters of the Universe*, *Willow* and *The Abyss*. During this time, Moebius also collaborated with American comic maestro Stan Lee on a two-part *Silver Surfer* miniseries entitled *Parable*.

Moebius's visionary work included the surreal series *The Airtight Garage* (1976) which he described the series as 'a research laboratory' for his ideas; each installment happily bearing no sign whatsoever of a traditional storyline. Then, too, there was *The Long Tomorrow*, a title that massively influenced the look of the film *Blade Runner*.

One of Moebius's most iconic titles was the stunning *Arzach*, a series depicting the adventures of a pterodactyl and its human rider.

Moebius had a profound interest in all things mystical and this sensibility is evident in every panel of his luminous, intricate, surreal and transporting images.

Moebius worked for fifty years as a comic book artist and he died in 2012.

But there is no question about his influence: European comic culture is wide and deep and fascinating; reminding us just how mind-altering science fiction and fantasy can be. Moebius was essential to the creative landscape of the comic book, over which his imagination soared.

'THEY SAVED LISA'S BRAIN' AIRED IN 1999

Theoretical physicist, Stephen Hawking, has become a real world geek hero. He is referenced in the sitcom *The Big Bang Theory* (2007–present) and in 1991 Steven Spielberg produced a documentary based on *A Brief History of Time* (1988). But Hawking's greatest accolade that he features in the *The Simpson's* episode 'They Saved Lisa's Brain'?

LONDON PREMIERE OF *2001: A SPACE ODYSSEY* IN 1968

Stanley Kubrick famously considered movies to be more akin to music than to literature and it's music that's so associated with his film *2001: A Space Odyssey*.

THE VERY LONG TIMELINE OF *2001*

NOVERMBER

OCTOBER

DECEMBER

SEPT

JANUARY

AUGUST

FEBRUARY

JULY

MARCH

JUNE

APRIL

MAY

AD 2002
Saturday 12 October: *Discovery One* is bound for Jupiter with a crew of scientists and pilots

4,000,000 BC: Ape-men discover a huge alien monolith.

AD 2003
AD 2002
AD 2001
4,000,000 BC

AD 2001
Thursday 26 April: Heywood Floyd travels to Clavius Base on the Moon and visits another mysterious artefact.

AD 2003 Friday 14 Feb: Onboard computer HAL 9000 suggests AE-35 electronics unit must be replaced or fail within 72 hours

AD 2003 Sunday 16 Feb: After no fault is found with the unit it is discussed that HAL 9000 is at fault instead, and the AI monitors this discussion using lipreading.

AD 2003 Monday 17 Feb: HAL first murders scientist Dr Frank Poole by cutting his airline, then while Dr David Bowman attempts a rescue, shuts off life-support to three other cryogenically frozen crew-members. Bowman is then forced to deactivate HAL by eliminating his higher intellectual functions.

AD 2003 Friday 13 June: David Bowman enters Jupiter's space to find an enormous monolith that sends him through a star-gate and then turns him into a Space Foetus.

THE SPACE RITUAL ALIVE IN LIVERPOOL AND LONDON WAS RELEASED IN 1973

In 1964, a young writer named Michael Moorcock secured the position of editor at *New Worlds* magazine. Moorcock revived the fortunes of this sci-fi periodical, which became essential to the new wave in science fiction. It was in *New Worlds* that his Jerry Cornelius stories were first published.

Moorcock's fantasy and science fiction is considered some of the very best of British work in the genres. His novel *Behold the Man* (1966) is about a time traveller who goes from 1970 to 28 AD to meet Jesus. His novels comprising *The Nomad of the Time Streams* series focus on the adventures of Captain Oswald Bastable. The trilogy of *Warlord of the Air*, (1971), *The Land Leviathan* (1974) and *The Steel Tsar* (1981) offers the chance for Moorcock to develop an allegory about colonialism. In Moorcock's writing the overarching concept is of the Eternal Champion, a character who has to keep confronting the presence of Chaos in various kinds of reality. Alongside his literary endeavours, Moorcock was also involved with the band Hawkwind, whose live double album *The Space Ritual Alive in Liverpool and London* includes Moorcock's song 'Sonic Attack'.

PULP FICTION DEBUTED IN 1994 AT CANNES

Six men in black suits, ties and shades stride together in the glare of the LA sun: they are the *Reservoir Dogs*, Quentin Tarantino's debut as screenwriter and director; a story of loyalties, broken and busted and soaked in blood.

The influence of the film has never gone away. Since then, Tarantino has written and directed just a handful of baroquely styled genre revisions: the crime dramas *Pulp Fiction* (1994) and *Jackie Brown* (1997); the martial arts female-centred revenge diptych *Kill Bill:* *Volume 1* (2003) and *Volume 2* (2004); the war film *Inglourious Basterds* (2009); and the westerns *Django Unchained* (2012) and *The Hateful Eight* (2015).

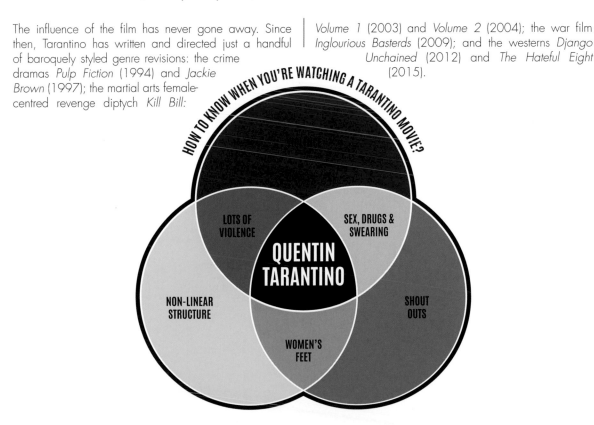

HOW TO KNOW WHEN YOU'RE WATCHING A TARANTINO MOVIE?

LOTS OF VIOLENCE

SEX, DRUGS & SWEARING

QUENTIN TARANTINO

NON-LINEAR STRUCTURE

SHOUT OUTS

WOMEN'S FEET

IN 1992 *THE THIEF AND THE COBBLER* WAS SHOWN TO WARNER BROS.

The Thief and the Cobbler is legendary as a lost animated movie that might just have been a classic. Directed by Richard Williams, it's a film that's emblematic of those films that never really happened. We can add to the list: the never made James Cameron version of *Spider-Man*, David Lynch's film *Ronnie Rocket* and Brad Bird's *Ray Gunn*. Then, too, there's the never- made Alejandro Jodorowsky version of *Dune*.

RONNIE ROCKET (David Lynch) : A three-and-a half-foot detective enters another dimension in which a teen is the victim of a surgical error and has to plug into electricity. He channels this to become a rockstar.

FRANKENSTEIN (David Cronenberg): In the early 1980s, Cronenberg was considering an adaptation and mulled on it over the years. A producer team got somewhat carried away and advertised the film as David Cronenberg's Frankenstein. What about Mary Shelley?

THE DEFECTIVE DETECTIVE (Terry Gilliam): A detective finds himself in a kid's fantasy world. Gilliam first announced the project in 1991. It has yet to be realized.

SUPERMAN LIVES (Tim Burton): Based broadly on the Superman comic *Death of Superman*. This would have starred Nicholas Cage in a story that featured Lex Luthor, Brainiac and Doomsday. Late 1990s.

RAY GUNN (Brad Bird): A science fiction noir in which the last human detective investigates an alleged infidelity. Bird had developed this idea from the following starting point: he had misunderstood the lyrics of a B52s song. He has expressed interest in reviving the project that he was originally working on in the 1990s.

ROBOPOCALYPSE (Steven Spielberg): A human resistance challenges a robot uprising. Spielberg put the project on hold during its development in 2015. The film would have been an adaption of Daniel H.Wilson's novel of the same name.

THE LOST PROJECTS

GEORGE LUCAS WAS BORN IN 1944

Lucas gloriously rebooted movie genres long-considered moribund: the space opera and the action adventure. *Star Wars* (1977) and *Raiders of the Lost Ark* (co-created with Spielberg, 1981) are all-American classics.

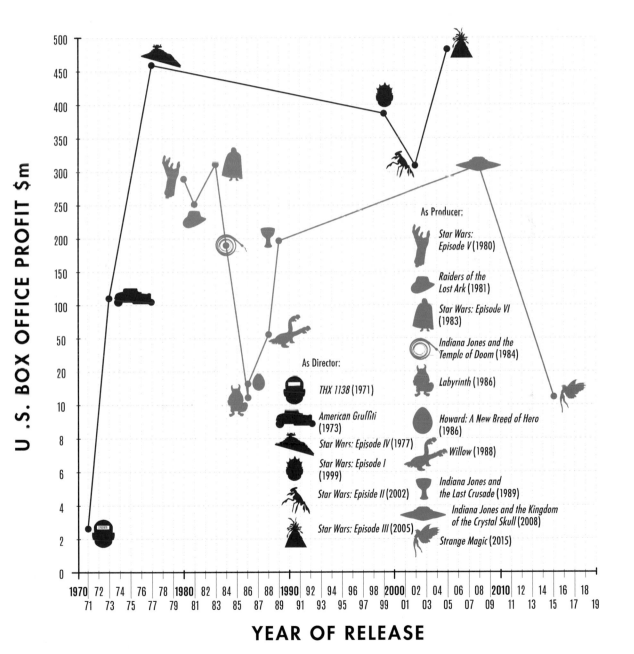

U.S. BOX OFFICE PROFIT $m

As Producer:

Star Wars: Episode V (1980)

Raiders of the Lost Ark (1981)

Star Wars: Episode VI (1983)

Indiana Jones and the Temple of Doom (1984)

Labyrinth (1986)

Howard: A New Breed of Hero (1986)

Willow (1988)

Indiana Jones and the Last Crusade (1989)

Indiana Jones and the Kingdom of the Crystal Skull (2008)

Strange Magic (2015)

As Director:

THX 1138 (1971)

American Graffiti (1973)

Star Wars: Episode IV (1977)

Star Wars: Episode I (1999)

Star Wars: Episide II (2002)

Star Wars: Episode III (2005)

YEAR OF RELEASE

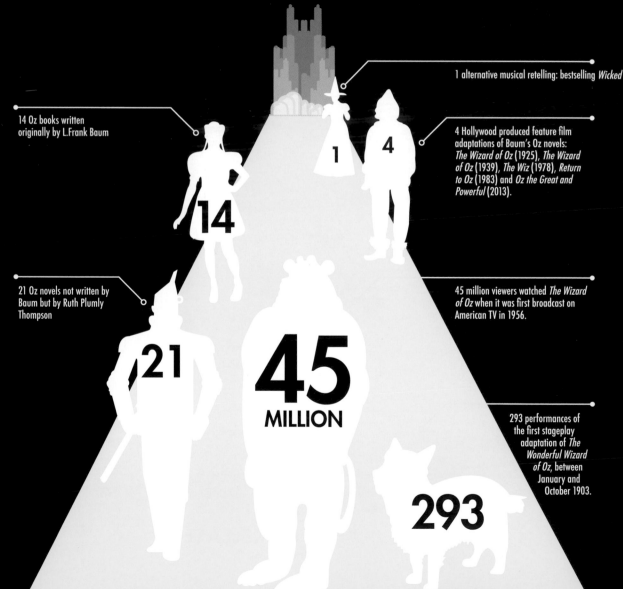

L.FRANK BAUM WAS BORN IN 1856.

Baum finally found his place in the world as a writer in his early 40s. In 1900, his novel *The Wonderful Wizard of Oz* was published. Critically, Baum's hero is a girl and not a boy. Where fairy tales has beasts, Baum gave us plenty of talking machines and in doing so identified Oz as a fantasy about the world of the new century.

During the McCarthy era of the 1950s in America, the film *The Wizard of Oz* was considered by many to be an example of subversive pop culture. It's songwriter, Yip Harburg, was even blacklisted.

This seems a huge contrast to the content of the novel, which is seen as an allegory about the American dream. It's popularity is such that it has been adapted by cinema and also for the theatre and for comics.

1 alternative musical retelling: bestselling *Wicked*

14 Oz books written originally by L.Frank Baum

4 Hollywood produced feature film adaptations of Baum's Oz novels: *The Wizard of Oz* (1925), *The Wizard of Oz* (1939), *The Wiz* (1978), *Return to Oz* (1983) and *Oz the Great and Powerful* (2013).

21 Oz novels not written by Baum but by Ruth Plumly Thompson

45 million viewers watched *The Wizard of Oz* when it was first broadcast on American TV in 1956.

45 MILLION

293 performances of the first stageplay adaptation of *The Wonderful Wizard of Oz*, between January and October 1903.

COMIC BOOK HERO *SPAWN* DEBUTED IN 1992

Spawn is the altar ego of American ex-soldier Al Simmons. Murdered by his Captain, Simmons makes a pact with a devil-like character named Malebolgia. Simmons discovers that he is, in fact, the new form of Hellspawn, and soon enough he's fighting crime in the grand tradition of comic book heroes.

Spawn was emotionally conflicted and his adventures became evermore elaborate and fantastical. Todd

McFarlane's creation is a comic-book symphony of dark fantasy.

IN 1995 THE FILM *CITY OF LOST* WAS RELEASED

Kids are everywhere in science fiction: from Dorothy Gale walking the Yellow Brick Road with the Tin Man and Tik-Tok, to Ender Wiggin in Orson Scott Card's hugely popular novel *Ender's Game*.

Kids in science fiction are typically open to the extraordinary events unfolding around them. Think of Barry in the film *Close Encounters of the Third Kind* (1977): when the aliens explore his house, Barry smiles and laughs and ultimately opens a door to the bright, pretty light just beyond it. In *E.T. the Extra-Terrestrial* (1982), it's children and not adults who are the source of friendship and solace for the visiting alien.

After the comedy horror of Gremlins, director Joe Dante directed the cult film *Explorers* (1985) in which three teenage boys build a spaceship and blast out of suburbia.

Kids in science-fiction films become emblems of the ever-appealing wish to leave behind our familiar lives in the knowledge that we'll always be able to come back home – just like Dorothy in *The Wizard of Oz*.

18
MAY

IN 2004 THE ANIME *STEAMBOY* WAS RELEASED IN THE US

EDWARDIAN ERA

FLYING GOGGLES

ROMANTIC

WHIMSY

VICTORIAN ERA / INDUSTRIALISM

EXPLORERS / SOLDIERS / COUNTESSES

Saberhagen wrote ten Dracula novels which reveal the close bond between the nineteenth century and science fiction and fantasy. Indeed, without the Victorian era's fascination with the possibilities of steam engines and global travel, Steampunk would not have evolved into what we know today.

THE OLD

THE NEW

19
MAY

IN 2005 THE FINAL GEORGE LUCAS-DIRECTED *STAR WARS* FILM WAS RELEASED

The *Star Wars* film *Revenge of the Sith* brought to a conclusion the 'prequel' series that was more historical drama than fast-paced action movie.

In the original *Star Wars* film of 1977, the conflict between Darth Vader and Obi-Wan Kenobi had been hinted at, and this film was finally able to depict the long awaited showdown between the two men. Director Lucas drafted in Steven Spielberg to help design the sequence prior to filming.

Set against an immense lava flow, the battle was intense, both physically and emotionally and struck the perfect note of tragedy at its conclusion. Its images of elemental rage in action were reinforced by John Williams's surging score, which expresses the tragedy of the Anakin's fall from grace, leaving a sense of utter loss.

FINALE OF *BUFFY THE VAMPIRE SLAYER* AIRED IN 2003

Buffy the Vampire Slayer wittily combined a vampire story with smalltown drama.
In Buffy Summers, Sarah Michelle Gellar embodied a new kind of female hero.

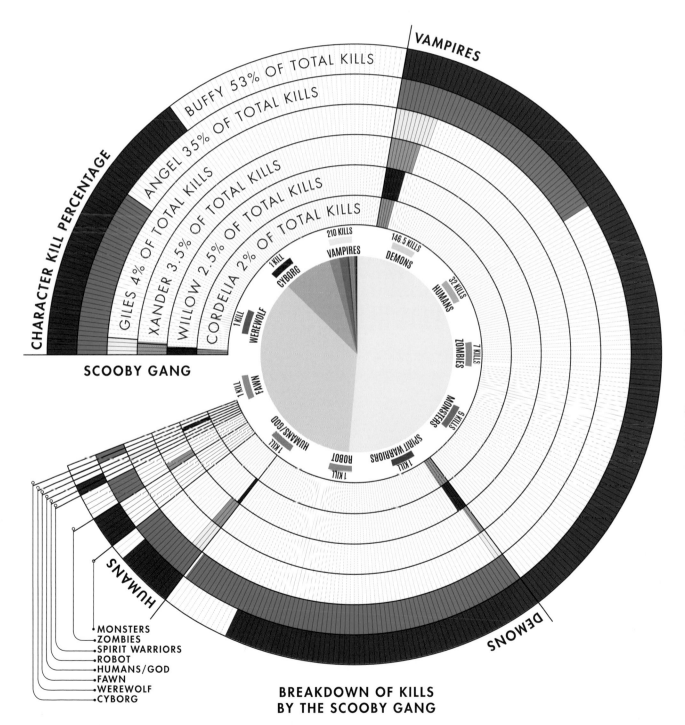

VAMPIRES

CHARACTER KILL PERCENTAGE

BUFFY 53% OF TOTAL KILLS

ANGEL 35% OF TOTAL KILLS

GILES 4% OF TOTAL KILLS

XANDER 3.5% OF TOTAL KILLS

WILLOW 2.5% OF TOTAL KILLS

CORDELIA 2% OF TOTAL KILLS

SCOOBY GANG

210 KILLS
VAMPIRES

146.5 KILLS
DEMONS

32 KILLS
HUMANS

7 KILLS
ZOMBIES

5 KILLS
MONSTERS

1 KILL
CYBORG

1 KILL
WEREWOLF

1 KILL
FAWN

1 KILL
HUMANS/GOD

1 KILL
ROBOT

1 KILL
SPIRIT WARRIORS

HUMANS
- MONSTERS
- ZOMBIES
- SPIRIT WARRIORS
- ROBOT
- HUMANS/GOD
- FAWN
- WEREWOLF
- CYBORG

DEMONS

**BREAKDOWN OF KILLS
BY THE SCOOBY GANG**

21
MAY

MARY ANNING WAS BORN IN 1799

Who could have foreseen that a young girl born on the south coast of England
at the end of the eighteenth century would become so vital to geekdom?

Ever since the late nineteenth century, dinosaurs have roamed through novels, comics, films, TV programmes and computer games. Mary Anning's 1811 discovery of the bones of an ichthyosaur at Lyme Regis in Dorset played a significant part in this.

Marvel's comic book release of 2015 Moon Girl and Devil Dinosaur rebooted the late 1970s Devil Dinosaur in which, in an alternative Earthly reality, a red T. Rex befriends a Neanderthal named Moon Boy. Dinosaurs have also stomped around the panels of DC's Danger: Dinosaurs and in the series Cadillacs and Dinosaurs from Dark Horse Comics.

It's in films, though, that dinosaurs loom especially large. In 2015 Pixar released The Good Dinosaur, and way back in 1988 Spielberg, Lucas and animation director Don Bluth took us to The Land Before Time. Then, too, there's been The Valley of Gwangi (1969), We're Back! A Dinosaur's Story (1993), the 1933 and 2005 versions of King Kong and of course, the Jurassic Park franchise (1993, 1997, 2001, 2015 and 2018).

In the world of literature, Jules Verne's Journey to the Centre of the Earth (1864), Arthur Conan Doyle's The Lost World (1912), Anne McCaffrey's Dinosaur Planet (1978), Ray Bradbury's Dinosaur Tales (1983), Jurassic Park by Michael Crichton (1990) and Greg Bear's Dinosaur Summer (1998) all tell dino-tales.

22
MAY

THE COMPUTER GAME *PAC-MAN* WAS RELEASED IN 1980

Pac-Man chomped his way through computer gaming in the early 1980s: the
yellow mouth moved around a maze, consuming the dots along the way.

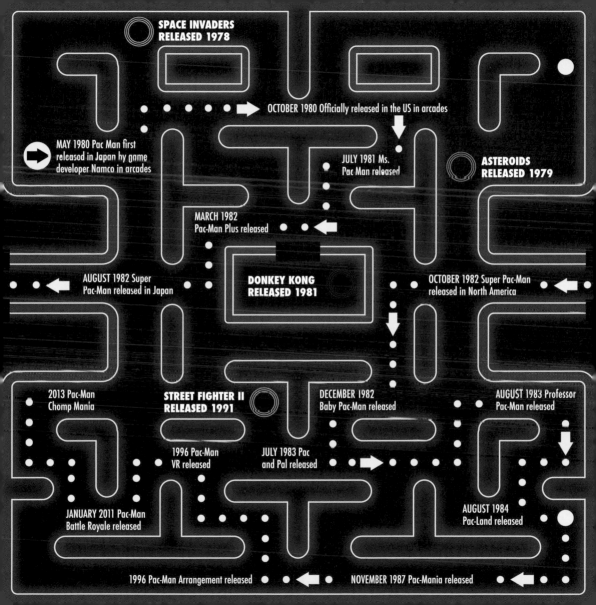

SPACE INVADERS RELEASED 1978

OCTOBER 1980 Officially released in the US in arcades

MAY 1980 Pac Man first released in Japan by game developer Namco in arcades

JULY 1981 Ms. Pac Man released

ASTEROIDS RELEASED 1979

MARCH 1982 Pac-Man Plus released

DONKEY KONG RELEASED 1981

AUGUST 1982 Super Pac-Man released in Japan

OCTOBER 1982 Super Pac-Man released in North America

2013 Pac-Man Chomp Mania

STREET FIGHTER II RELEASED 1991

DECEMBER 1982 Baby Pac-Man released

AUGUST 1983 Professor Pac-Man released

1996 Pac-Man VR released

JULY 1983 Pac and Pal released

JANUARY 2011 Pac-Man Battle Royale released

AUGUST 1984 Pac-Land released

1996 Pac-Man Arrangement released

NOVEMBER 1987 Pac-Mania released

SUSAN COOPER WAS BORN IN 1935

Susan Cooper's novel sequence *The Dark Is Rising* (1965–1977) is a vital part of the British fantasy landscape and could well be the book that got you hooked on all things geek. The story focuses on a boy who discovers that he can use magic and, sure enough, becomes embroiled in a battle of good and evil.

The Dark Is Rising is a five-novel series that relishes in the allure of Arthurian myth, as does T.H. White's *The Once and Future King* (1958). As an undergraduate student, Cooper had a particularly appropriate experience: she was taught by both Tolkien and C.S. Lewis at Oxford.

THE FANTASY NOVELIST'S MENAGERIE

THE COMPUTER GAME *OVERWATCH* PREMIERED IN 2016

A well-received team-based-multiplayer online first- person-shooter, *Overwatch* was been a huge success, selling over 7 million copies within a week of its launch.

Its colourful imaginative characters and non-dystopic future setting immediately appealed, and even before the game was released, a huge amount of fan art was created. Blizzard's intention with the game was to combine the fast-moving characters and expansive arenas of games like *Team Fortress 2* (2007), with the co-operative gameplay and reduced focus of popular MOBAs (Multiplayer Online Battle Arena) games like Dota 2 (2013).

As is common in these games, the teams are organised around offence, defence, tank and support, but they are represented in interesting and unique ways, from a Shakespeare-quoting gorilla named Winston to the popular Tracer, a British adventurer suffering from chronal disassociation. Blizzard are also continually releasing new characters into the game, cleverly seeding their eventual appearance with little hints in the game's backstory and graphics, building anticipation among the lively and largely positive fan-base. This was further helped by Blizzard releasing many documents featuring over 360 designs of the games' entire selection of characters and their accessories, so that those creating fan-art and costumes could do so as accurately as possible.

One of the key reasons *Overwatch* has been so immediately popular is its teams' commitment to diversity in its characters' designs, ages, ethnicity, body-type and sexuality, as well as being receptive to fan's comments about aspects of this that need improvement. Their commitment to giving each character a unique identity even extends to the sounds of their footsteps, so attentive players can tell who is coming around the corner. Unless they are Zenyatta, who of course doesn't actually touch the ground.

STAR WARS WAS RELEASED IN AMERICAN CINEMAS IN 1977

The release of the first *Star Wars* film was a seminal moment in geek history. It would go on to become one of the most significant franchises in history and create its own complex web of connections.

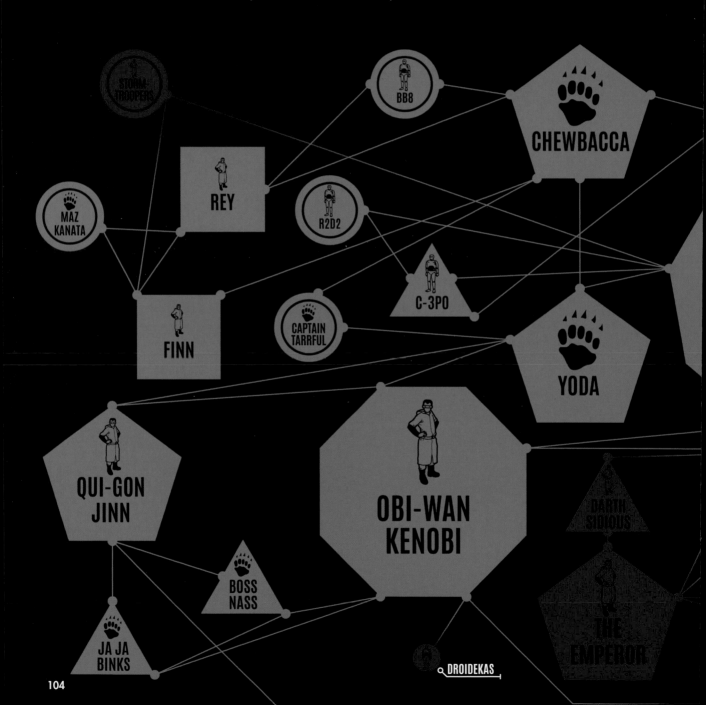

ANDREAS BRANDHORST WAS BORN IN 1956

German novels and movies have a rich connection and history with science fiction and Andreas Brandhorst stands as a major contemporary author in the genre, focused particularly on capturing the excitements of space opera.

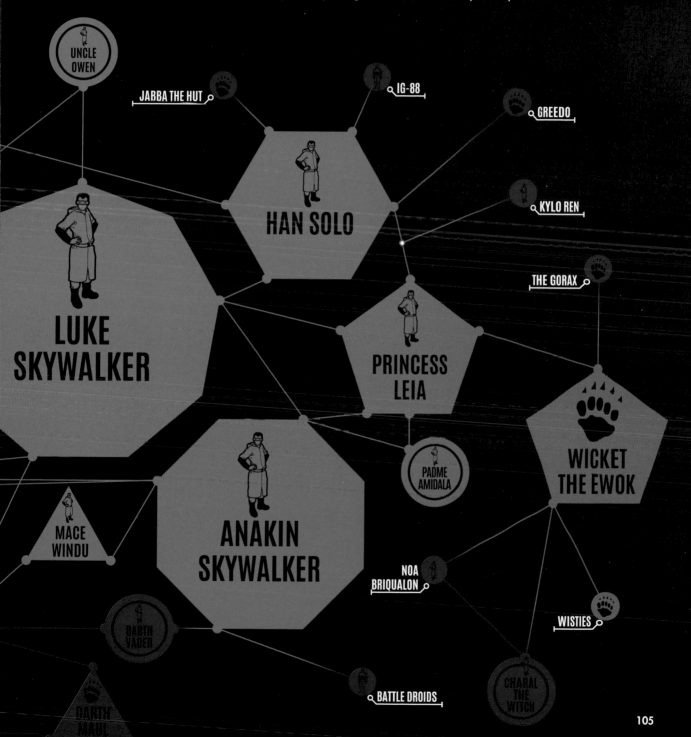

SPACE MOUNTAIN OPENS IN 1977 AT DISNEYLAND

Walt Disney saw the possibility of theme parks as an extension of the worlds depicted in the films produced so successfully by his studio in the first half of the 20th century. Disneyland was the first to open, in 1955), and was followed by Disneyworld, EuroDisney (now Disneyland Paris), Disneyland Tokyo and Disneyland Shanghai – all of them making the fantasy real.

For Walt, the theme park was a place to create a utopia, and the theme park areas of Tomorrowland and EPCOT speak to Disney's futurist ambitions. For many, a Disney theme park visit is a restorative experience.

1975
SPACE MOUNTAIN DEBUTS AT THE MAGIC KINGDOM AT WALT DISNEY WORLD. ORIGINALLY CONCEIVED IN 1964, DISNEY HAD TO WAIT OVER 10 YEARS FOR THE TECHNOLOGY TO CATCH UP TO THE VISION

30
NUMBER OF TWO-CAR TRAINS AVAILABLE ON THE RIDE

26
FEET – DROP ON THE RIDE

5
NUMBER OF DISNEY PARKS THAT FEATURE SPACE MOUNTAIN. THE ONLY EXCEPTION IS THE SHANGHAI DISNEYLAND RESORT

3196
FEET IS THE LENGTH OF THE ALPHA TRACK AT WALT DISNEY WORLD. THE OMEGA TRACK IS 3186 FEET

$18MILLION
TOTAL COST OF BUILDING THE ORIGINAL SPACE MOUNTAIN, DISNEYLAND, WHICH OPENED IN 1955

28
MILES PER HOUR – TOP SPEED THE RIDE REACHES

4,029,019
US PATENT NUMBER ISSUED FOR THE TUBULAR STEEL TRACK DESIGN FOR THE RIDE AT DISNEYLAND

185,500
RECORD-BREAKING NUMBER OF VISITORS TO DISNEYLAND FOR THE MEMORIAL DAY WEEKEND WHEN SPACE MOUNTAIN OPENED

2005, 2015 & 2017
DATES FOR REFURBISHMENT OF THE RIDE AT DISNEYLAND PARIS

DOCTOR WHO CAME FACE TO FACE WITH HIMSELF ON THIS DAY IN AN EPISODE THAT AIRED IN 2011

In this episode of *Doctor Who* (portrayed by Matt Smith) entitled 'The Almost People', the good Doctor encounters his double.

BRITISH WRITER T.H.WHITE WAS BORN IN 1906

Best known for the all-out fantasy classic, *The Sword in the Stone* (1938), White also wrote a number of novels that suit the science-fiction moniker: including a sequence of books called *Earth Stopped* (published in 1934 and 1935) and *The Master: An Adventure Story* (1957).

The *Earth Stopped* stories are threaded with an apocalyptic subject that's so often been a rewarding staple of the science fiction genre. However, it's White's fantasy serial of five novels, bracketed together as *The Once and Future King* (1958), that is his most famous contribution to the genres of speculative fiction. They're imbued with a sense of wonder. These novels chart the youth and adulthood of King Arthur in a dazzling combination of drama, comedy, fantasy, sentiment and a delight in ideas.

MILTON BRADLEY DIED IN 1911

The 1980s remains a moment in time that is rich with geek treasures,
many of which are still out there to be found in our online world.

During that decade, toys, games and puzzles existed in an exciting 'twilight zone' between traditional and the new world of entertainment offered by the microprocessor. Milton Bradley games were a byword for such entertainment.

Milton Bradley's Big Trak was a lavishly realized toy that suggested what would one day become all the more possible for computer-based home entertainment.

Released in 1979, Big Trak was sci-fi in its design, tapping into the late 1970s and early 1980s fascination with robots and quantum leaps in technology. A programmable toy, it had six (big) wheels and a keypad with which you could all rather excitingly punch in up to sixteen commands that would set a series of turns that Big Trak could make in journey from a start point to a finish point.

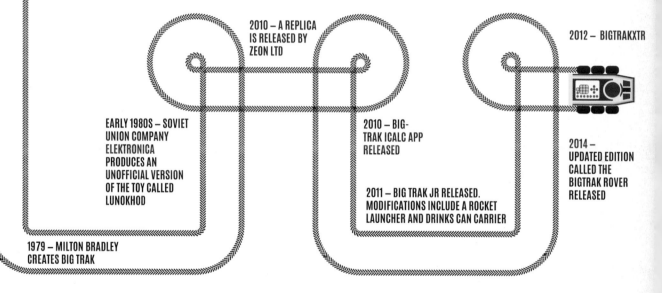

2010 – A REPLICA IS RELEASED BY ZEON LTD

2012 – BIGTRAKXTR

EARLY 1980S – SOVIET UNION COMPANY ELEKTRONICA PRODUCES AN UNOFFICIAL VERSION OF THE TOY CALLED LUNOKHOD

2010 – BIG-TRAK ICALC APP RELEASED

2014 – UPDATED EDITION CALLED THE BIGTRAK ROVER RELEASED

2011 – BIG TRAK JR RELEASED. MODIFICATIONS INCLUDE A ROCKET LAUNCHER AND DRINKS CAN CARRIER

1979 – MILTON BRADLEY CREATES BIG TRAK

RAN PREMIERED IN 1985 IN TOKOYO

Broadly speaking, the classic Akira Kurosawa movie *Ran* is a film-geek classic, its samurai speaking to an interest in Japan's feudal era. Comic books have certainly treated samurai with zeal. *Lone Wolf and Cub* (1970), created by Kazuo Koike and Goseki Kojima, tells of a disgraced samurai (the titular Lone Wolf) and his three-year-old son (the Cub).

By contrast, *Usagi Yojimbo* (1984–present) by Stan Sakai tells the adventures of a samurai rabbit in an animal-only world that reimagines Japan's Edo period.

Then, too, there is the much-loved animated American TV series *Samurai Jack* (2001–17), created by Genndy Tartakovsky. A young samurai finds himself in the future, and from there he returns to restore order to the world he left, which has been destroyed by a nefarious wizard.

SPACE INVADERS WAS RELEASED IN 1978

The late 1970s was a flashpoint for science fiction as it moved towards mainstream pop culture. A high point was when the Space Invaders arcade video game was released, marking the moment when the brave new world of computer gaming revealed its potential for world domination.

Created by Japanese games designer Tomohiro Nishikado, *Space Invaders* tapped into the fascination with real and imaginary ventures in space and brought extraterrestrial adventure to the suburbs' arcades.

Originally, the game had focused on players shooting down waves of enemy airplanes. However, when Nishikado had difficulty in animating airplanes he looked to the recently released *Star Wars* for inspiration and suddenly those airplanes became spaceships. Nishikado spliced into the mix the Martian forms from the H. G.

Wells novel *The War of the Worlds* and the now iconic pesky pixelated *Space Invaders* came to be.

By 1980, 300,000 *Space Invaders* arcade consoles had been sold. The computer gaming industry was born, as was global *Space Invader* mania: a boy in Japan even held up a bank with a shotgun because wanted the money for playing in the arcade.

Space Invaders marks the moment when the fusion between reality and the virtual reality of gaming took a quantum leap into the future.

```
SCORE <1>        HI-SCORE        SCORE <2>
  2703             1978
```

110'510 highest score achieved in the arcade game

$2 billion in quarters grossed by the end of 1932

360'000 arcade games sold

$2000-3000 average price for each arcade machine in 1980

1978 First released as an arcade game

$600 million grossed by the end of 1978 in Japan

2 MILLION copies of home console sold, 1981

```
CREDIT 00
```

THE SPIRIT BY WILL EISNER DEBUTED IN 1940

Will Eisner's work has influenced the likes of Brad Bird, Frank Miller and Michael Chabon. There's even an award named for Eisner and his book *Comics and Sequential Art* is a must read.

In 1978, at the age of 61, Eisner published the graphic novel *A Contract With God* that became vital to establishing the commercial prospects of the format. Of the project Eisner wrote in 2004 that 'At an age when I could have "retired", I chose instead to create literary comics…'

The Spirit, a masked detective in a film noir-like world, is Eisner's most famous creation. In 1987, actor Sam Jones portrayed Spirit in a shortlived series on American tv. In the 1950s, Eisner left behind the world of comics and headed into commercials. However, by the 1970s, he was sufficiently encouraged to return to comics.

With his heavy ink work, Eisner produced material from 1930 until the 2000s and was an infuence on Jack Kirby, Wally Wood, Bob Kane and Jules Feiffer.

In the 1980s, animator Brad Bird developed an approach to an animated feature adaptation, giving the following credit to Eisner's work: 'It was cinematic. I loved the angles, the use of shadow and the fact that its characters were expressive.'

WORLD OF *WARCRAFT: LEGION* WAS RELEASED IN 2016 IN SPAIN

After a decade of popularity as an online game, *Warcraft* became a movie telling the story of a dispossessed orc tribe who come into contact with humans. Directed by Duncan Jones, *Warcraft* was essentially an animated movie combined with live action elements, featuring dazzling character and environment work by visual effects specialists Industrial Light & Magic. Whilst the film struggled to find an audience in America and Europe, it was hugely popular in China.

WENDY PINI (NÉE FLETCHER) IS BORN ON THIS DAY IN 1951

In 1965, the authorised edition of *The Lord of the Rings* trilogy of novels was first published in the USA. Its success fed into a growing subculture that geeked out for fantasy and science fiction. Combined with a longstanding comic book culture, this made conditions just right for publication of an expansive, high fantasy comic series – and in 1978, the *Elfquest* comic was published. It continues to be published and is overseen by the same husband and wife team that created it: Richard and Wendy Pini. There are wolf-riding elves, distinctive tribes and magical powers in abundance, all focused around three characters: Cutter, Leetah and Skywise. *Elfquest* is marked by a seriousness of tone and its storylines are intricately woven across an expansive scale. *Elfquest* is epic storytelling.

FERRIS BUELLER TOOK THE DAY OFF IN 1985

Teens in geek movies go back to at least *I Was A Teenage Werewolf*. It's a connection that's worked well. Geek-movie teens are smart (*Explorers*), smart-ass (*The Goonies*), sensitive (*Super 8*), no-nonsense (*Buffy the Vampire Slayer*) and always brave. Sometimes they're not quite of this earth either: just watch *The Lost Boys* in which a horde of vampire teens lurk in the shadows of a Californian coastal town. The original conception for the film owed more of a developed debt to J.M.Barrie's *Peter Pan*.

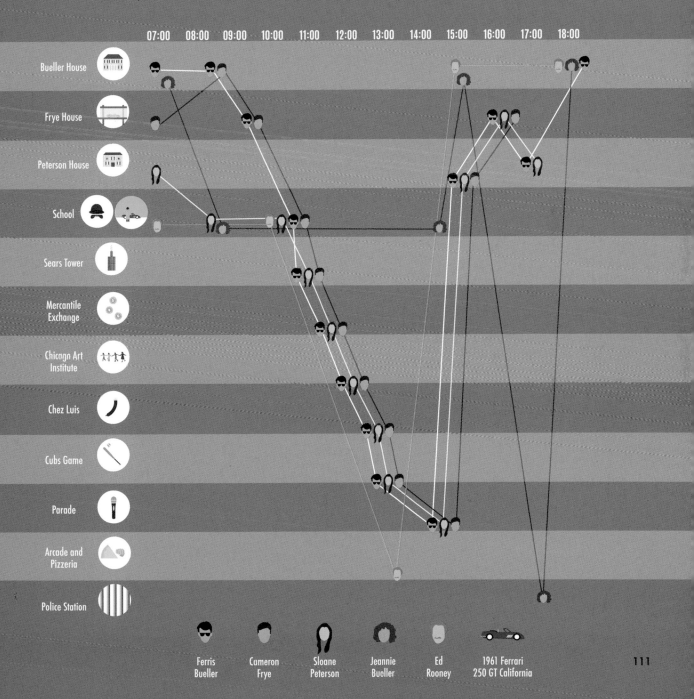

| | Ferris Bueller | Cameron Frye | Sloane Peterson | Jeannie Bueller | Ed Rooney | 1961 Ferrari 250 GT California |

BONELAND PUBLISHED IN PAPERBACK IN 2013

Alan Garner's fantasy novels have a rich connection with the English countryside and the folklore and legend that rises up from it, particularly from around the Cheshire countryside of the UK where Garner grew up and where he has deep ancestral roots. His novels *The Weirdstone of Brisingamen* (1960) and *The Moon of Gomrath* (1963) are brooding, whimsical and utterly believable and have been completed by the third installment, *Boneland*.

Garner's fantasy novels explore the interplay of distant past on fleeting present and, as predominantly children's novels, focus on young people confronting quite fearful challenges. His novel *Elidor* (1965) focuses on four children who venture into a parallel world where they win various treasures which they must then keep safe in this world. Garner has said that 'My background is deep and set in deep time… ' That ability to reach back to something ancient and weave it into the modern world is where Garner's fantasies find their power. Garner's work has influenced much British literary children's fantasy over the past forty years.

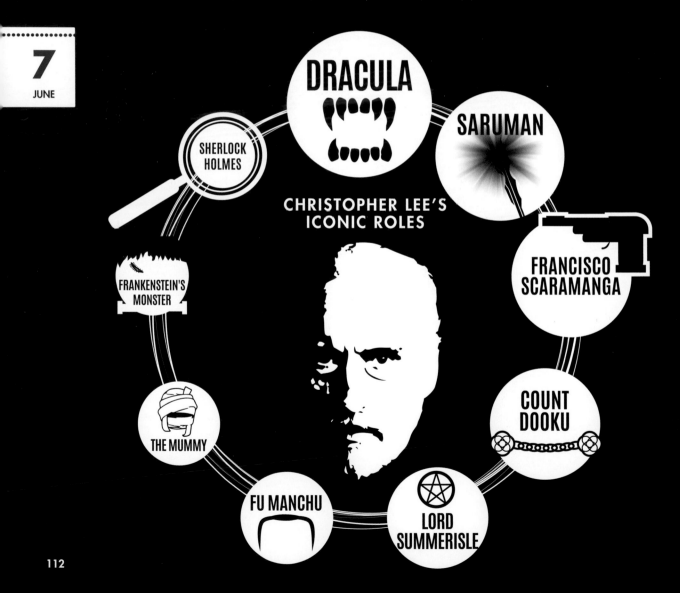

CHRISTOPHER LEE'S
ICONIC ROLES

DRACULA

SHERLOCK HOLMES

SARUMAN

FRANCISCO SCARAMANGA

FRANKENSTEIN'S MONSTER

COUNT DOOKU

THE MUMMY

FU MANCHU

LORD SUMMERISLE

CHRISTOPHER LEE DIED IN 2015

Christopher Lee's movie legacy is rich with classic genre performances, famously including *Dracula*. More recently, he portrayed Saruman in *The Lord of the Rings* trilogy (2001–03) and *The Hobbit* trilogy (2012–2014); and in *Star Wars: Episode II – Attack of the Clones* (2002) and *Star Wars: Episode III – Revenge of Sith* (2005) as suave Sith, Count Dooku.

IN 1949 GEORGE ORWELL'S *NINETEEN EIGHTY-FOUR* WAS PUBLISHED

Originally entitled *The Last Man in Europe*, the book now seems ever more prescient with its story of a world of constant surveillance and totalitarian rule.

In early 2017, the novel surprisingly re-entered the bestseller charts. An early Cold War-informed novel, Orwell brought to the story of a man named Winston Smith who rebels against a totalitarian regime, known as Big Brother. In 1984, a well-regarded film adaptation of the novel was released.

WRITER PIERCE ASKEGREN WAS BORN IN 1955

It's a niche within a niche for sure, but Pierce Askegren occupied it well before dying at the young age of 51: he wrote novels based on licensed properties. These included the Spider-Man *Dooms Day* series, *Fantastic Four: Countdown to Chaos*, *Alias* (with J J.Abrams), *Angel: The Longest Night, Volume 1* and *Buffy the Vampire Slayer: After Image*. In addition to his work on licensed material, Askegren also wrote a science-fiction trilogy entitled *Inconstant Moon*.

10
JUNE

MAURICE SENDAK WAS BORN IN 1928

Where the Wild Things Are (1963) is surely one of the most recognized children's picture books. Its author, Maurice Sendak's work for this book has been emblazoned not only on book pages but merchandise, too. *Where the Wild Things Are* is Sendak's most well known story and its style echoes in a detail of Sarah's bedroom in Jim Henson's *Labyrinth* (1986).

Sendak's story of a boy who ventures to an island of beasts to get away from the demands of life at home and relishes the chance to play and abandon the rules of daily domestic life has been adapted numerous times. Spike Jonze directed an affecting live action film adaptation of *Where The Wild Things Are* in 2009, from a screenplay by Dave Eggers, and in the early 1980s John Lasseter, during his career as an animator at Disney, had combined cel animation and rudimentary computer-generated environments in a test animation short film. The story that he used as a premise for the project was *Where The Wild Things Are*.

11
JUNE

JURASSIC PARK WAS RELEASED IN AMERICAN CINEMAS IN 1993

Cloning has functioned as a great source of material for science fiction. In the novel (1990) and its film adaptation of *Jurassic Park*, the cloning and DNA manipulation of dinosaur DNA allows these mighty beasts to be re-engineered in the 20th century.

Never Let Me Go (2010), based on Kazuo Ishiguro's novel, is set in an alternative version of the 1990s, in which several young people, Kathy, Tommy and Ruth, have been cloned in order to serve as organ donors. A compelling film adaptation, that has a stillness about it, was directed by Mark Romanek.

IN 1987 *PREDATOR* WAS RELEASED IN AMERICA

Predator turbo-charged the action movie genre that had proved so popular in the 1980s. A key entry in the genre, *Predator* told of a military unit besieged in a jungle by the titular Predator. The beast was designed and articulated by the late great Stan Winston and his crew.

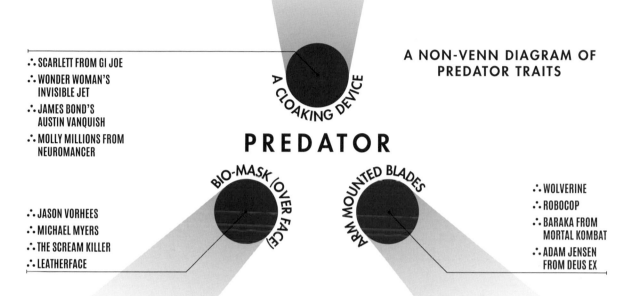

A NON-VENN DIAGRAM OF PREDATOR TRAITS

∴ SCARLETT FROM GI JOE
∴ WONDER WOMAN'S INVISIBLE JET
∴ JAMES BOND'S AUSTIN VANQUISH
∴ MOLLY MILLIONS FROM NEUROMANCER

A CLOAKING DEVICE

PREDATOR

BIO-MASK (OVER FACE)

ARM MOUNTED BLADES

∴ JASON VORHEES
∴ MICHAEL MYERS
∴ THE SCREAM KILLER
∴ LEATHERFACE

∴ WOLVERINE
∴ ROBOCOP
∴ BARAKA FROM MORTAL KOMBAT
∴ ADAM JENSEN FROM DEUS EX

RALPH MCQUARRIE WAS BORN IN 1929

When artist Ralph McQuarrie painted twelve images to aid filmmaker George Lucas in explaining to Hollywood studio heads what he was trying to achieve in imagining *Star Wars*, how could he have forseen the landmark, watershed work that he was rendering?

The lyricism that often permeated his work was very present in his cover image for Isaac Asimov's book *Robot Dreams* (1986). For this piece, McQuarrie's sci-fi imaginings have clearly been inspired by the 19th-century painting entitled 'Flaming June' (1985).

ALLEGED UFO DEBRIS FOUND AT ROSWELL IN 1947

First reported by farmer Mack Brazel, the UFO landing at Roswell, New Mexico has fuelled much speculation about what might be out in the stars and just who or what may have visited us here on Earth.

While the American government denied anything extraordinary, speculation persists and this has fuelled the spirit of the TV series *The X-Files* (1993–2002, 2016) and even played its part in some of the Indiana Jones lore.

15
JUNE

THE FIRST PEZ DISPENSER CONVENTION HELD IN 1991

Sometimes it's the very little things that make a big impact. What
could be more modestly scaled than a PEZ sweet dispenser?

It was on this day in 1991 that the first ever PEZ convention
was held in Ohio for enthusiasts and collectors of the
sweet dispenser.

As well as being a geek enthusiasm in its own right,
PEZ has become synonymous with movie merchandise,
including licensed properties such as: *Star Wars*, *Disney*,
Marvel and *Super Mario Bros*.

16
JUNE

THE ALBUM *THE RISE AND FALL OF ZIGGY STARDUST AND THE SPIDERS FROM MARS* WAS RELEASED IN 1972 IN THE UK

Ziggy was David Bowie's alter ego for a period of time,
representing a somewhat messianic figure, come to earth
to preach harmony. The name Ziggy was prompted by the
name of a tailor's shop that Bowie sighted from a train.

The album included tracks such as 'Suffragette City'
and 'Rock 'n' Roll Suicide"' and was very much a sci-fi
-inspired rock album and it hasn't been the only one. Of
the work's otherworldly vibe, Bowie explained to writer
William Burroughs in an interview for *Rolling Stone*
magazine that 'Ziggy is advised in a dream by the
infinites to write the coming of a starman … this amazing
spaceman who will be coming down to save the Earth.'

For Bowie, later albums allowed him to continue
expressing his sci-fi interests: 'Glass Spider' from his

album *Never Let Me Down* is one such example and his
song 'Blackstar' from his final album of the same name
has an accompanying music video that refers to Bowie's
Major Tom character.

So potent was Bowie's image as a 'starman' that
several years later he was cast in the Nic Roeg science
fiction film *The Man Who Fell To Earth* (1976). Bowie's
album now stands as a classic title; not only in terms of
his discography but in the annals of British pop music of
the 1970s.

ANNE MCCAFFREY INDUCTED BY THE SCIENCE FICTION HALL OF FAME IN 2006

Like Ursula K. Le Guin and Octavia Butler, McCaffrey has been essential to the profile of female voices in a male-dominated world.

McCaffrey broke through in 1967 with a short story set in the dragon-filled world of Pern. These dragons, had been biologically engineered by humans, the two species striking up a strong bond. The third novel in the series, *The White Dragon* (1978) became one of the first hardcore science fiction novel to be a mainstream. bestseller.

THE FOUR-DIMENSIONAL HUMAN WAS PUBLISHED IN THE UK IN 2015

Subtitled *Ways of Being in the Digital World*, Laurence Scott's non-fiction book explores the emotional impression that digital technology can make on us. This digital technology becomes what Scott identifies as the portal to another reality.

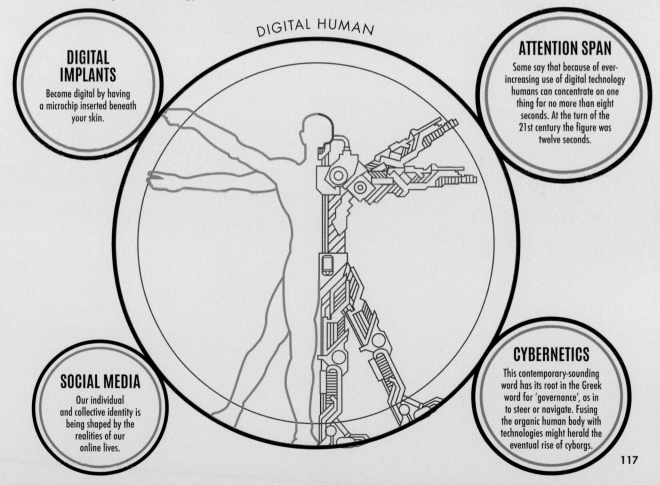

DIGITAL HUMAN

DIGITAL IMPLANTS
Become digital by having a microchip inserted beneath your skin.

ATTENTION SPAN
Some say that because of ever-increasing use of digital technology humans can concentrate on one thing for no more than eight seconds. At the turn of the 21st century the figure was twelve seconds.

SOCIAL MEDIA
Our individual and collective identity is being shaped by the realities of our online lives.

CYBERNETICS
This contemporary-sounding word has its root in the Greek word for 'governance', as in to steer or navigate. Fusing the organic human body with technologies might herald the eventual rise of cyborgs.

19
JUNE

ZOE SALDANA WAS BORN IN 1978

Saldana has become a major presence in science-fiction movies: starring as Uhura in the J.J.Abrams directed and produced series of *Star Trek* films: *Star Trek* (2009), *Star Trek Into Darkness* (2013) and *Star Trek Beyond* (2016). She has also starred as Neytiri in James Cameron's *Avatar* (2009) and as Gamora in *Guardians of the Galaxy* and *Guardians of the Galaxy Vol. 2* (2017).

20
JUNE

JAWS WAS RELEASED AT CINEMAS IN AMERICA IN 1975

The brooding sense of terror and the toothsome predator of *Jaws* have an almost sci-fi quality about them, resonant of *Alien* (1979). Both films set the benchmark for the science fiction/horror movie fusion

If science fiction is fascinated by what happens to our sense of humanity when technology meets human beings and their thoughts and feelings, then horror's about the return of repressed feeling, events and characters. With its visceral beasts and flurry of bloody shocks, *Alien* mostly feels like horror. Its sequel, *Aliens* (1986) goes much more for a horror-war movie vibe, while *Alien³* (1992) and *Alien: Resurrection* (1997) stay more true to straight horror. The sci fi/horror splicing also characterizes *Prometheus* (2012) and *Covenant* (2006).

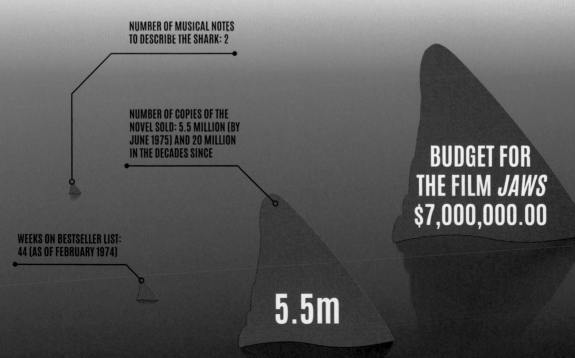

NUMBER OF MUSICAL NOTES TO DESCRIBE THE SHARK: 2

NUMBER OF COPIES OF THE NOVEL SOLD: 5.5 MILLION (BY JUNE 1975) AND 20 MILLION IN THE DECADES SINCE

BUDGET FOR THE FILM *JAWS* $7,000,000.00

WEEKS ON BESTSELLER LIST: 44 (AS OF FEBRUARY 1974)

5.5m

CHRIS PRATT WAS BORN IN 1979

To date, Chris Pratt has proved hugely appealing as two somewhat geeky but very heroic characters: Star-Lord in the *Guardians of the Galaxy* films (2014, 2017 and as Owen in *Jurassic World* (2015). Pratt's characterizations have just the right balance of ordinariness and cockiness.

JEAN-MARC LOFFICIER WAS BORN IN 1954

French author Lofficier has written for books, television, films and comics. Since he usually collaborates with his wife Randy Lofficier, they are often credited as R.J.M. Officier.

BOX OFFICE OF THE FILM:
$260,000,000.00

TIMELY PUBLICATIONS WAS ESTABLISHED IN 1939

23
JUNE

Timely Publications. Never heard of it Have you heard of Marvel ?
Well, Timely Publications would be the progenitor of Marvel.

Timely Comics' first *Marvel Comics* was dated October 1939. In 1941, Timely introduced Captain America, and it was only in the early 1960s that Marvel Comics became the publisher's new name.

In that twenty-year interval, Timely established so much of the storytelling DNA of superhero comics. Running in parallel with DC Comics, Marvel created heroes notable for how they related to other characters in very ordinary ways: Spider-Man, Iron Man and the Hulk all had something appealingly familiar about them, and this quality extended to stories developed by the publisher that brought real-world issues to all that fantasy.

24
JUNE

IN 1987 THE MEL BROOKS-DIRECTED PARODY *SPACEBALLS* WAS RELEASED IN THE US

Starring Rick Moranis, Bill Paxton and John Candy *Spaceballs* is a warm-hearted spoof of the kind of space opera that was best embodied in *Star Wars*.

25
JUNE

PATENT REGISTERED FOR THE FIRST TEXAS INSTRUMENTS HANDHELD CALCULATOR IN 1974

Maths and the realms of science fiction and of fantasy have made a neat fit. Famously, *Alice in Wonderland* plays with the logic that maths embodies. There are many other examples, including Robert A. Heinlein's short story '– And He Built A Crooked House –' (1941). In Carl Sagan's novel *Contact* it's mathematics that contains the otherworldly message that propels the story.

RICHARD GARFIELD WAS BORN IN 1963

Phenomenally popular, *Magic the Gathering*, created by Richard Garfield, who was intrigued about the possibility of creating a game in which players made their own decks of cards, is a fantasy-orientated strategic role playing card game that launched in 1993.

The cards feature lavish illustrations and detailed instructions on how each one functions in the game. The game is rich in the traditions of high fantasy characters, conflicts, landscapes and minutiae of the genre. An ever-expanding world, *Magic the Gathering* is loaded with statistical delights.

In an interview with *Vice* online, Richard said of the game's allure that 'The game bleeds into real life. There's this whole world of how you get the cards, and how the cards circulate among people.'

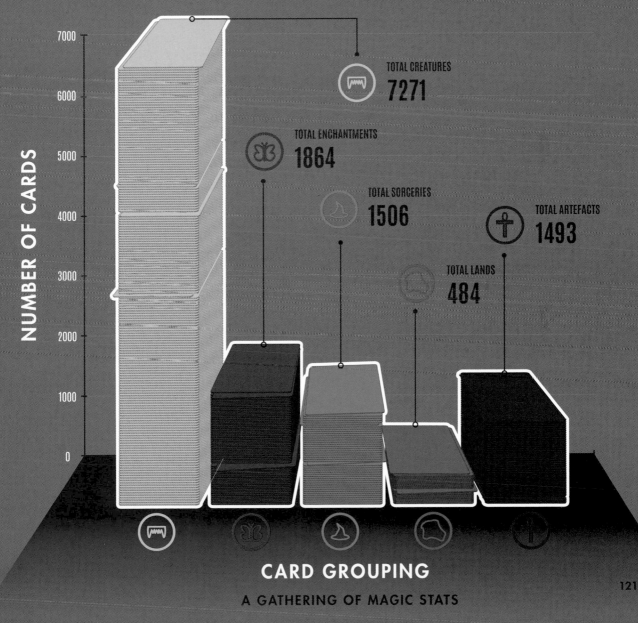

NUMBER OF CARDS

TOTAL CREATURES
7271

TOTAL ENCHANTMENTS
1864

TOTAL SORCERIES
1506

TOTAL ARTEFACTS
1493

TOTAL LANDS
484

CARD GROUPING

A GATHERING OF MAGIC STATS

J.J. ABRAMS WAS BORN IN 1966

Lost (2004–10), *Star Trek* reboots (2009, 2013, 2016), *Star Wars: The Force Awakens* (2015) and *Super 8* (2011) all attest to Abrams' enthusiasm for science fiction and fantasy.

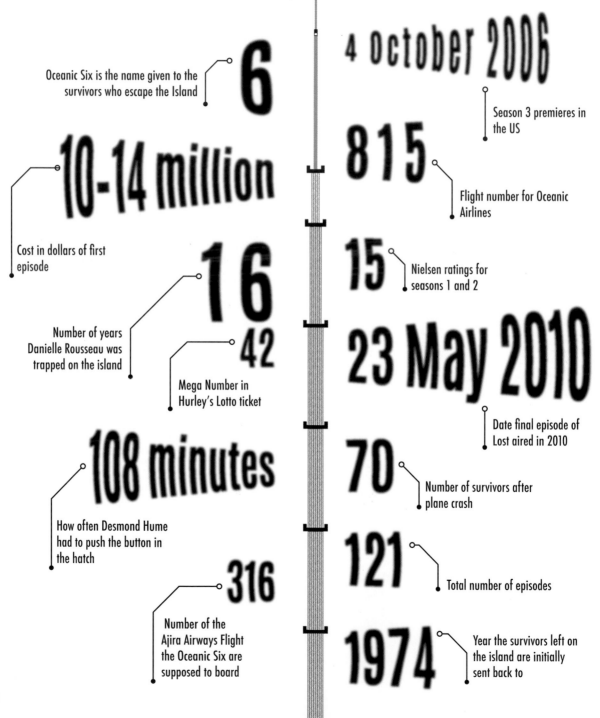

6
Oceanic Six is the name given to the survivors who escape the Island

4 october 2006
Season 3 premieres in the US

10-14 million
Cost in dollars of first episode

815
Flight number for Oceanic Airlines

16
Number of years Danielle Rousseau was trapped on the island

15
Nielsen ratings for seasons 1 and 2

42
Mega Number in Hurley's Lotto ticket

23 May 2010
Date final episode of Lost aired in 2010

108 minutes
How often Desmond Hume had to push the button in the hatch

70
Number of survivors after plane crash

121
Total number of episodes

316
Number of the Ajira Airways Flight the Oceanic Six are supposed to board

1974
Year the survivors left on the island are initially sent back to

PHILIPPE DRUILLET WAS BORN IN 1944

28
JUNE

France has been critical to the evolution and increasing sophistication of the comic-book form, or, to use the French term: *bandes dessinées*. In France, comics are wide-ranging in subject and genre, and certainly don't confine themselves to superheroes. The broader European take on comics and what might constitute geek culture makes for a useful variation on what we know from the American wellspring.

Phillip Druillet's comic work was first published in 1966 in the form of the story of Lone Sloane, *Le mystère des abîmes*.

Druillet's images are dense with detail and vividly deploy colour. There's an intriguing *Star Wars* image he drew in the 1970s that shows Darth Vader and stormtroopers. You might think the film is more a horror piece than a feelgood space adventure.

During the 1970s, his illustrations of fantastical structures and architecture attracted particular recognition. In 1974, with Jean 'Moebius' Giraud and comic-writer Jean-Pierre Dionnet, Druillet published *Métal Hurlant* (*Screaming Metal*), an anthology of science fiction and fantasy material.

RAY HARRYHAUSEN WAS BORN IN 1920

29
JUNE

In the Pixar movie *Monsters, Inc.*, there's a scene set in a restaurant. If you look closely, you'll see that the setting is named Harryhausen's. It's a nod to the impact of Harryhausen on fantasy filmmaking with his ingenious, detailed and expressive stop-motion animation effects.

Harryhausen's creations famously included the skeleton army in *Jason and the Argonauts* (1963), Kali in *The Golden Voyage of Sinbad* (1973), Mighty Joe Young in the 1949 film of the same name and the Greek myth-inspired Medusa and Kraken in *Clash of the Titans* (1981).

Harryhausen's creatures are not just believably proportioned, detailed and lit, but they movie with such subtlety. They became the touchstone for such effects right through the 1970s and 1980s, when Harryhausen's example informed the work of visual effects creative, such as Phil Tippett, Dennis Muren and Ken Ralston.

USAGI TSUKINO WAS BORN IN 1994 IN THE STORYWORLD OF *SAILOR MOON*

Usagi is best known as Sailor Moon herself and she is just one of many anime and manga female heroes.

Anime and manga are suffused with vividly realized female protagonists and one of the most recognizable and emblematic of both formats is Nausiccaä, the titular protagonist of *Nausiccaä of the Valley of the Wind* 1982–94). Her name, though, takes its inspiration not from Japanese culture but from the Greek epic, the Odyssey.

British comic book hero *Tank Girl* (1988) connects well to the example of Nausiccaä.

THE SAILOR SOLAR SYSTEM

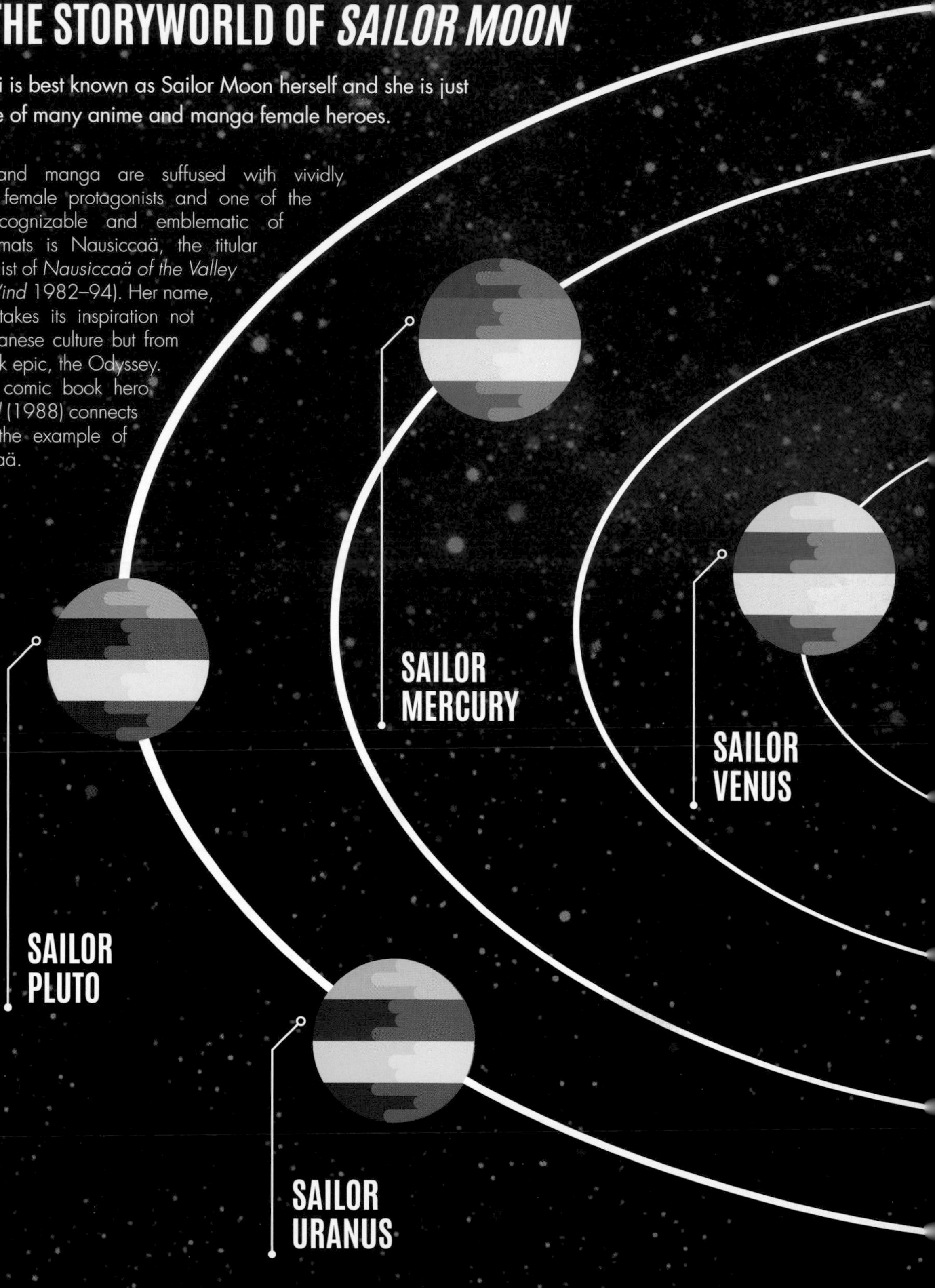

SAILOR MERCURY

SAILOR VENUS

SAILOR PLUTO

SAILOR URANUS

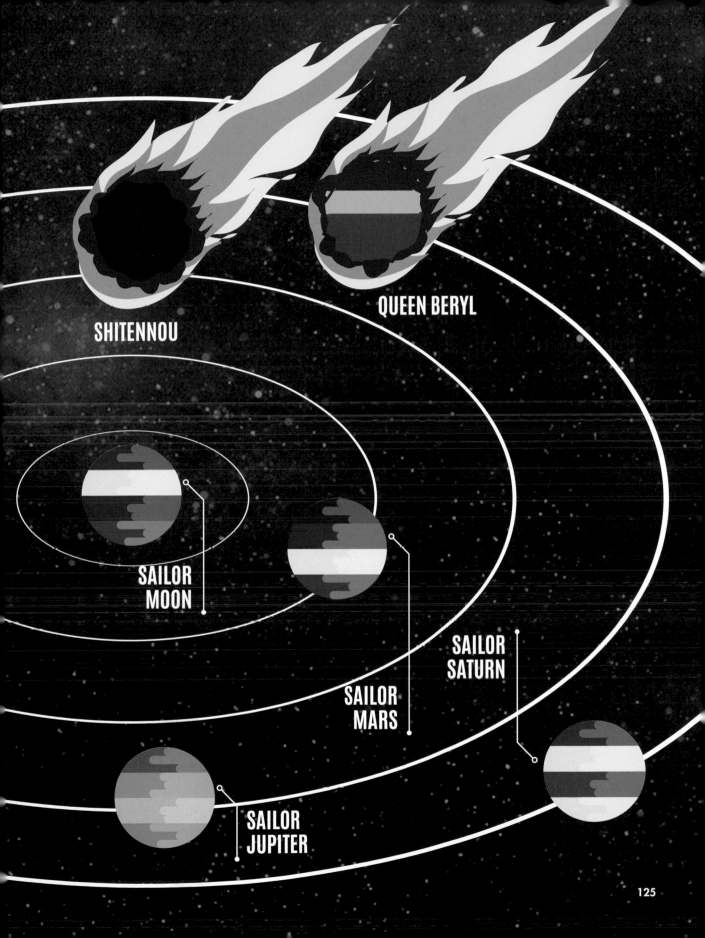

HENRY JONES JR. WAS BORN IN 1899

'Indiana' Jones's passion for history and his efforts to outwit his usually Fascist enemies fuel his determined quests as he rough and tumbles his way around the world with his fedora and bullwhip.

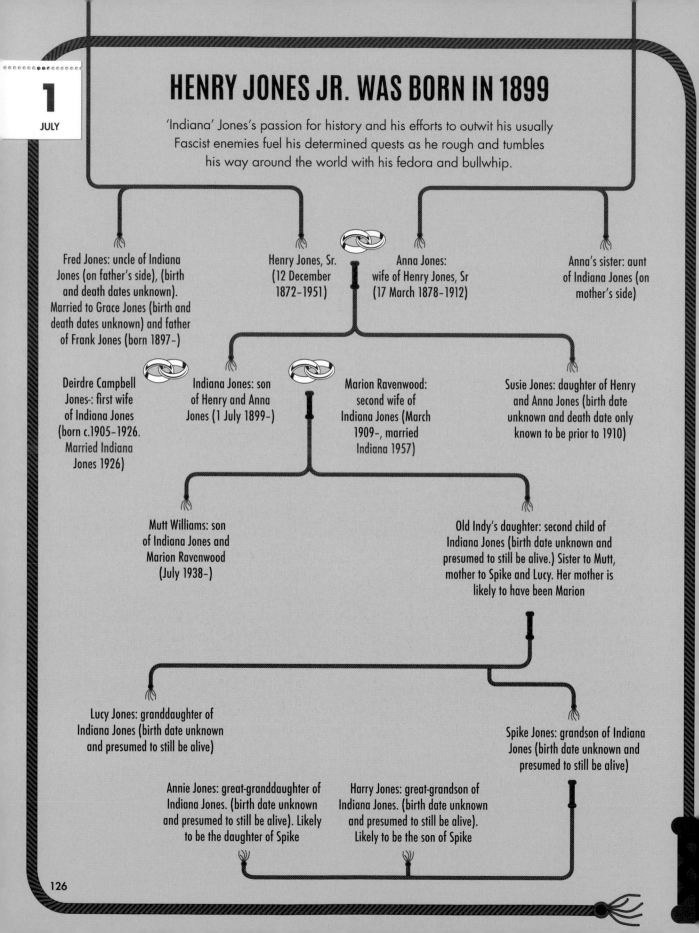

Fred Jones: uncle of Indiana Jones (on father's side), (birth and death dates unknown). Married to Grace Jones (birth and death dates unknown) and father of Frank Jones (born 1897–)

Henry Jones, Sr. (12 December 1872–1951)

Anna Jones: wife of Henry Jones, Sr (17 March 1878–1912)

Anna's sister: aunt of Indiana Jones (on mother's side)

Deirdre Campbell Jones–: first wife of Indiana Jones (born c.1905–1926. Married Indiana Jones 1926)

Indiana Jones: son of Henry and Anna Jones (1 July 1899–)

Marion Ravenwood: second wife of Indiana Jones (March 1909–, married Indiana 1957)

Susie Jones: daughter of Henry and Anna Jones (birth date unknown and death date only known to be prior to 1910)

Mutt Williams: son of Indiana Jones and Marion Ravenwood (July 1938–)

Old Indy's daughter: second child of Indiana Jones (birth date unknown and presumed to still be alive.) Sister to Mutt, mother to Spike and Lucy. Her mother is likely to have been Marion

Lucy Jones: granddaughter of Indiana Jones (birth date unknown and presumed to still be alive)

Spike Jones: grandson of Indiana Jones (birth date unknown and presumed to still be alive)

Annie Jones: great-granddaughter of Indiana Jones. (birth date unknown and presumed to still be alive). Likely to be the daughter of Spike

Harry Jones: great-grandson of Indiana Jones. (birth date unknown and presumed to still be alive). Likely to be the son of Spike

SCI-FI COMEDY MOVIE *MEN IN BLACK* WAS RELEASED IN US CINEMAS IN 1997

A cult comic created by Lowell Cunningham and Sandy Carruthers, *Men In Black* was originally published in black and white and subsequently adapted into a popular film trilogy.

TOM CRUISE WAS BORN IN 1962

Tom Cruise has starred in a number of films set squarely in the science-fiction genre: *Minority Report* (2002), *War of the Worlds* (2005), *Oblivion* (2013) and *Edge of Tomorrow* (2014).

In *Oblivion*, Cruise portrays Jack Harper, a technician maintaining the drones that watch over a fallen earth, the population having gone to establish a new colony somewhere else. *Edge of Tomorrow* is a large-scaled, event-movie adaptation that realises the Japanese novel *All You Need is Kill* by Hiroshi Sakurazaka (2005). It centres on humans who wear armour that is body-encompassing, 'transforming' the soldier into a cyborg of sorts. As John Anderton in *Minority Report*, Cruise captures the character's angst in a world where law and justice have gone awry. In *War of the Worlds* Cruise plays Ray Ferrier, making good use of his screen persona as a 'blue collar' star.

IN 1776 INDEPENDENCE DAY WAS FIRST DECLARED IN THE UNITED STATES

Stories about societies in which life, liberty and the pursuit of happiness are not easily enjoyed have made rich material for comic book readers.

In Alan Moore and David Lloyd's *V For Vendetta* (1989), the England of the future is ruled by a totalitarian regime. Only a man in a mask, resembling Guy Fawkes, makes a stand. American speculative fiction author Orson Scott Card's novels *Empire* and *Hidden Empire* imagine a future American in which a second American Civil War rages.

MEREDITH ANN PIERCE WAS BORN IN 1958

Pierce's fantasy novels include those comprising *The Darkangel Trilogy* (1982–1990) and *The Firebringer Trilogy* (1985–1996). Pierce's work is bound together by an exploration of mythological tropes combined with vivid world-building that draws inspiration from cultures including Native American.

6
JULY

LAWYER, PHILOSOPHER AND HUMANIST THOMAS MORE DIED IN 1535

How could More have known that his idea of a Utopia would work its way into plenty of geek material many centuries later?

For More, a utopia was a republic (no monarchy here) and marked by an adherence to reason as the basis for the culture's intellectual and daily life. That's a little different to what we might now think of a utopia – a place without difficulty – but the thread of More's idea is still with us. Aldous Huxley's novel *Brave New World* (1932) and H.G. Wells's The Shape of Things To Come (1933) both attest to utopian ideas. In more comic fashion Woody Allen's film *Sleeper* (1973) takes a lively look at life in the 22nd century, while *Gattaca* (1997) offers a nuanced take on what a dystopia could mean.

In 2015, Disney released the lavishly produced *Tomorrowland*, which centred on a parallel reality fashioned around a utopian ideal of inclusion and inspiration.

7
JULY

THE BRITISH MUSEUM ESTABLISHED IN AN ACT OF PARLIAMENT IN 1753

With their celebration of all things historical and exhibits far beyond of our immediate experience, it's not hard to see how the setting of a museum is ripe for adaptation into novels, films and comics. In *Alice in Wonderland* (1865), the still then-new world of museums and cabinets of curiosities inspired some of Lewis Carroll's imaginings.

8
JULY

FINAL EPISODE OF AMERICAN TV SERIES *FREAKS AND GEEKS* AIRED IN 2000

It's in the title of this book. It's become a readily used term and a badge of pop culture honour for millions. Maybe you consider yourself one of this tribe.

What does the word actually mean, though? Typically, *geek* was a term of derision and disparagement: a pejorative term used to indicate someone physically weak and socially clumsy.

If being a little clumsy, a little quirky, a little bit outside the ordinary are deficits, then so be it. Geeks have an often startling knowledge of their subject and their loyalty to their tribe is strong. In the film *The Lost Boys* (1987), it's that very geekiness that allows the two young boys to emerge as heroes of the story.

In contemporary 'real' life, the likes of Bill Gates, Steven Spielberg, Simon Pegg and Mayim Bialik (who also portrays a geek in *The Big Bang Theory*) all encapsulate that appealing sense of geeks as those who communicate sheer enthusiasm for the subject they care about.

Whoever would have foreseen geek-focused film trailers becoming a key moment in each year's annual Superbowl broadcast on American TV?

TRON IS RELEASED AT CINEMAS IN AMERICA IN 1982

The movie *Tron* was written and directed by Steven Lisberger. Released in 1982, it became a cult favourite and in 2010 a sequel was released, entitled *Tron: Legacy*.

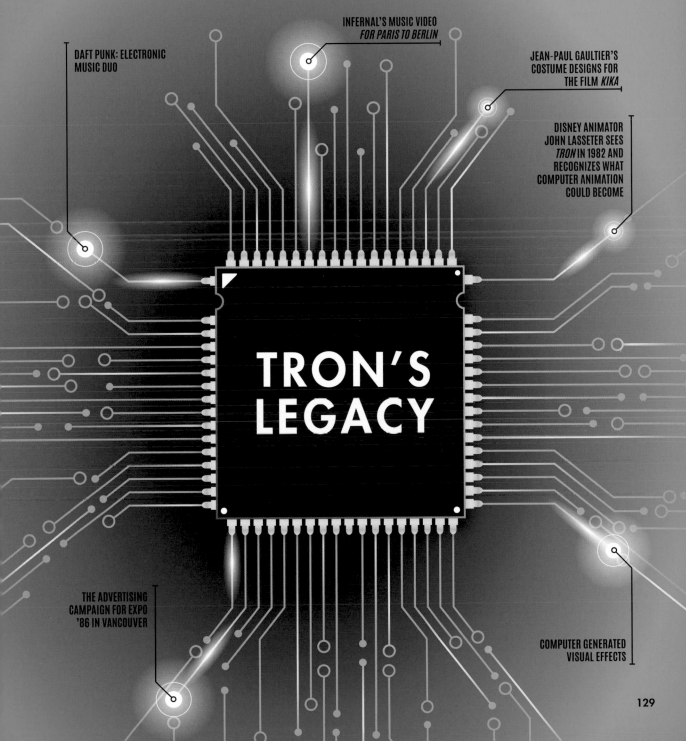

INFERNAL'S MUSIC VIDEO *FOR PARIS TO BERLIN*

DAFT PUNK: ELECTRONIC MUSIC DUO

JEAN-PAUL GAULTIER'S COSTUME DESIGNS FOR THE FILM *KIKA*

DISNEY ANIMATOR JOHN LASSETER SEES *TRON* IN 1982 AND RECOGNIZES WHAT COMPUTER ANIMATION COULD BECOME

TRON'S LEGACY

THE ADVERTISING CAMPAIGN FOR EXPO '86 IN VANCOUVER

COMPUTER GENERATED VISUAL EFFECTS

THE SCOPES MONKEY TRIAL BEGAN IN 1925

Science fiction has been able to explore evolution quite readily. The Scopes trial was about the right to teach evolution in American schools but science fiction has been able to explore evolution quite readily, with frequent discussion on the relationships between religion and science.

THE FILM *THE LEAGUE OF EXTRAORDINARY GENTLEMEN* WAS RELEASED IN AMERICA IN 2003

The League of Extraordinary Gentleman was a film adaptation of the Alan Moore comic series. Comprising several volumes to date, the original six issue miniseries was published between 1999 and 2000. So highly regarded is the first volume of the series that a copy is archived in The British Library in London.

Like Moore's *Watchmen* (1986–87), this comic project emphasised a certain faith in the reader's awareness of established generic characters and themes. The first volume draws together a number of iconic characters from Victorian novels: including Mina Harker from Bram Stoker's *Dracula* (1897) (now under her maiden name of Murray) and Allan Quatermain from H. Rider Haggard's *King Solomon's Mines* (1885). The original volume captures the distinct pleasures of the steampunk sensibility and the most recent volume brings the world Moore and artist Kevin O'Neill have created way up into 1969 and beyond.

BUCKMINSTER FULLER WAS BORN IN 1895

The gloriously named Buckminster Fuller was a thinker, a writer and a futurist. Perhaps his most captivating idea was that of Spaceship Earth, a collective entity travelling around the universe. Bucky's idea is marvellously hopeful. Fuller's also responsible for coining the now oft-used term *synergy*.

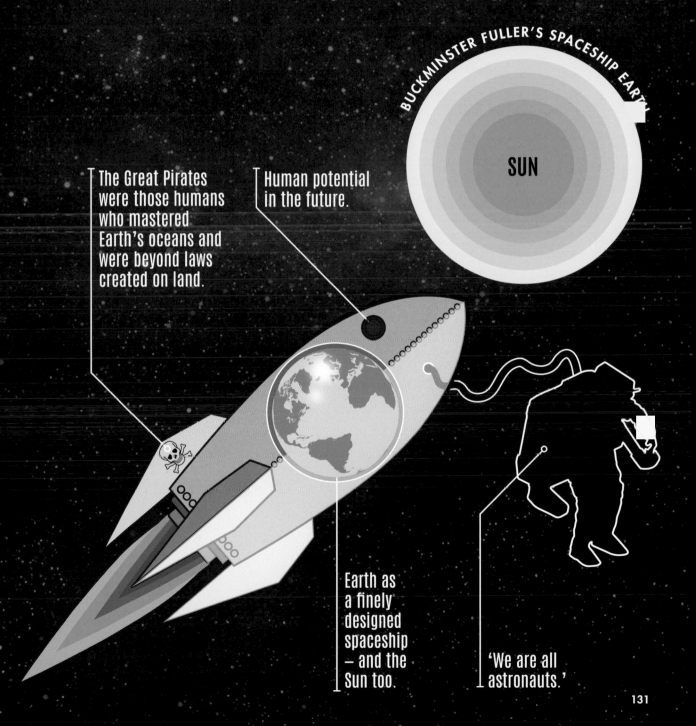

BUCKMINSTER FULLER'S SPACESHIP EARTH

SUN

The Great Pirates were those humans who mastered Earth's oceans and were beyond laws created on land.

Human potential in the future.

Earth as a finely designed spaceship – and the Sun too.

'We are all astronauts.'

THE MOVIE *THE LAST STARFIGHTER* WAS RELEASED IN 1984

The film was not a smash success, but thanks partly to the VHS generation *The Last Starfighter* did find an audience that endures to this day. The story turns on the idea of a teenager arcade game-playing ace being recruited to serve in an actual intergalactic war, using his game-playing skills to help win the day. *The Last Starfighter*'s great hero is a geek.

IN 1910 WILLIAM HANNA WAS BORN

With Joe Barbera, he would go on to establish the Hanna-Barbera animation studio. The studio produced a number of series and characters that remain widely recognised today: *The Flintstones* (1960–2001), *Hong Kong Phooey* (1974), *Scooby-Doo* (1969–2002) and *Wacky Races* (1968–69).

IN 1994, THE FIRST EPISODE OF ARTHUR C.CLARKE'S TV SERIES *ARTHUR C.CLARKE'S MYSTERIOUS UNIVERSE* WAS BROADCAST

The series examined stories of the unexplained, Clarke approaching often fabulous-sounding scenarios with a healthy scepticism. The series included investigations into giants, psychic behaviour, extra-terrestrial intelligence and the Bermuda Triangle.

THE CHINESE FANTASY ACTION MOVIE
MONSTER HUNT WAS RELEASED IN 2015

Monster Hunt stands as one of the biggest-ever box office hits in Chinese cinema. It is the story of a civil war between monsters, which spills over into the human realm.

Drawing on the *Classic of Mountains and Seas* (or *Shan Hai Jing*), which has its origins in texts dating to the fourth century BC, the film captured the Chinese film-going audience's imagination. It didn't find a sizeable audience overseas, however.

WUBA IS A CUTE BABY MONSTER BORN TO HUMAN PARENTS BUT DESTINED TO BECOME KING

BOX OFFICE: CHINA AND OTHER TERRITORIES
$385,252,051

BOX OFFICE: AMERICA
$32,766.00

A MONSTROUS BOX OFFICE COMPARISON

ROBOCOP WAS RELEASED IN 1987

RoboCop was a violent, occasionally cynical, science-fiction action movie that examines modern law and order, and the potential for humans to become technology.

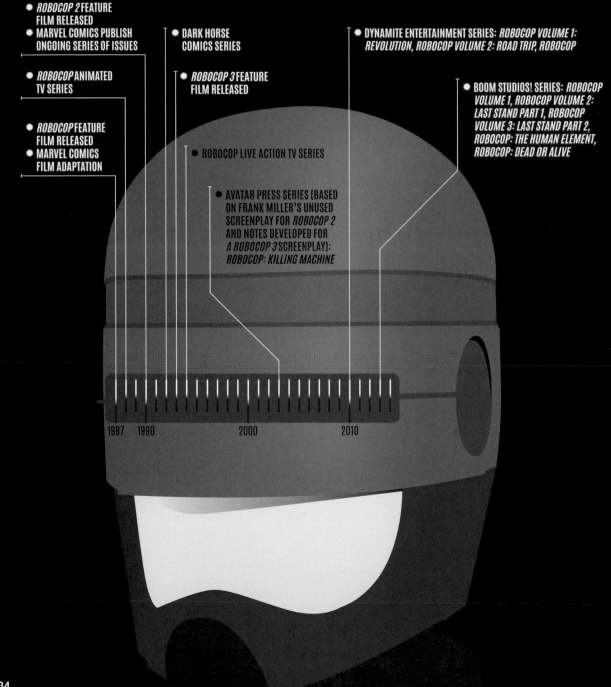

* *ROBOCOP 2* FEATURE FILM RELEASED
* MARVEL COMICS PUBLISH ONGOING SERIES OF ISSUES

* *ROBOCOP* ANIMATED TV SERIES

* *ROBOCOP* FEATURE FILM RELEASED
* MARVEL COMICS FILM ADAPTATION

* DARK HORSE COMICS SERIES

* *ROBOCOP 3* FEATURE FILM RELEASED

* ROBOCOP LIVE ACTION TV SERIES

* AVATAR PRESS SERIES (BASED ON FRANK MILLER'S UNUSED SCREENPLAY FOR *ROBOCOP 2* AND NOTES DEVELOPED FOR A *ROBOCOP 3* SCREENPLAY): *ROBOCOP: KILLING MACHINE*

* DYNAMITE ENTERTAINMENT SERIES: *ROBOCOP VOLUME 1: REVOLUTION, ROBOCOP VOLUME 2: ROAD TRIP, ROBOCOP*

* BOOM STUDIOS! SERIES: *ROBOCOP VOLUME 1, ROBOCOP VOLUME 2: LAST STAND PART 1, ROBOCOP VOLUME 3: LAST STAND PART 2, ROBOCOP: THE HUMAN ELEMENT, ROBOCOP: DEAD OR ALIVE*

1987 1990 2000 2010

SYD MEAD WAS BORN IN 1933

Part of the pleasure of enjoying science-fiction films is enjoying the artwork that informed their creative development. Syd Mead is key to that conceptual art tradition, creating images and designs for Star Trek: *The Motion Picture* (1979), *Blade Runner* (1982), *Tron* (1982), *2010* (1984), *Aliens* (1986), *Elysium* (2013) and *Tomorrowland* (2015).

GARTH NIX WAS BORN IN 1963

Garth Nix's novels for young readers are an ideal place from which to start venturing into the realms of speculative fiction. The Australian writer is a fantasy specialist whose writing includes the series *Keys to the Kingdom* (1995–2003) and *Old Kingdom* (1995–2016). At the age of nineteen he sold his first story, a short piece entitled 'Sam, Cars and the Cuckoo' to *Warlock* magazine in 1984.

His breakthrough came with *Sabriel* (1995), the first in the *Old Kingdom* series in which the living and the dead share worlds. This charts Sabriel's quest to find her father, aided by a cat named Mogget and a young magician named Touchstone. The series also includes *Lirael* (2001) and *Abhorsen* (2003).

In the science fiction novel *Shade's Children* (1997), he created a future world in which children are hunted by a sinister machine. Several children ally themselves with a stranger named Shade to thwart them.

Nix is a role-playing enthusiast and he's made the point that playing *Dungeons & Dragons* since it was first released in 1974 had an important role in developing his storytelling sensibility.

NEIL ARMSTRONG WALKS ON THE MOON ON IN 1969

Films set specifically in our solar system carry a particular fascination: relatively speaking, the planets orbiting the sun are within our reach (kind of). Films and TV programmes set on and around the Moon are even closer to home. Just a few to explore are *Moon* (2009), *2001: A Space Odyssey* (1968, the IMAX documentary *Magnificent Desolation: Walking on the Moon 3D* (2005) and the mini-series *From the Earth to the Moon* (1998).

GUARDIANS OF THE GALAXY IS RELEASED IN 2014

It was a smash hit, despite being based on a relatively little known Marvel Comic, first published in 1969 in Marvel Super Heroes, issue number 18. This original team was very different to the team depicted in the film.

PLAN 9 FROM OUTER SPACE WAS RELEASED IN 1959

Ed Wood's ultra-low budget films of the 1950s have become ultra-cult films. Memorably, the film director Tim Burton collaborated with film star Johnny Depp to bring Ed Wood to the screen with their film *Ed Wood* (1993). Wood's most famous low budget film was *Plan 9 From Outer Space* (1959).

COMPUTER GAME *MONKEY ISLAND* IS RE-RELEASED FOR THE iPHONE IN 2009

In 1984, having made his mark on science-fiction and fantasy cinema with the *Star Wars* trilogy and as co-creator of *Raiders of the Lost Ark* (1981), George Lucas's Lucasfilm Games (later Lucasarts) launched its first two titles: *Ballblazer* and *Rescue on Fractalus!* These were followed in 1985 by *Koronis Rift* and *The Eidolon*.

The company continued publishing titles, and in 1990 had perhaps its most well remembered success with the release of *The Secret of Monkey Island*, followed by *Monkey Island 2: LeChuck's Revenge* in 1991. The *Monkey Island* games were point and click adventure games set in the world of pirates, and they are widely considered to be amongst the very best such computer games of their era.

IN 2012 GEEK SHOPPING HAVEN *FORBIDDEN PLANET* RELOCATES ITS STORE IN NEW YORK

The big box of delights that is the shop Forbidden Planet has become an essential destination across the UK and in New York, too.

This writer recalls quite clearly the pokey, slightly shadowy upstairs and downstairs of London's Forbidden Planet when it was on New Oxford Street in the late 80s and early 1990s. Now the store on Shaftesbury Avenue is spacious, brightly lit – and stocked with so many books, comics, toys, games, clothes and trading cards.

From the moment you enter the store to the moment you leave, you are in the company of your fellow geek brothers and sisters.

Established in 1978, on Denmark Street in Soho, Forbidden Planet was set up by Nick Landau who had once been sub editor of *2000AD* and the war comic *Battle*, Mike Lake and Mike Luckman.

Opened at that now seemingly critical juncture in the space-time continuum for so many things fantasy, sci-fi and horror, Forbidden Planet tapped into a world that had been introduced the previous year (1977) to *2000AD*, *Star Wars* and *Close Encounters of the Third Kind*.

With guests coming to sign their work, Forbidden Planet became a central hub around which British geekdom was able to happily turn.

THE MODERN-DAY SERIES OF *SHERLOCK HOLMES* BEGAN ON THE BBC IN 2010

Starring Benedict Cumberbatch and Martin Freeman (who'd also share the screen in *The Hobbit: The Desolation of Smaug*, 2013), the new Holmes iteration attested to the character's malleability, allowing his mental agility and charm to shine through. Written by *Dr Who* showrunner Steven Moffat and Mark Gattis, the show was witty, tense and sincere.

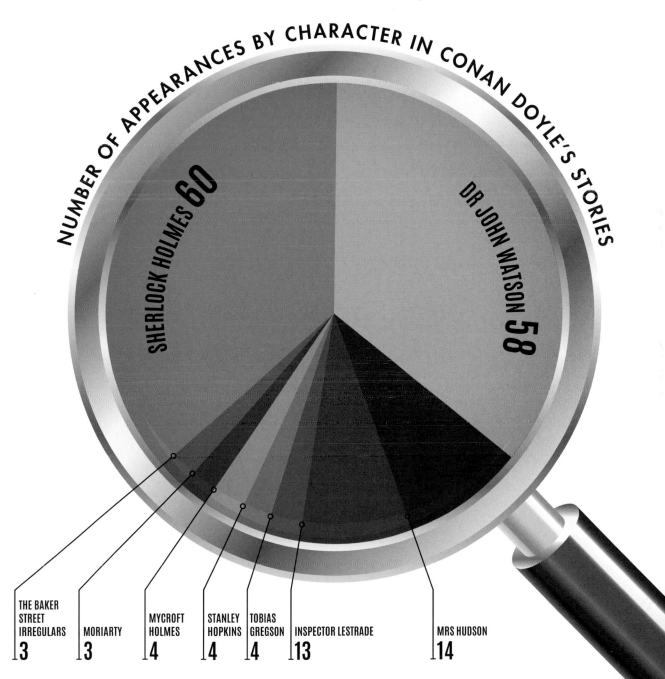

NUMBER OF APPEARANCES BY CHARACTER IN CONAN DOYLE'S STORIES

SHERLOCK HOLMES **60**

DR JOHN WATSON **58**

THE BAKER STREET IRREGULARS **3**

MORIARTY **3**

MYCROFT HOLMES **4**

STANLEY HOPKINS **4**

TOBIAS GREGSON **4**

INSPECTOR LESTRADE **13**

MRS HUDSON **14**

26 JULY

ALDOUS HUXLEY WAS BORN IN 1894

Huxley would write *Brave New World* (1932), a key sci-fi novel that's informed plenty of other literary and cinema geek titles such as *THX 1138* (1971) and *Logan's Run* (1976).

Huxley took his title for the novel from Shakespeare's play *The Tempest* (1611). Huxley's world is the antithesis of Wells' utopian future. Set in the twenty-sixth century, Huxley's novel is a cautionary tale about consumerism and the infantilization of adults.

27 JULY

THE TV SERIES *STARGATE: SG1* PREMIERED ON AMERICAN TV IN 1997

Fresh from the success of science fiction adventure movie *Stargate* (1994), the spin-off series utilised the feature film's portal concept as a device allowing for plenty of adventures into unknown worlds.

THE FIRST WORLD WAR BEGAN IN 1914

The trauma of this war eventually seeded some wondrously imaginative writing, which laid so many foundations for what we now think of as geek classics.

Tolkien and Lewis both served during the War, as did composer Ralph Vaughan Williams. His pastoral music has influenced the work of John Williams: his theme for the Grail Knight in Indiana Jones and the Last Crusade is suffused with sound of Vaughan Williams.

Reality and an escape from it go hand-in-hand and in his essay 'On Fairy-Stories'(1947), Tolkien writes eloquently on this subject.

J.R.R.TOLKIEN

SERVES ON THE FRONT LINE IN THE SOMME VALLEY. TOLKIEN WAS NOT IN THE FIRST SOMME ASSAULT. HE SERVED AS APPOINTED BATTALION SIGNALING OFFICER IN THE TRENCHES. OCTOBER 1916: GOES TO SERVE AT YPRES. BUT, A LOUSE BITE SEES HIM RETURN HOME TO THE UK.

JOHN MASEFIELD

SERVES IN THE RED CROSS, WORKING AS A HOSPITAL ORDERLY AT CHATEAU OF ARC-EN-BARROIS IN THE HAUTE-MARNE.

WALT DISNEY

SERVES IN THE RED CROSS AMBULANCE CORPS AT LE HAVRE.

C.S.LEWIS

SERVES ON THE FRONT LINE IN THE SOMME VALLEY ON HIS 19TH BIRTHDAY. ON 15 APRIL 1918, LEWIS IS WOUNDED ON MOUNT BERECHON DURING THE BATTLE OF ARRAS.

29 JULY

IN 1994 THE FILM *THE MASK* WAS RELEASED

An adaptation of the *Dark Horse* comic, the film stars Jim Carrey as humble Stanley Ipkiss, who discovers an ancient mask that transforms the wearer into a comic, high-energy soul. The film's notable, too, for being Cameron Diaz's debut and marking her capacity for working with comedy. ILM's visual effects for the film rekindle the aesthetic of Tex Avery and Chuck Jones.

30 JULY

FILM DIRECTOR AND SCREENWRITER CHRISTOPHER NOLAN WAS BORN IN 1970

Bringing a certain seriousness to genre material, Nolan makes films that are key to contemporary film geek culture. His *Batman* trilogy (2005, 2008, 2012) and his 'puzzle films' (*Memento*, 2000, and *The Prestige*, 2006) are vividly realised while *Inception* (2010) and *Interstellar* (2014) are science-fiction movies that relish the chance to dramatize moral choices.

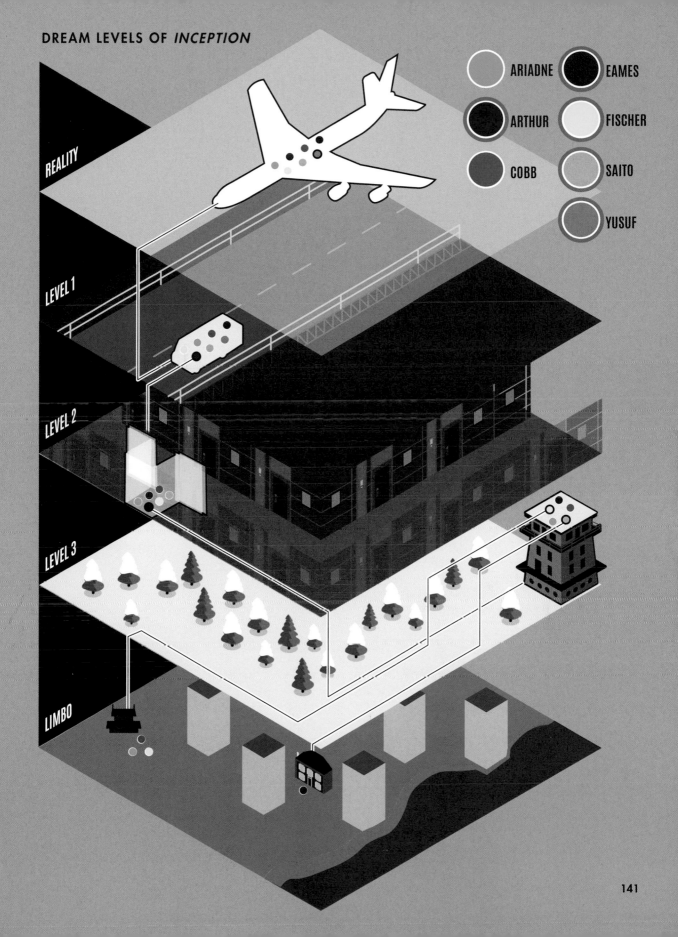

DREAM LEVELS OF *INCEPTION*

ARIADNE   EAMES
ARTHUR   FISCHER
COBB   SAITO
YUSUF

REALITY

LEVEL 1

LEVEL 2

LEVEL 3

LIMBO

HARRY POTTER WAS BORN IN 1980

The *Harry Potter* saga is a dazzling reminder of the allure of the hero's journey. Published in 1997, J.K. Rowling's first Harry Potter novel affirmed the value of fantasy as a powerful way to explore reality.

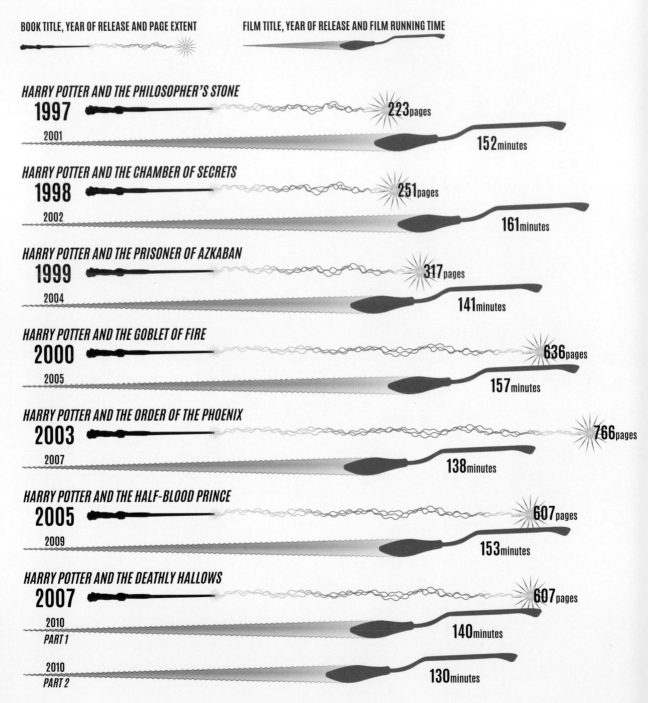

BOOK TITLE, YEAR OF RELEASE AND PAGE EXTENT

FILM TITLE, YEAR OF RELEASE AND FILM RUNNING TIME

HARRY POTTER AND THE PHILOSOPHER'S STONE
1997 — 223 pages
2001 — 152 minutes

HARRY POTTER AND THE CHAMBER OF SECRETS
1998 — 251 pages
2002 — 161 minutes

HARRY POTTER AND THE PRISONER OF AZKABAN
1999 — 317 pages
2004 — 141 minutes

HARRY POTTER AND THE GOBLET OF FIRE
2000 — 636 pages
2005 — 157 minutes

HARRY POTTER AND THE ORDER OF THE PHOENIX
2003 — 766 pages
2007 — 138 minutes

HARRY POTTER AND THE HALF-BLOOD PRINCE
2005 — 607 pages
2009 — 153 minutes

HARRY POTTER AND THE DEATHLY HALLOWS
2007 — 607 pages
2010 *PART 1* — 140 minutes
2010 *PART 2* — 130 minutes

DUNE WAS PUBLISHED IN 1965

The 1960s witnessed a growing conversation about ecology, and Frank Herbert's novel *Dune* saga tapped into that. Dune charts the experiences of Paul Atreides, a young prince seeking to return to power after a feud between families. Five further *Dune* novels from Herbert followed (1969, 1976, 1981, 1984 1985), continuing the eco-theme and infused further with the influence of Carl Jung's writing.

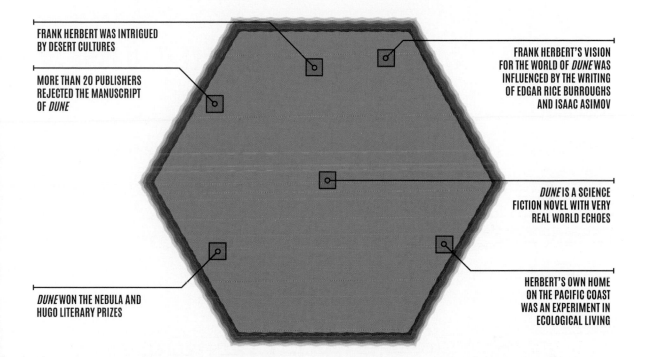

FRANK HERBERT WAS INTRIGUED BY DESERT CULTURES

MORE THAN 20 PUBLISHERS REJECTED THE MANUSCRIPT OF *DUNE*

FRANK HERBERT'S VISION FOR THE WORLD OF *DUNE* WAS INFLUENCED BY THE WRITING OF EDGAR RICE BURROUGHS AND ISAAC ASIMOV

DUNE IS A SCIENCE FICTION NOVEL WITH VERY REAL WORLD ECHOES

DUNE WON THE NEBULA AND HUGO LITERARY PRIZES

HERBERT'S OWN HOME ON THE PACIFIC COAST WAS AN EXPERIMENT IN ECOLOGICAL LIVING

THE SIXTH SENSE PREMIERED IN 1999

M.Night Shyamalan's films have explored the dynamics of science fiction, horror and fantasy. His thoughtful and moving superhero film *Unbreakable* (2000) grapples with comic book lore.

A NEAR COMPLETE NEANDERTHAL MAN IS UNEARTHED IN FRANCE IN 1908

Things primaeval and prehistoric have been a rich source for science fiction, fantasy and horror. *One Million Years B.C.* (1966) is a classic film of the prehistoric genre. Quite different in tone is *The Clan of the Cave Bear* (1986), which adapts the Jean M. Auel novel.

HANS CHRISTIAN ANDERSEN DIED IN 1875

Danish writer Hans Christian Andersen, ungainly in appearance and manner, but never more elegant than in his writing, gave us so much that now forms the fabric of fairy-tale films.

We live in a moment when many of the most popular blockbusters have been derived from fairy tales. Disney's *Frozen* (2103) reframes Andersen's *The Snow Queen* (1844) and the studio's take (1992) on his story 'The Little Mermaid' (1837) contributed to the Disney studio's animation revival.

Fairytale geek films include Ridley Scott's *Legend* (1985), Jean Cocteau's *La Belle et la Bête* (1946) and the animated films of Lotte Reiniger (1899–1981).

THE PIPER AT THE GATES OF DAWN RELEASED 1967

The title of Pink Floyd's debut studio album is taken from the chapter of the same name in the novel *The Wind in the Willows* (1908). The psychedelic rock album combines instrumental pieces that were improvised, such as 'Insterstellar Overdrive' and 'Pow R. Toc H', with songs written by Syd Barrett, Pink Floyd's original guitarist and frontman.

The Piper at the Gates of Dawn marks quite a moment for geek rock music. Other such albums include The Flaming Lips' *Yoshimi and the Pink Robots* (2002), in which the songs tell stories of human/robot interaction, and They Might Be Giants's *Apollo 18* (1992). Other albums deserving of a namecheck are: Thomas Dolby's *The Golden Age of Wireless* (1982), Weezer's *Blue Album* (1994), Devo's *Duty Now for the Future* (1979) – and, coming full circle, Pink Floyd's *Dark Side of the Moon* (1973), which got to musical grips with the big stuff: mortality, conflict and mental health.

DWARVES WAS PUBLISHED IN ENGLISH IN 2009

Back in 2011, *The Hollywood Reporter* noted that the film rights to Markus Heitz's series of *Dwarves* novels had been bought. A bestseller in Germany, the *Dwarves* stories follow in the tradition of Tolkien and other high fantasy practitioners like David Gemmell and Terry Brooks.

Set in a world called Girdlegard, the novel focuses on Tungdil, a young dwarf who becomes embroiled in a war with the Orcs. The series of novels comprises *The War of the Dwarves* (2004), *The Revenge of the Dwarves* (2005), and *The Fate of the Dwarves* (2008). Heitz's writing communicates a vividly thought-through fantasy world, and his own familiarity with the world of role-playing that became so popular during the 1970s and '80s. Heitz has gone on to write *The Legends of the Älfar* series (2009–14), among others. In a sure sign of the popularity of the *Dwarves* series, it has been adapted into a computer game.

AUTHOR YASUMI KOBAYASHI WAS BORN IN 1962

Yasumi is relatively unknown in Europe and America but is a major voice in science fiction and fantasy (and horror, too) in his home country of Japan. Yasumi's novels include *Alpha and Omega* (2001) and the brilliantly titled *Phantasia of the Nephilim Super-Vampires* (2004). Somewhat more modestly titled is Yasumi's volume of short stories, *The Man Watching the Sea* (2011).

TERRY NATION WAS BORN IN 1930

Whilst the creation of *Doctor Who* was the work of Canadian Sydney Newman, (who had also created the TV series *The Avengers* 1961–69), without Terry Nation, the landscape of British science-fiction TV would be very different.

As well as creating the Doctor's most famous nemesis, Nation also created two classics of 1970s science-fiction. *Blake's 7* (1978–81) came along in the wake of *Star Wars* (1977) and ran for four series, focusing on a band of intergalactic outsiders. *Survivors* (1975–77) was a post-apocalyptic series, and Nation's interest was in charting the moral dilemmas faced by his characters.

IN 1973 E.E. 'DOC' SMITH'S NOVEL *GREY LENSMAN* WAS RERELEASED IN PAPERBACK IN ENGLISH

Space opera is a sub-genre of science fiction which tends towards the melodramatic. Often focusing on warfare in space, if we're lucky, there's a welcome shot of human dilemma fuelling the drama, too.

The *Lensman* saga by E. E. 'Doc' Smith stands as critical piece of space opera literature. For this set of novels, Smith (who had a PhD, hence 'Doc') established a number of space-opera must-haves.

In 1928, *The Skylark of Space* was serialised in *Amazing Stories*. Its genius hero, Richard Seaton, makes a spaceship from a newly-discovered element and a rescue adventure ensues when Seaton realises that his nemesis has kidnapped his girlfriend.

Following *Skylark*, Smith began work on the *Lensman* stories, in which two hyper-intelligent races, the peace-loving Arisians and the less peace-loving Eddorians, are in conflict. A Galactic Patrol of humans and other races are gifted by the Arisians with lenses that allow them to channel extrasensory abilities and powers.

SPIDER-MAN DEBUTS IN 1962

First seen in issue number 15 of Marvel's *Amazing Fantasy* and created by Stan Lee and Steve Ditko, *Spider-Man* remains one of the most significant and recognizable American comic book heroes.

In his ordinary life, Peter Parker is a student. Bitten by a spider, Peter's body evolves with the ability to climb walls, spin webs and move at high speed. So popular was his debut appearance that by 1963 he had his own comic: *The Amazing Spider-Man*. Artists Steve Ditko and John Romita in succession evolved Spider-Man's physique, tending towards a more muscular presentation of the hero.

Over the decades various comic line spin-offs have followed including: *Peter Parker The Spectacular Spider-Man*, *Web of Spider-Man*, *Avenging Spider-Man*, *The Superior Spider-Man*.

Sam Raimi's bright, energetic and sincerely felt Spider-Man movie trilogy (2002, 2004 and 2007) are classics of the comic book movie canon.

ALLIES

J

MF

BC

AC

MW

MJ

T

SS

M

EB

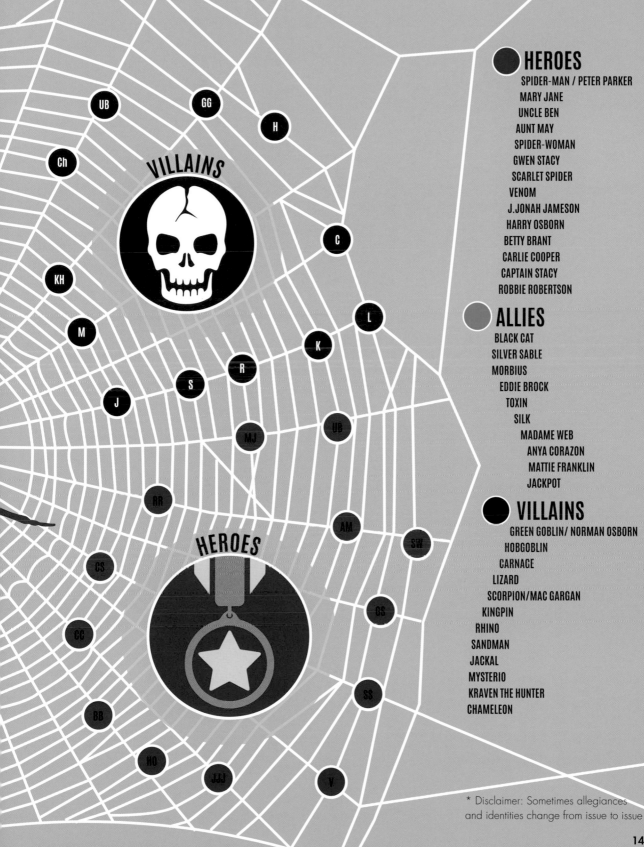

HEROES

SPIDER-MAN / PETER PARKER
MARY JANE
UNCLE BEN
AUNT MAY
SPIDER-WOMAN
GWEN STACY
SCARLET SPIDER
VENOM
J. JONAH JAMESON
HARRY OSBORN
BETTY BRANT
CARLIE COOPER
CAPTAIN STACY
ROBBIE ROBERTSON

ALLIES

BLACK CAT
SILVER SABLE
MORBIUS
EDDIE BROCK
TOXIN
SILK
MADAME WEB
ANYA CORAZON
MATTIE FRANKLIN
JACKPOT

VILLAINS

GREEN GOBLIN/ NORMAN OSBORN
HOBGOBLIN
CARNAGE
LIZARD
SCORPION/MAC GARGAN
KINGPIN
RHINO
SANDMAN
JACKAL
MYSTERIO
KRAVEN THE HUNTER
CHAMELEON

VILLAINS

HEROES

* Disclaimer: Sometimes allegiances
and identities change from issue to issue

THE *GHOSTBUSTERS* SONG HIT NUMBER 1 IN THE US IN 1984

When the punchy synths and guitar intro of Ray Parker Jr's theme song for Ghostbusters play, you'll either be ectoplasmed back to 1984, or, at least, you'll know that spooks and chuckles in good combination are close at hand.

The box office hit of summer 1984, *Ghostbusters* proved the appeal of fantasy comedy. This feature film, set in New York, had just the right contemporary feel and four geeks at its centre. Enhancing the visual effects and comedy was Elmer Bernstein's perfectly judged playfully spooky musical score.

The film's sequel (1989) revisited the same premise as the first film, a supernatural force imperilling our heroes and the wider world. So successful were these films that a cartoon series and accompanying toys proved very popular. In 2016, amid unnecessary reservations expressed about an all-female team of Ghostbusters, a new film was released.

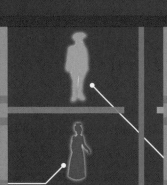

LIBRARY GHOST (FROM 1984 FILM): CLASS 4 SEMI-ANCHORED ENTITY

SLIMER (FROM 1984 AND 2016 FILM): CLASS 5 FULL ROAMING VAPOUR

BOX OF EGGS (FROM 1984 FILM): CLASS 2 ANIMATED OBJECT

ECTOPLASM: CLASS 1 SUPERNATURAL SECRETION

TERROR DOGS (FROM 1984 FILM): CLASS 6 ENTITY

TIMES SQUARE BATTLE GHOST (FROM 2016 FILM): CLASS 3 ANIMATING SPECTRE

STAY-PUFT MARSHMALLOW MAN (FROM 1984 FILM): CLASS 7 OUTSIDER AVATAR

SUPERNATURAL CLASSIFICATIONS

WADE WATTS WAS BORN IN 2024

In 2011, a modestly promoted novel was published and garnered something of a cult following. In 2015, when Warner Bros. announced that Steven Spielberg would be directing the feature film adaptation, interest in the novel skyrocketed. The novel was *Ready Player One*, written by Ernest Cline, and its take on the connection between real and virtual worlds echoes William Gibson's classic novel *Neuromancer* (1984).

Cline's story is set in a dismal future and takes the form of a quest for treasure in the virtual world, undertaken by teenager Wade Watts and his virtual world friends Art3mis and Aech.

The novel is marinated in an uber-geeky fascination with the pop culture artefacts of the 1970s and '80s, a point that has attracted much comment.

IN 1876, RICHARD WAGNER'S *THE RING* PREMIERED

Whether it's Thor bolting around the world with his hammer in a Marvel comic, Bilbo Baggins and the dwarves trekking to the Lonely Mountain or *Warhammer*'s gameplay, there's something that binds them all together: a creative debt to the influence of European mythology.

Wagner's *The Ring of the Nibelung*, a cycle of four epic operas, demonstrated the popular allure of the mythology of ancient Europe, and its stories and images have been almost endlessly used and reworked in sword and sorcery stories, space opera and high fantasy.

WIM WENDERS WAS BORN IN 1945

Sombre German filmmakers of the 1980s may not immediately come to mind in relation to fantasy films, but *Wings of Desire*, directed by Wim Wenders, is one of the very best.

Shot in black-and-white, it tells of angels above Berlin and their interactions with the humans below. In terms of subject matter and execution, it's right up there with the Hollywood classics *A Guy Named Joe* (1943) and *It's A Wonderful Life* (1946) and with British fantasy favourite *A Matter of Life and Death* (1946).

JENNIFER LAWRENCE WAS BORN IN 1990

Part futuristic thriller, part adventure story, *The Hunger Games* novels by Suzanne Collins achieved bestseller status before being adapted as hugely popular feature films, which star actress Jennifer Lawrence as Katniss Everdeen. Like many other geek ideas referenced in this book, *The Hunger Games* takes an imaginary world and uses it to make salient points about current world issues.

IN 1898 THE FIRST ROLLERCOASTER WAS PATENTED

16 AUGUST

'Rollercoaster movies' – a term used to describe the kind of films that tend to appeal to geek audiences. *Indiana Jones and the Temple of Doom* (1984) takes the comparison to its logical extreme during one sequence in the film, and sure enough rollercoasters have worked as location and story element in a number of geek films.

Rollercoasters and theme parks have played a useful role in plenty of films: in *Zombieland* (2009) a ride offers escape from a horde of zombies below. In *Something Wicked This Way Comes* (1983, based on Ray Bradbury's novel, 1962), a carnival ride has the power to make you grow older or younger. *Final Destination 3* (2006) begins with a bad ride, and the animated short 'Roller Coaster Rabbit' gives us a Roger Rabbit spin on the ride.

To date, perhaps *Westworld* – both the film from 1973 and the TV series that began in 2016 – takes the theme park idea to its most elaborate conclusion.

BRITISH WRITER TED HUGHES WAS BORN IN 1930

17 AUGUST

The Iron Giant (1999) stands as a modern animated classic: it was based on Ted Hughes's novel for children, entitled *The Iron Man*, published in 1968. It was the first of several geek film favourites to be directed by Brad Bird, the others including *The Incredibles* (2004) and *Tomorrowland: A World Beyond* (2015). One of Bird's earliest projects was as a writer for *batteries not included* (1987) in which a group of mechanical aliens help to save a building from destruction.

THE HUGO AWARDS ANNOUNCED ITS RETRO 1941 HUGO AWARDS WINNERS IN 2016

18 AUGUST

Victors at the ceremony included the late Isaac Asimov for his Best Short Story winner *Robbie*, first published in *Super Science Stories* in September 1940.

The Best Novel Hugo for this retrospective awards ceremony went to A.E.Van Vogt's novel *Slan*, which had originally been published in December 1940. The retro 1941 Hugo Awards were made as there had originally never been a Hugo Award ceremony in that year.

THE SECOND DAY OF THE PENDLE WITCHES TRIAL IN 1612 IN LANCASHIRE, ENGLAND

Eighty years later, in colonial Massachusetts, the Salem Witch Trials of 1692–3 also carried real power.

The fascination with witchcraft is complex and deep, and we can certainly look to the influence of fairy tales and folklore. Since 1997, witches have re-entered pop culture with particular force in the context of the *Harry Potter* novels. In comics, witches have been showcased in *Sabrina the Teenage Witch* from Archie Comics, and in Stan Lee and Jack Kirby's creation Karnilla and DC Comics' Raven.

On television, programming with a witchy focus has included the suburban comedy of *Bewitched* (1964–72), the 60s *Gothic of Dark Shadows* (1966–71), the Southern Gothic of *True Blood* (2008–14) and the Victorian menace of *Penny Dreadful* (2014–16).

The Witches of Eastwick (1987, adapting John Updike's novel of the same name, 1984) and *The Craft* (1996) are notable film entries.

WRITER H.P. LOVECRAFT WAS BORN IN 1890

Lovecraft's fantasy horror writing has flowed into the bloodstream of geek culture quite powerfully, his influence hugely important to Stephen King and obvious in the work of Clive Barker and Neil Gaiman and the films of Guillermo del Toro.

Lovecraft's writing began finding a home in the world in 1919 in *The Vagrant* magazine, which published his short story 'Dagon' about drug-using sailors recalling horrific events during the First World War.

It was *Weird Tales* magazine, though, where Lovecraft's work found its wider platform. Here Lovecraft published 'The Call of Cthulhu' (1928), 'The Dunwich Horror' (1929), 'The Silver Key' (1929), *The Whisperer in Darkness* (1931), 'The Strange High House in the Mist' (1931) and 'The Dreams in the Witch House' (1933).

Lovecraft's creation of The Ancient Ones allowed him to characterise the mystery of the universe and its chaotic nature.

Perhaps his most well-regarded piece is *At the Mountains of Madness*; initially published in serial form (in 1936) before being issued as a single volume.

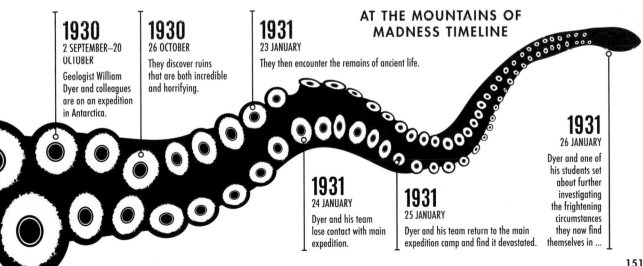

AT THE MOUNTAINS OF MADNESS TIMELINE

1930
2 SEPTEMBER–20 OCTOBER

Geologist William Dyer and colleagues are on an expedition in Antarctica.

1930
26 OCTOBER

They discover ruins that are both incredible and horrifying.

1931
23 JANUARY

They then encounter the remains of ancient life.

1931
24 JANUARY

Dyer and his team lose contact with main expedition.

1931
25 JANUARY

Dyer and his team return to the main expedition camp and find it devastated.

1931
26 JANUARY

Dyer and one of his students set about further investigating the frightening circumstances they now find themselves in ...

21 AUGUST

HORROR FILM *BLADE* PREMIERED IN 1998

The *Blade* film franchise adapted the comic book series for the screen across three films (1998, 2002, 2004). Blade is the name of a vampire slayer who first appeared in Marvel Comics's *Tomb of Dracula Volume 1* in 1973. Blade is immune to a vampire's bite and he brings martial arts skills to bear on his encounters with the undead. The second Blade film, *Blade II*, was directed by Guillermo del Toro.

22 AUGUST

IN AD 565 THE LEGEND OF LOCH NESS WAS FIRST RECORDED

Submarine beasts have found a home in geek culture. In *The Abyss* and *Leviathan* (both 1989 releases) otherworldly creatures prove both benevolent and malevolent. Then, too, there's *Jaws* (1975), *Piranha* (1978), and *The Beast from 20,000 Fathoms* (1953).

23 AUGUST

THE FILM *TEEN WOLF* WAS RELEASED IN 1985

Teen werewolves enjoyed a moment in the 1950s with films such as *I Was A Teenage Werewolf* (1957), and the subgenre had a moment of resurgence with *Teen Wolf*, starring Michael J. Fox.

A warm-hearted comedy about adolescence, *Teen Wolf* remains a favourite. In 2010, a lavish retelling of the werewolf lore was realised in *The Wolfman* which revisited the 1941 film starring Lon Chaney. *Wolf* (1994), starring Jack Nicholson and Michelle Pfeiffer, the *Twilight* films (2010, 2102, 2103) and *True Blood* TV series (2008–14) also showcased the werewolf's allure.

24 AUGUST

HIDEO KOJIMA WAS BORN IN 1963

Hideo Kojima is the director of the computer game series *Metal Gear Solid*. Notable for being key to the popularity of the stealth genre in computer gaming, MGS is set in a world of genetics. A rebel unit go up against the United States government in order to decommission an immense robotic weapons setup. Solid Snake is commissioned by the US government to stop Liquid Snake's rebel unit. Solid's Snake's alter egos include the name Iroquois Pliskin – surely a nod to the cult action movie *Escape from New York* (1981).

IN 1978 THE FIRST YELLOW LEGO MINIFIGURE WAS RELEASED

Lego and geekdom go hand in hand. Recently *The LEGO Movie* (2014) and *The LEGO Batman Movie* (2017) have proved irresistible.

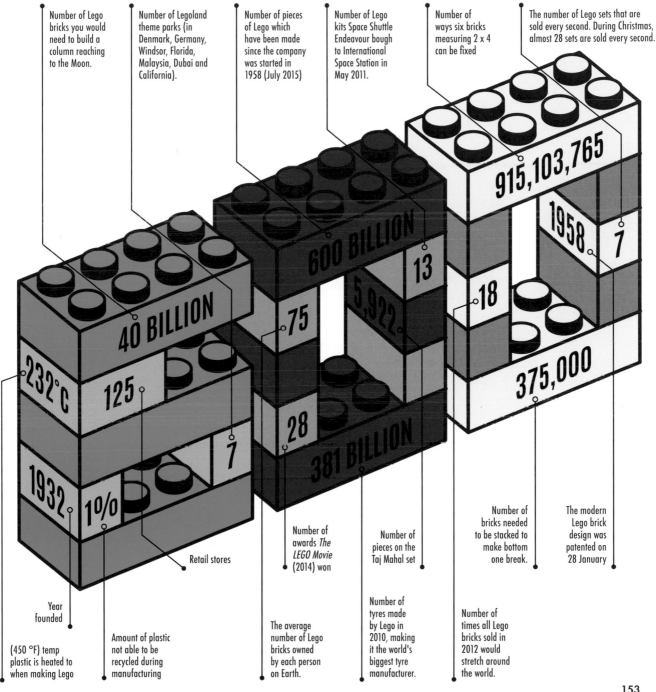

Number of Lego bricks you would need to build a column reaching to the Moon.

Number of Legoland theme parks (in Denmark, Germany, Windsor, Florida, Malaysia, Dubai and California).

Number of pieces of Lego which have been made since the company was started in 1958 (July 2015)

Number of Lego kits Space Shuttle Endeavour bough to International Space Station in May 2011.

Number of ways six bricks measuring 2 x 4 can be fixed

The number of Lego sets that are sold every second. During Christmas, almost 28 sets are sold every second.

915,103,765

600 BILLION

13

1958

7

75

5,922.

18

40 BILLION

232°C

125

28

381 BILLION

375,000

1932

1%

7

Retail stores

Number of awards *The LEGO Movie* (2014) won

Number of pieces on the Taj Mahal set

Number of bricks needed to be stacked to make bottom one break.

The modern Lego brick design was patented on 28 January

Year founded

(450 °F) temp plastic is heated to when making Lego

Amount of plastic not able to be recycled during manufacturing

The average number of Lego bricks owned by each person on Earth.

Number of tyres made by Lego in 2010, making it the world's biggest tyre manufacturer.

Number of times all Lego bricks sold in 2012 would stretch around the world.

RALPH BAKSHI'S FILM *FIRE AND ICE* WAS RELEASED IN 1983

Bakshi's name and work deserves to be more widely known. It was central to the American fantasy filmmaking boom of the 1970s and 1980s. Working just a little outside the mainstream, Bakshi had directed the adult animated film *Fritz the Cat* (1972) before going on to direct the fantasy movies *Wizards* (1977), a somewhat truncated adaptation of *The Lord of the Rings*, and *Fire and Ice*.

IN 2003 MARS MADE ITS CLOSEST APPROACH TO EARTH

Mars passed by Earth at 34,646,418 miles (55,758,005 km) distance, making its closest approach in 60,000 years. The planet has long been a fascination for sci-fi, including, *The Sirens of Titan* by Kurt Vonnegut (1959), 'Ananke' by Stanislaw Lew (1982) and of course, *The War of the Worlds* (1898) by H.G. Wells.

SATOSHI TAJIRI WAS BORN IN 1965

Released in late 1996 and an immediate global geek phenomenon, *Pokémon* was the brainchild of Satoshi Tajiri. There were 150 Pokémon (or pocket monsters) to be caught in the game. *Pokémon* was recently given an augmented reality twist in 2016 as *Pokémon Go*.

COMPARATIVE POKÉMON
POWER SCALES

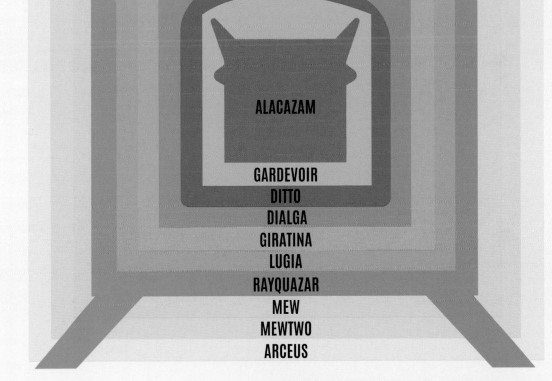

ALACAZAM

GARDEVOIR
DITTO
DIALGA
GIRATINA
LUGIA
RAYQUAZAR
MEW
MEWTWO
ARCEUS

POWER SCALE

UNDER THE SKIN DEBUTED IN 2013

Under the Skin, written and directed by Jonathan Glazer, and adapted from Michel Faber's novel of the same name (2000), debuted on this day in 2013. It already stands as one of the great science fiction films to be produced in Britain. The film follows an alien, appearing as a woman, who lures men to her. The film, then, uses its genre trappings to powerfully explore gender issues.

MARY SHELLEY IS BORN ON THIS DAY IN 1797

With her novel *Frankenstein: or, The Modern Prometheus* (1818), Mary Shelley unleashed the potency of science fiction as a channel through which to deal with the essentials of human life: knowledge, power, science, responsibility.

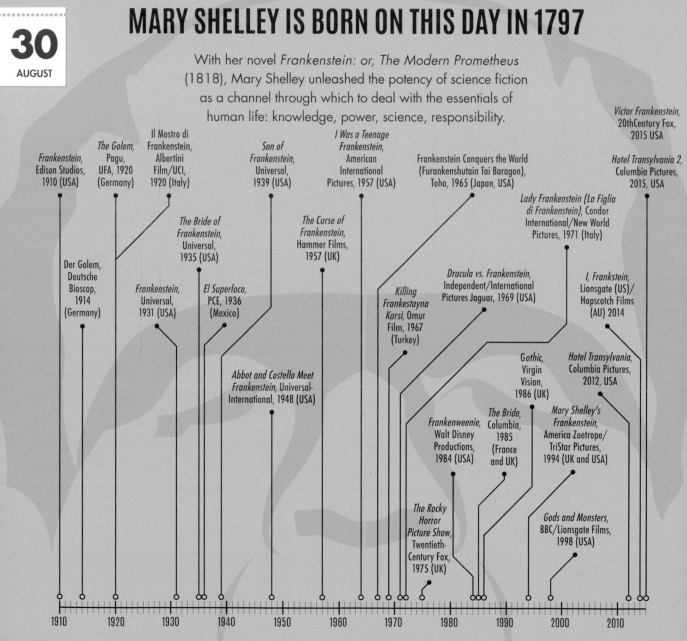

Frankenstein, Edison Studios, 1910 (USA)

The Golem, Pagu, UFA, 1920 (Germany)

Il Mostro di Frankenstein, Albertini Film/UCI, 1920 (Italy)

Son of Frankenstein, Universal, 1939 (USA)

I Was a Teenage Frankenstein, American International Pictures, 1957 (USA)

Frankenstein Conquers the World (Furankenshutain Tai Baragon), Toho, 1965 (Japan, USA)

Victor Frankenstein, 20thCentury Fox, 2015 USA

Hotel Transylvania 2, Columbia Pictures, 2015, USA

Der Golem, Deutsche Bioscop, 1914 (Germany)

The Bride of Frankenstein, Universal, 1935 (USA)

The Curse of Frankenstein, Hammer Films, 1957 (UK)

Lady Frankenstein (La Figlia di Frankenstein), Condor International/New World Pictures, 1971 (Italy)

Frankenstein, Universal, 1931 (USA)

El Superloco, PCE, 1936 (Mexico)

Killing Frankestayna Karsi, Omur Film, 1967 (Turkey)

Dracula vs. Frankenstein, Independent/International Pictures Jaguar, 1969 (USA)

I, Frankstein, Lionsgate (US)/ Hopscotch Films (AU) 2014

Abbot and Costello Meet Frankenstein, Universal-International, 1948 (USA)

Gothic, Virgin Vision, 1986 (UK)

Hotel Transylvania, Columbia Pictures, 2012, USA

Frankenweenie, Walt Disney Productions, 1984 (USA)

The Bride, Columbia, 1985 (France and UK)

Mary Shelley's Frankenstein, America Zoetrope/ TriStar Pictures, 1994 (UK and USA)

The Rocky Horror Picture Show, Twentieth-Century Fox, 1975 (UK)

Gods and Monsters, BBC/Lionsgate Films, 1998 (USA)

1910   1920   1930   1940   1950   1960   1970   1980   1990   2000   2010

RICHARD BASEHART WAS BORN IN 1914

Basehart starred as Admiral Harriman Nelson in the subaquatic science fiction series *Voyage to the Bottom of the Sea* (1964–68) – which, like *Lost in Space* (1965–68), *Time Tunnel* (1966–67) and *Land of the Giants* (1968–70), was produced by Irwin Allen.

A TRIP TO THE MOON DEBUTED IN 1902 IN FRANCE

If you've seen Martin Scorsese's film *Hugo* (2011) then you've encountered something of French filmmaker George Méliès: the creative world he made for himself and the work that emerged from that.

One of the earliest science-fiction movies and essential viewing, *A Trip to the Moon* (1902) was George Méliès's most well known work. Produced at his studio in Paris and starring Méliès's as the heroic scientist Professor Barbenfouillis, the film has given us the iconic image of a space rocket that has crashlanded into the face of the Man on the Moon. It's an image that is so well known that it forms the basis for the design of the Visual Effects Society's logo.

Méliès's film satirizes conservative science in its densely packed eleven-minute running time and was inspired by many sources, including the Jules Verne story *From the Earth to the Moon* (1865).

The Village Voice newspaper in the USA placed *A Trip to the Moon* at no. 84 in its list of the 100 greatest films of the 20th century. If another indicator of the film's reputation is needed then we can namecheck the band The Smashing Pumpkins whose music video for their song 'Tonight, Tonight' references *A Trip to the Moon*.

2

SEPTEMBER

IN 1962 BRIAN W. ALDISS WON A HUGO AWARD

Brian W. Aldiss is a titan of British science fiction and his work includes the short story 'Supertoys Last All Summer Long' (1968) which Stanley Kubrick developed and which Steven Spielberg brought to fruition as the film *A.I. Artificial Intelligence* (2001).

Born in Norfolk in 1925, Aldiss's output includes more than twenty science fiction novels and 320 short stories.

Aldiss, like his contemporary J.G. Ballard, was central to the British science fiction novel boom of the 1960s. Just ahead of that moment, in 1958 his first science-fiction novel, entitled *Non-Stop*, was published. The 1960s saw him on a seriously productive roll, with titles including *Greybeard* (1964) about an England in which there are no children after a plague has ravaged the land and

Hothouse (for which he won the Hugo Award). His other writing includes *Earthworks* (1962), *Frankenstein Unbound* (1973), the *Helliconia* trilogy (1982–85), *Dracula Unbound* (1990) and *Squire Quartet* (1980–94).

Aldiss's work has notably explored subjects such as memory, religion and the natural world. His *Helliconia* novels are influenced by James Lovelock's Gaia Hypothesis and tell the story of the rise and fall of a civilization in a world akin to Earth.

3

SEPTEMBER

DREW STRUZAN ANNOUNCED HIS RETIREMENT IN 2008

Between the mid 1970s and the early 2000s, Struzan's work was essential to a panoply of films that have become classics. His posters for the *Back to the Future* trilogy (1985, 1989, 1990), the *Indiana Jones* movies and novels (1981, 1984, 1989, 2008), Blader Runner (1982), and the *Star Wars* saga are all elegantly composed. Struzan's work typically captures the combination of drama and mystery and offers the promise of some kind of wonderment.

4

SEPTEMBER

EDMOND HALLEY OBSERVES THE COMET THAT WILL BE NAMED FOR HIM IN 1682

Comets and asteroids in movies have featured as a useful nemesis. *Armageddon* sent a crew into space to destroy and incoming asteroid, as did the film *Deep Impact*, each released in summer 1998.

5

SEPTEMBER

IN 1983 *HE-MAN AND THE MASTERS OF THE UNIVERSE* PREMIERED

He-Man and the Masters of the Universe (1983–85) was an animated show that took high fantasy, sword and sorcery and pitched it squarely at kids. He-Man and his friends Man-at-Arms, She-Ra and Teela lived in Eternia engaged in an endless conflict with the evil Skeletor. The toys were hugely popular and the show was part of the 80s run of animated fantasy cartoon programming.

THE FILM *ALIEN* WAS RELEASED IN THE UK IN 1979

Alien was not only a landmark combination of horror and science fiction but it also launched a major feminist movie icon in the character of Ellen Ripley.

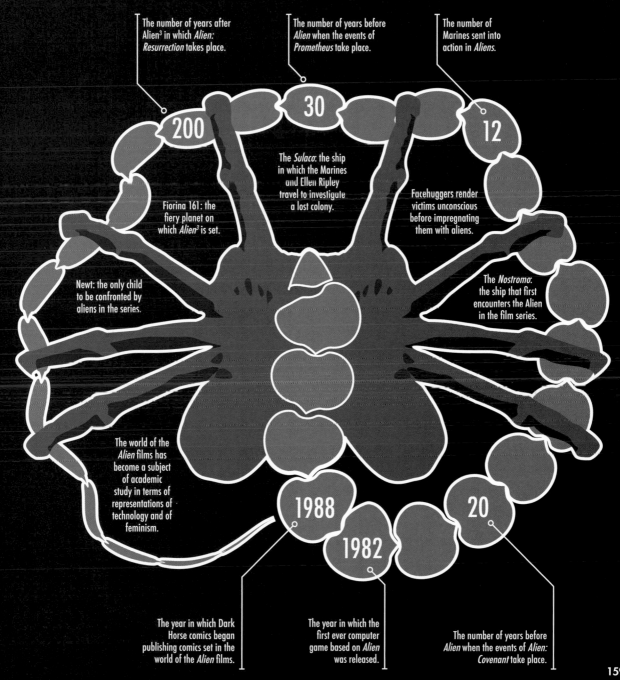

The number of years after *Alien³* in which *Alien: Resurrection* takes place.

The number of years before *Alien* when the events of *Prometheus* take place.

The number of Marines sent into action in *Aliens*.

200

30

12

Fiorina 161: the fiery planet on which *Alien³* is set.

The *Sulaco*: the ship in which the Marines and Ellen Ripley travel to investigate a lost colony.

Facehuggers render victims unconscious before impregnating them with aliens.

Newt: the only child to be confronted by aliens in the series.

The *Nostromo*: the ship that first encounters the Alien in the film series.

The world of the *Alien* films has become a subject of academic study in terms of representations of technology and of feminism.

1988

1982

20

The year in which Dark Horse comics began publishing comics set in the world of the *Alien* films.

The year in which the first ever computer game based on *Alien* was released.

The number of years before *Alien* when the events of *Alien: Covenant* take place.

IN 1984 *THE BROTHER FROM ANOTHER PLANET* WAS RELEASED IN AMERICAN CINEMAS

Science fiction and fantasy have a good record of reframing reality and *The Brother From Another Planet* is one of the great 1980's sci-fi movies that seems hardly ever to be spoken about.

Set in Manthattan, the film tells the story of a man, portrayed by Joe Morton, who cannot talk, but who has the ability to read peoples' minds. The Brother reflects back our world to us. The film was written and directed by John Sayles who had written the screenplay for *Battle Beyond the Stars* (1980).

STAR TREK'S FIRST REGULAR EPISODE, 'THE MAN TRAP', AIRED ON THIS DATE IN 1966

With Kirk, McCoy, Spock, Uhura, Scotty, Sulu and Chekov all in place, this first episode introduced audiences to the characters who still perhaps remain most synonymous with the immense *Star Trek* world that has evolved over the past fifty-odd years. Beyond the fantasy of its premise, *Star Trek* had a sharp eye on where American society was in the mid- and late 1960s and acknowledged in its allegorical way the diversity of human experience at a time when the Civil Rights movement in America was proving so powerful.

STARFLEET UNIFORM DESIGNS

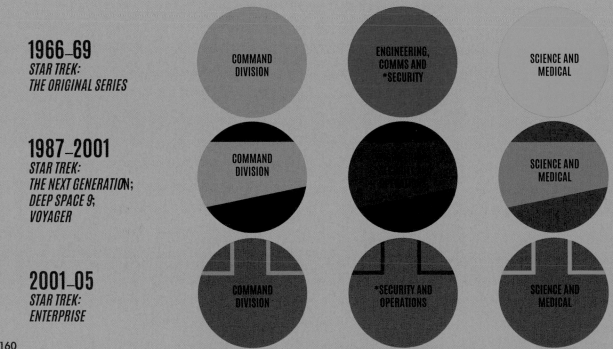

1966–69
*STAR TREK:
THE ORIGINAL SERIES*

COMMAND DIVISION

ENGINEERING, COMMS AND *SECURITY

SCIENCE AND MEDICAL

1987–2001
*STAR TREK:
THE NEXT GENERATION;
DEEP SPACE 9;
VOYAGER*

COMMAND DIVISION

SCIENCE AND MEDICAL

2001–05
*STAR TREK:
ENTERPRISE*

COMMAND DIVISION

*SECURITY AND OPERATIONS

SCIENCE AND MEDICAL

ILLUSTRATOR PAULINE BAYNES WAS BORN IN 1922

This book is replete with the names of creators that have become synonymous with their work. Not so, though, for Pauline Baynes, and it's about time that her name enjoys much wider recognition. Baynes is the illustrator who pictured C.S.Lewis's *The Chronicles of Narnia* (1950–56) novels and also provided images for an illustrated edition of J.R.R.Tolkien's charming novella *Farmer Giles of Ham* (1949) and the poetry collection, *The Adventures of Tom Bombadil* (1962).

Baynes always considered herself to be more a designer than an illustrator. Her work includes maps for *The Lord of the Rings* and *The Hobbit* produced as posters, as well as material for *A Map of Middle-Earth*, inspired by Tolkien's work. Baynes' illustration for the Narnia books are widely considered definitive in visualising the places, characters, situations and feelings of C.S.Lewis fantasy world but she also influenced artists such as Arthur Rackham, Edmund Dulac and Gustave Doré.

Working in pen and ink or in paint, Pauline Baynes's work has a fluid and clear quality. Her work for Lewis and Tolkien is notable for the vivid use of colour and elegance of line.

Of her landmark work for Tolkien's lesser-known stories, including 'Smith of Wootton Major' and 'Leaf by Niggle', the author said that it was 'more than illustrations, they are a collateral theme.'

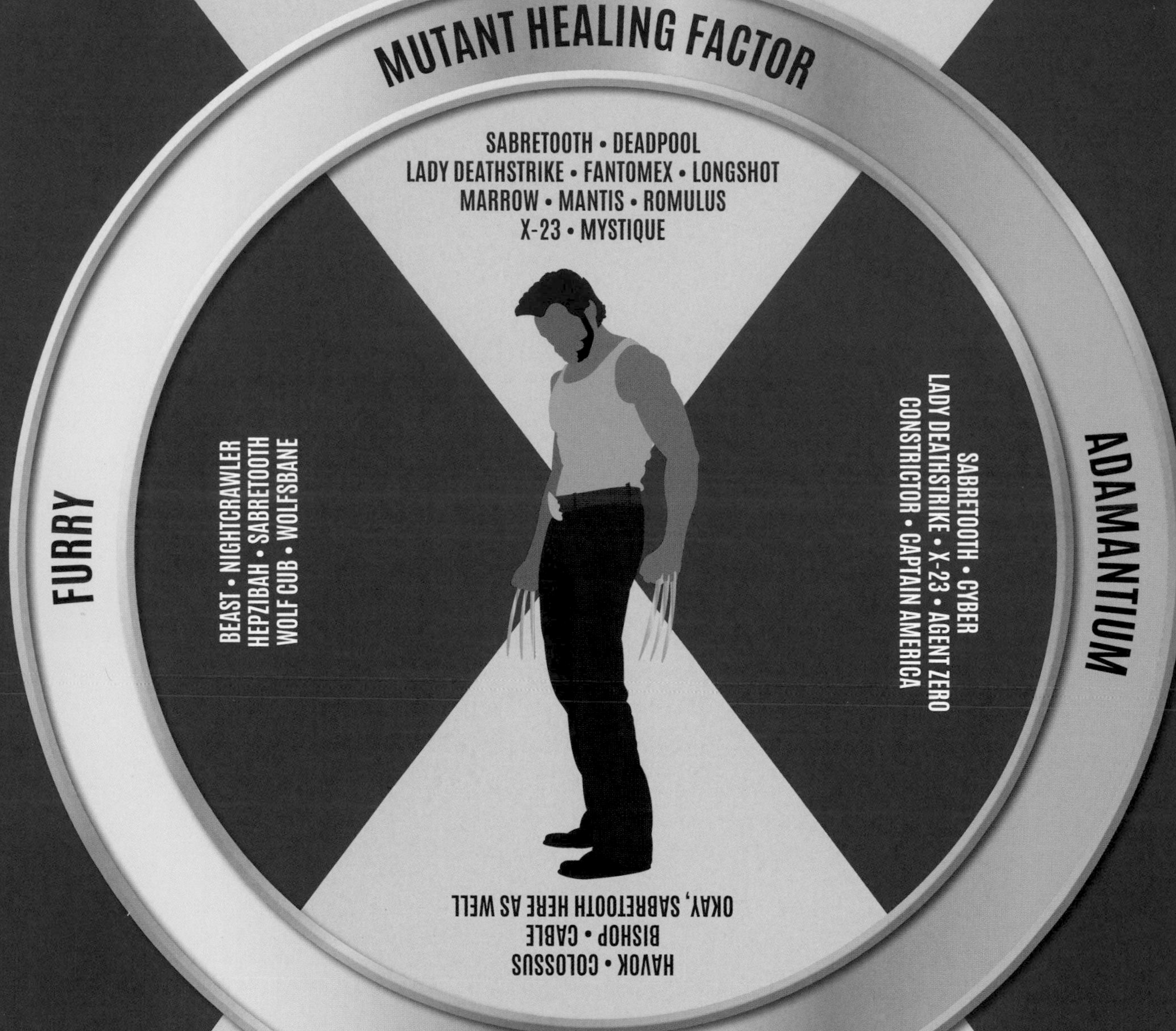

MUTANT HEALING FACTOR

SABRETOOTH • DEADPOOL
LADY DEATHSTRIKE • FANTOMEX • LONGSHOT
MARROW • MANTIS • ROMULUS
X-23 • MYSTIQUE

FURRY

BEAST • NIGHTCRAWLER
HEPZIBAH • SABRETOOTH
WOLF CUB • WOLFSBANE

ADAMANTIUM

SABRETOOTH • CYBER
LADY DEATHSTRIKE • X-23 • AGENT ZERO
CONSTRICTOR • CAPTAIN AMERICA

GRUMPY

HAVOK • COLOSSUS
BISHOP • CABLE
OKAY, SABRETOOTH HERE AS WELL

WOLVERINE'S TRAITS

THE X-MEN COMIC WAS FIRST PUBLISHED IN 1963

Jack Kirby is known as The King. He created the *Fantastic Four* with artist Stan Lee and, again with Lee, he created *The X-Men*.

We take *The X-Men*'s presence in comics and on cinema screens somewhat for granted now, but initially the mutants found it a challenge to garner an audience. In the early 1970s, *The X-Men* comic line was cancelled. However, when fans of the original run expressed their wish to see the stories continue, *The X-Men* was relaunched in 1975 with Chris Claremont, David Cockrum and John Byrne revising the concept.

In the 1990s, *The X-Men* became increasingly popular and in 2000 the first of several *X-Men* films, and their spinoffs, was released to great success. Clearly its conceit of outsiders as heroes has enduring appeal to readers and cinema-goers worldwide.

JEAN-CLAUDE FOREST WAS BORN IN 1930

11
SEPTEMBER

Sex has long threaded through science fiction and perhaps never more memorably than in the French comic strip *Barbarella* created by Jean-Claude Forest. First published in France in *V Magazine* in 1962, *Barbarella* is most well known because of the 1968 film adaptation, travelling outer space with confidence in herself.

WRITER JUDITH MERRIL DIED IN 1997

12
SEPTEMBER

Esteemed writer, editor and political activist, Judith Merril was often described as 'the little mother of science fiction', and at a time when men dominated the genre, Merrill quickly made her mark. Her first published work 'That Only a Mother', a short story about nuclear radiation, was published in 1948 and unsettled and challenged readers.

Merril's novels are: *Shadow on the Hearth* (1950), *Gunner Cade* (1952), *Outpost Mars* (1952) and *The Tomorrow People* (1960). Merril also wrote poetry and radio scripts and translated Japanese science fiction into English.

She wrote more than 300 pieces of critical writing in the form of essays, commentaries, reviews and introductions. Significantly, she also wrote a 12,000-word survey of speculative fiction entitled 'What Do You Mean, Science? Fiction?', first published in 1956.

SUPER MARIO BROS. WAS FIRST RELEASED IN 1985

Mario and Luigi's adventures began in 1985 when they first appeared in the game *Donkey Kong*. They are now one of the bestselling computer games in history.

Super Mario Bros. have become a staple of the computer gaming universe. Numerous computer games depict their endless adventures which see Mario and Luigi dashing through the Mushroom Kingdom, rescuing Princess Peach and competing with their adversary, Bowser.

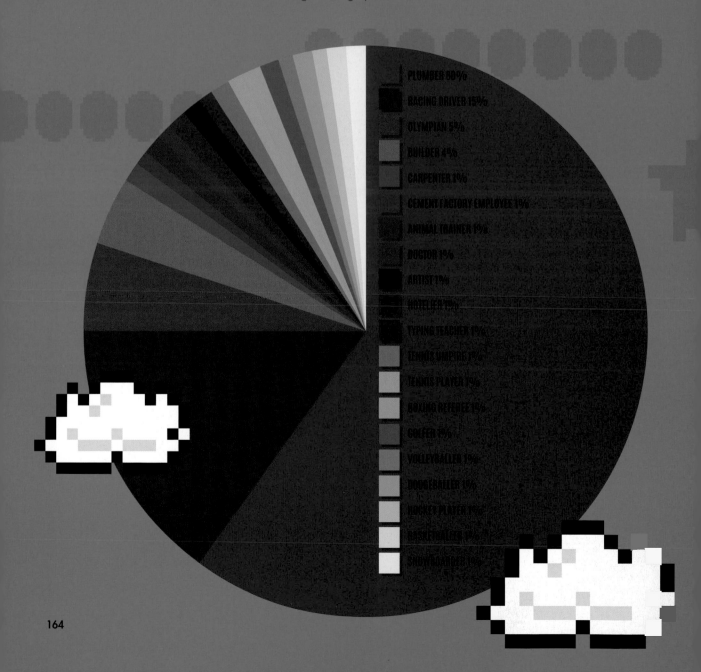

PLUMBER 60%
RACING DRIVER 15%
OLYMPIAN 5%
BUILDER 4%
CARPENTER 1%
CEMENT FACTORY EMPLOYEE 1%
ANIMAL TRAINER 1%
DOCTOR 1%
ARTIST 1%
HOTELIER 1%
TYPING TEACHER 1%
TENNIS UMPIRE 1%
TENNIS PLAYER 1%
BOXING REFEREE 1%
GOLFER 1%
VOLLEYBALLER 1%
DODGEBALLER 1%
HOCKEY PLAYER 1%
BASKETBALLER 1%
SNOWBOARDER 1%

ACTOR WALTER KOENIG WAS BORN IN 1936

14 SEPTEMBER

When Koenig played the Russian Pavel Chekov aboard the Starship *Enterprise* in the *Star Trek* series and the first series of *Star Trek* feature films, the possibility for intercultural connections found a visible emblem. Certainly, *Star Trek* has always promoted that intercultural angle, and Nichelle Nichols as Uhura was one of the first African-American characters in a TV series not to be a servant.

NOVELIST ANDREAS ESCHBACH WAS BORN IN 1959

15 SEPTEMBER

Andreas Eschbach has been described as being akin to American novelist Michael Crichton. Like Crichton, Eshcbach is a bestselling author; indeed, he is the biggest selling science-fiction author in Germany. Eschbach's first science-fiction novel was *Die Haarteppichknüpfer* (*The Carpet Makers*, 1995) and his other novels include *Solarstation* (1996), *Kelwitts Stern* (*Kelwitt's Star*, 1995), *Quest* and *Der Letzte seiner Art* (*The Last of his Species*, 2005).In much of his work there's a tangible space-opera influence at play.

THE TV SERIES *THE OUTER LIMITS* WAS FIRST BROADCAST IN 1963

16 SEPTEMBER

The Outer Limits TV series began as a distinctly science-fiction focused series, but increasingly its storylines skewed towards horror and an emphasis on the power of the subconscious.

One of the notable writers on the series was Harlan Ellison and his story 'Soldier' became the focus of a settlement in 1984 when *The Terminator* was released: the premise of the film was considered by some to be very close to the Ellison concept. If you look at the end credits on *The Terminator*, you'll see that Ellison is acknowledged.

THE TRANSFORMERS FIRST AIRED IN 1984

The Transformers, the first of many shows to featured the Transformers,
was an animated show for US TV that ran from 1984–87.

In 1974, American G.I. Joe toys were given a Japanese sci-fi spin and sold as Henshin Cyborg. In turn they became Micronauts and then, in spring 1984, the Transformers were ready to be unleashed. Toys (arriving in toy shops in September 1984), cartoons, comics and films followed quickly. Audiences were swift to respond to Optimus Prime (originally named Orion Pax), the leader

of the Autobots, against the villainous Decepticons led by Megatron. A range of toy variations have followed over the decades, and in 2007 a new era for Transformers arrived with the release of a new film, the latest of which is 2017's *Transformers: The Last Knight*. Peter Cullen who memorably voiced Prime in the animated TV series returned to voice Prime in the new film series.

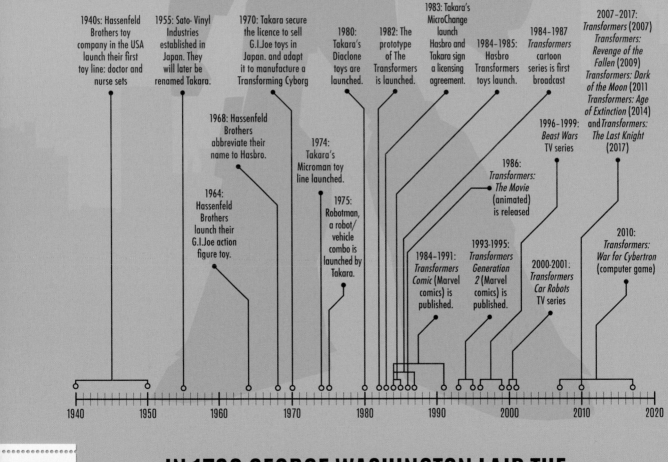

1940s: Hassenfeld Brothers toy company in the USA launch their first toy line: doctor and nurse sets

1955: Sato- Vinyl Industries established in Japan. They will later be renamed Takara.

1970: Takara secure the licence to sell G.I.Joe toys in Japan. and adapt it to manufacture a Transforming Cyborg

1980: Takara's Diaclone toys are launched.

1982: The prototype of The Transformers is launched.

1983: Takara's MicroChange launch Hasbro and Takara sign a licensing agreement.

1984–1985: Hasbro Transformers toys launch.

1984–1987 *Transformers* cartoon series is first broadcast

2007–2017: *Transformers* (2007) *Transformers: Revenge of the Fallen* (2009) *Transformers: Dark of the Moon* (2011 *Transformers: Age of Extinction* (2014) and *Transformers: The Last Knight* (2017)

1968: Hassenfeld Brothers abbreviate their name to Hasbro.

1974: Takara's Microman toy line launched.

1996–1999: *Beast Wars* TV series

1964: Hassenfeld Brothers launch their G.I.Joe action figure toy.

1975: Robotman, a robot/ vehicle combo is launched by Takara.

1986: *Transformers: The Movie* (animated) is released

2010: *Transformers: War for Cybertron* (computer game)

1984–1991: *Transformers Comic* (Marvel comics) is published.

1993-1995: *Transformers Generation 2* (Marvel comics) is published.

2000-2001: *Transformers Car Robots* TV series

1940   1950   1960   1970   1980   1990   2000   2010   2020

IN 1793 GEORGE WASHINGTON LAID THE CORNERSTONE OF THE CAPITOL IN D.C.

Alien destruction of human monuments have provided jaw-dropping images. The *Transformers* films revel in it, *Independence Day* (1996) famously brought down the White House and in *Superman 2* (1980), Superman retstores the White House after it's been destroyed.

THE NOVEL *THE AMAZING ADVENTURES OF KAVALIER AND CLAY* WAS PUBLISHED DAY IN 2000

19
SEPTEMBER

In the American writer Michael Chabon, lovers of comics and films and fantasy have a wonderfully eloquent spokesperson and defender.

The Amazing Adventures of Kavalier and Clay is a hefty novel about comic books, its plot focusing on two teenage boys in 1930s New York who create a comic superhero

The Escapist to counter fascism. The Escapist eventually got his own comic, written by Michael Chabon.

THE TV SERIES *FIREFLY* PREMIERED ON AMERICAN TV IN 2002

20
SEPTEMBER

Like the original series of *Star Trek*, the *Firefly* TV series was shortlived yet much loved.

Created by Joss Whedon, it crystallised much of his appeal and enjoys a cult following. With Whedon at the helm, witty, sharp dialogue was a feature of the series along with a sense of humour and Western-inflected characters, costumes and tone. When *Firefly* was cancelled, Whedon was able to conclude the story with a modestly budgeted feature film entitled *Serenity* (2002).

Whedon also created the landmark series *Buffy the Vampire Slayer* (1997–2003) and the web series *Dr Horrible's Sing-Along Blog* (2008), and he directed an inventive adaptation of Shakespeare's play *Much Ado About Nothing* (2012). He has also written for the *Astonishing X-Men* comic and most recently wrote and directed *The Avengers* (2012) and the sequel *Avengers: Age of Ultron* (2015).

NOVELIST STEPHEN KING WAS BORN IN 1947

21
SEPTEMBER

For more than 40 years, Stephen King has dominated geek fiction. His breakthrough as a novelist came with *Carrie* (1974) and he then followed this up with *Salem's Lot* (1978). There's no question, however, that King's profile has been reinforced by the range of TV and film adaptations of his work.

His novels range from one-offs to interconnected installments in elaborately conceived worlds, as is the case with *The Dark Tower* series (1998–2004).

With the novella *Rita Hayworth and Shawshank Redemption* (1982) and the novel *The Green Mile* (initially published in monthly installments in 1996), King has made prison a setting in which ideas of faith and goodness in cruel worlds can play out.

With *The Talisman* (1984), King collaborated with Peter Straub to craft an odyssey across all-American terrain and a parallel fantasy world as a boy named Jack Sawyer embarks on a quest to save his dying mother.

King's novels take the most ordinary of humans and confront them with situations perilous and wondrous, unknowable and unsettling

LAND OF THE GIANTS FIRST BROADCAST IN 1968

If you want a taste of the work that John Williams was composing for the science fiction and fantasy genres before he became a household name for *Star Wars*, check out his themes for *Lost in Space* (1965–68), *Time Tunnel* (1966–67) and *Land of the Giants* (1968–70).

Land of the Giants was the Irwin Allen series that replaced his previous science fiction project, *Voyage to the Bottom of the Sea* (1964–68). Set in the far future of 1983, *Land of the Giants* focused on the crew and passengers of the spaceship *Spindrift*, which crashed on a planet populated by immense creatures. Simple visual tricks sold the differences in size between humans and giants.

23

SEPTEMBER

THE JETSONS FIRST BROADCAST IN 1962

Influenced by the popularity of *The Flintstones* (1960–66) and also produced by Hanna-Barbera animation studio, *The Jetsons* applied a very 1960s family dynamic to the year 2062. There was also *Jetsons: The Movie* (1990) and a new animated series was broadcast in America between 1985 and 1987.

PREDICTED BY THE JETSONS

VIDEOPHONES

ROBOT SERVANTS

DRONES

DOG TREADMILLS

A WATCH THAT PLAYS TV

3D PRINTED FOOD

DIGITAL NEWSPAPERS

TANNING BEDS

POLLUTION

FLAT SCREEN TVS

HOLOGRAMS

JIM HENSON WAS BORN IN 1936

Puppeteer, director and producer, Jim Henson's TV and film geek favourites was massive. He bridged the moment between Disney and Lucas.

He began with his TV series *The Muppets* (1976–81), but his affinity for fuller, highly realised fantasy was manifested in his two films as director: *The Dark Crystal* (1982) and *Labyrinth* (1986). Then, too, there is his astonishing TV series *The Storyteller* (1988). Key to Henson's appeal is the sense of optimism and joy expressed by his characters.

NAUSICAÄ WAS PUBLISHED IN 1982

Hayao Miyazaki was born in 1941 and grew up during the atomic age, which has arguably been a massive influence on much Japanese animation of the last 20 years.

It was in the 1980s that Miyazaki began to establish his credentials and legacy. In 1984 he made the film *Nausicaä of the Valley of Wind*, based on the manga of the same name, which he had drawn. Studio Ghibli (pronounced jee-blee) was established off its success.

As a director Miyazaki has always been more hands-on than an animation director might usually be, even redrawing frames if necessary. For an insight into his process, the documentary *The Kingdom of Dreams and Madness* (2013) is essential viewing.

In his treatment for *Princess Mononoke* (1997) Miyazaki described his aim as 'To depict what constructs the unchanged basis of human throughout time ... The main characters will be the people who don't appear in the centre stage of history ...'

Miyazaki is committed to a refreshing humanism in his animation, evident in the fantasy of *Spirited Away* (2001) as much as in the reality of *The Wind Rises* (2013)

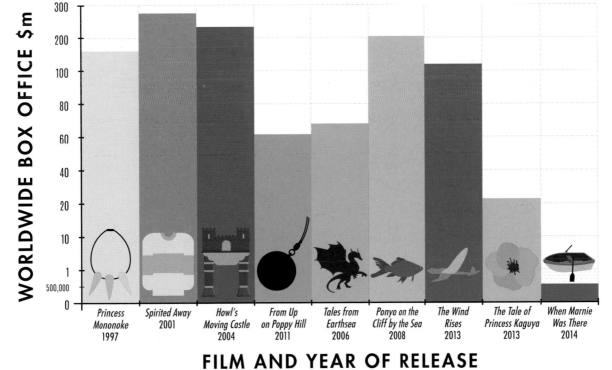

WORLDWIDE BOX OFFICE $m

FILM AND YEAR OF RELEASE

26
SEPTEMBER

IN 1869 ILLUSTRATOR AND ANIMATOR WINSOR MCCAY WAS BORN

Tragically, Winsor McCay's name is little known today, yet he contributed so much to popularizing animation as a form.

In 1909, McCay set about laying the groundwork for the American take on animation. McCay found the time to make 4,000 drawings which, when filmed and projected, brought to life his comic strip creation *Little Nemo*.

In 1914, he completed work on the landmark animated short *Gertie the Dinosaur*. The film creates a believable animated character expressing a range of emotions, and integrates live action and animation. Funny and wondrous throughout, it got a hat tip from Steven Spielberg in his film *Jurassic Park* (1993). By the time of *Gertie*, McCay was aware of his standing and in a title card described himself as 'America's Greatest Cartoonist'. Tellingly, he does not use the word animator.

27
SEPTEMBER

IN 2016 *SONIC BOOM: FIRE & ICE,* THE MOST RECENT ITERATION OF THE COMPUTER GAME *SONIC THE HEDGEHOG* WAS RELEASED IN NORTH AMERICA

There is a Mount Olympus of computer game characters that have have become iconic, recognized even by those who have never ever played their game. Pac-Man is one, as too are the Super Mario Bros. The other is Sonic the Hedgehog. This blue little guy, with his red sneakers, has been a major computer game hero since 1991.

Subtitled *A Personal Journey*, Carl Sagan's TV sereies *Cosmos* brought popular science to American TV

Sagan had been an astronomy professor at Cornell University and part of the NASA team working on robotic missions but he was also a brilliant communicator and the series became a landmark in popular science progamming. In the run-up to *Cosmos*, he was a regular guest on the *The Tonight Show with Johnny Carson*, though his ease with the mainstream media didn't always sit well with his colleagues in academia.

Sagan so perfectly encapuslated the scale of the cosmos when he described Earth in such a way that you can't help but recognize our human fragility. Earth, he said, was 'a mote of dust suspended in a sunbeam.'

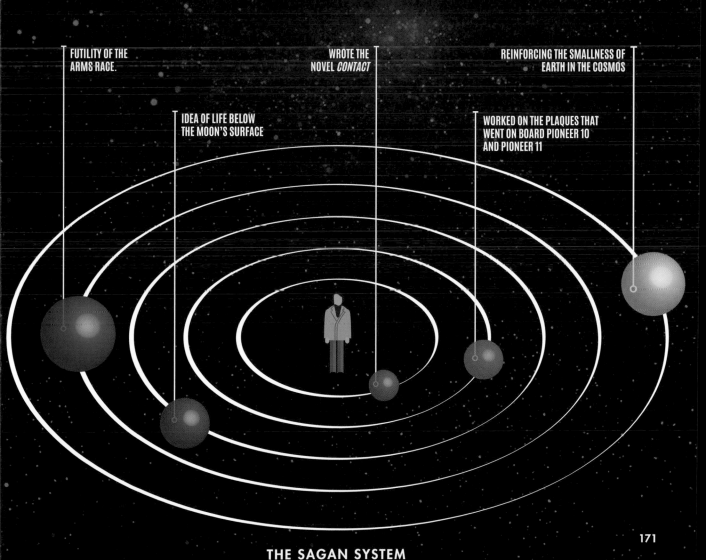

FUTILITY OF THE ARMS RACE.

WROTE THE NOVEL *CONTACT*

REINFORCING THE SMALLNESS OF EARTH IN THE COSMOS

IDEA OF LIFE BELOW THE MOON'S SURFACE

WORKED ON THE PLAQUES THAT WENT ON BOARD PIONEER 10 AND PIONEER 11

THE SAGAN SYSTEM

29
SEPTEMBER

THE CULT ANIMATED FILM *TWICE UPON A TIME* WAS RELEASED ON DVD IN 2015

Some of the most fascinating geek classics are by creators who veered off the beaten track, and the world of animation filmmakers is no exception.

First released in 1983, *Twice Upon a Time* was a fantasy piece about two factory workers who foil the plans of a tyrannical oaf named Synonamess Botch, the story takes a fairy-tale kind of approach to its plot and characterisations.

The film's visual style is highly distinctive. Director John Korty employed a technique that he described as lumage: cutout designs that were lit from below on a light table.

Henry Selick, David Fincher and Harley Jessup all worked on this film and would go on to become major American fantasy filmmakers in animation and live action.

In an era of photorealistic animation, it's worth invoking the refreshing example of *Twice Upon A Time*.

30
SEPTEMBER

THE NOVELIST ALFRED BESTER DIED IN 1987

In 1939, Bester's first piece of science fiction was published: a short story entitled 'The Broken Axiom' in the periodical *Thrilling Wonder Stories*. Bester would go on to write for *Superman* and the *Green Lantern* comic books and it was in the 1950s that he returned to science fiction prose.

In 1953, he published *The Demolished Man* about telepathic murder. In 1956, his most famous novel was published: the beautifully named *The Stars My Destination*. It was an inspiration for cyberpunk novelist William Gibson, author of *Neuromancer*.

1
OCTOBER

TIM BURTON'S SHORT FILM *VINCENT* PREMIERED IN 1982

Tim Burton's films celebrate the outsider, whether that's brooding *Batman* (1989, 1992) or the ever-hopeful *Alice in Wonderland* (2010). Their vividly imagined, cartoon Gothic sensibility is a bit satirical, a bit offbeat and a bit sentimental. Burton's lifelong enthusiasm for monster movies, fantasy and horror imbues his films with a B-movie nostalgia.

THE FIRST EPISODE OF *THE TWILIGHT ZONE* WAS BROADCAST ON AMERICAN TV IN 1959

When autumn brings darkness, TV screens light up with stories and, for five years in America, there was perhaps no more profound an impact than that made by *The Twilight Zone*. So well recognised is the show's music by Marius Constant that its opening notes are famously mimicked by Robin Williams in *Good Morning, Vietnam* (1968) and many others.

The Twilight Zone was the brainchild of Rod Serling and audiences ventured into it for the first time on this day in 1959. The very first episode, penned by Serling, was entitled 'Where Is Everybody?'.

Maybe it's a little hard to remember the impact of it all now, but the show certainly made an impression on filmmakers like Steven Spielberg, Joe Dante, George Miller and John Landis, all of whom directed installments of the homage, *Twilight Zone: The Movie* (1983). Spielberg continued to honour the spirit of the show with his own anthology series, *Amazing Stories* (1985–87).

The Twilight Zone has long been recognised for Serling's on-camera introductions to episodes and for its sense of irony. For a sense of that unsettling, ironic take, you only have to watch the episode 'Time Enough At Last' about a far-sighted bookworm who finally has time to read, only to break his glasses. The show also managed to work its way into the American education system with the episode 'The Shelter' about nuclear holocaust.

Serling contributed to another totem of geek culture, with his work on the screenplay of the first film version of *Planet of the Apes* (1968).

MAPLE STREET 300

TWILIGHT ZONE ECHOES

THE ANIME SERIES *SUPER DIMENSION FORTRESS MACROSS* FIRST AIRED IN 1982

Anime TV series sprawl across the past fifty years. With their sci-fi emphasis they are geek gold dust, their Japanese aesthetic hugely appealing around the world.

In the late 1980s, anime began to find and build an audience in America and Europe and certainly the release of the anime feature film *Akira* (1988) was key to this. Prior to this a fairly niche geek community had already been hooked on anime TV series, including *Science Ninja Team Gatchaman* (1972–74), *Space Battleship Yamato* (1974–74) and *Dragon Ball* (1986–89).

Anime is a rich and diverse world, produced for both adult and young audiences. The earliest commercial anime appeared in 1917, but it was in the late 1960s that anime as we know it best came into being.

It was then and into the 1970s that the association of anime and of science fiction was really made. *Space Battleship Yamato*, *Gundam* (from 1979) and *Akira* form the spine of science-fiction anime's evolution. *Yamato*, particularly, marked the moment when science fiction and anime became more widely recognized and fanclubs developed around the series.

With home video in the 1980s came the growing international access to anime. As the 1990s progressed, the Pokémon franchise provided the necessary next jolt of interest, and in the late 1990s Studio Ghibli's movie *Princess Mononoke* positioned its director Hayao Miyazaki as an major fantasy and science fiction filmmaker: his work has become increasingly well known since and served as an entry point to other anime creations.

NOVELIST ANNE RICE WAS BORN IN 1941

Anne Rice's vampire novels, focused on the vampire Lestat, have been very popular and *Interview with a Vampire* (1976) is the standout title. It was adapted into a film (1994) starring Tom Cruise.

IN THE STORYWORLD OF MIKE MIGNOLA'S COMIC BOOK *HELLBOY*, THE TITULAR CHARACTER WAS CONCEIVED IN 1617

Hellboy is an essential character of the American comic renaissance of the early 1990s. A paranormal investigator, Hellboy is the child of a demon and a witch.

BIRTHDAY OF RAJ KOOTHRAPPALI
IN *THE BIG BANG THEORY*

6
OCTOBER

The Big Bang Theory (2007–present) tells the stories of four geek
scientists as they navigate the adventure of real life and romance.

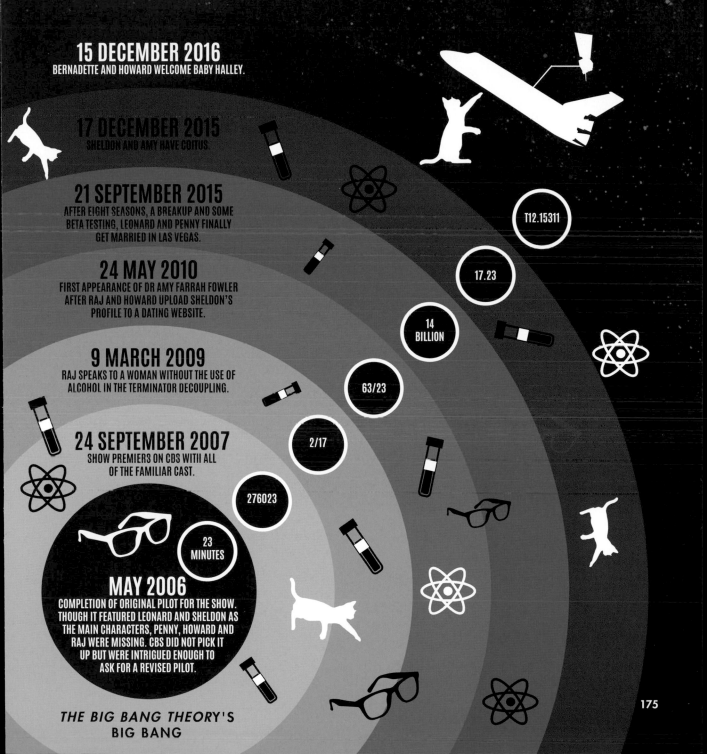

15 DECEMBER 2016
BERNADETTE AND HOWARD WELCOME BABY HALLEY.

17 DECEMBER 2015
SHELDON AND AMY HAVE COITUS.

21 SEPTEMBER 2015
AFTER EIGHT SEASONS, A BREAKUP AND SOME
BETA TESTING, LEONARD AND PENNY FINALLY
GET MARRIED IN LAS VEGAS.

24 MAY 2010
FIRST APPEARANCE OF DR AMY FARRAH FOWLER
AFTER RAJ AND HOWARD UPLOAD SHELDON'S
PROFILE TO A DATING WEBSITE.

9 MARCH 2009
RAJ SPEAKS TO A WOMAN WITHOUT THE USE OF
ALCOHOL IN THE TERMINATOR DECOUPLING.

24 SEPTEMBER 2007
SHOW PREMIERS ON CBS WITH ALL
OF THE FAMILIAR CAST.

T12.15311

17.23

14
BILLION

63/23

2/17

276023

23
MINUTES

MAY 2006
COMPLETION OF ORIGINAL PILOT FOR THE SHOW.
THOUGH IT FEATURED LEONARD AND SHELDON AS
THE MAIN CHARACTERS, PENNY, HOWARD AND
RAJ WERE MISSING. CBS DID NOT PICK IT
UP BUT WERE INTRIGUED ENOUGH TO
ASK FOR A REVISED PILOT.

THE BIG BANG THEORY'S
BIG BANG

COMIC BOOK ARTIST HOWARD CHAYKIN WAS BORN IN 1950

Chaykin made his comic book debut in 1971 and by the late 1970s his profile had risen thanks to his work on Marvel's comic adaptation of the first *Star Wars* (1976) movie. Chaykin's distinctive visuals have been part of an ongoing effort to treat the comic book mode with a certain kind of sophistication. His work includes *The Divided States of Hysteria* (2017), *American Flagg!* (1983–89), *Satellite Sam* (2013–2015) and *Blackhawk* (1983 and 1988).

ACTRESS SIGOURNEY WEAVER WAS BORN IN 1949

Sigourney Weaver has the distinction of portraying several globally recognised characters from hugely popular films: Ellen Ripley in the *Alien* franchise (1979, 1986, 1992 and 1997), Dana Barrett in the *Ghostbusters* series (1982 and 1989, with a special appeareance in the 2016 film as Dr. Rebecca Gorin), Gwen De Marco in *Galaxy Quest* (1999), and Dr Grace Augustine in *Avatar* (2009).

As in the *Alien* films, Weaver embodied a breakthrough portrayal of a woman in a large scale science fiction/horror fusion. Ripley was resolute and resourceful and has become synonymous with the saga. Images of Ripley confronting the Xenomorph in James Cameron's *Aliens* are especially striking. In *Ghostbusters*, Weaver is the the dramatic centre around which the comic heroics of Zeddemore, Stantz, Spengler and Venkman play out. Weaver's performances in this body of science fiction and fantasy material brings a certain emotional grounding to the chaos that's unfolding with ghosts and beasts and alternative realities.

FILMMAKER GUILLERMO DEL TORO WAS BORN IN 1964

Guillermo del Toro's baroque fantasies bring the wonder and the horror of life into one stunningly realised body of work that draws on the great traditions of science fiction, fantasy and horror.

Primarily a feature film writer and director, he has also branched out into producing film and TV and collaborating on books. He even cameos in the computer game *Death Stranding* (2019)

Arguably, del Toro's most highly regarded film is *Pan's Labyrinth* (2006). Set in Spain, it exhibits strong traces of its makers' Mexican origins: we see the influence of Catholic image-making and the aesthetics of Mexican murals.

Del Toro is aware of the violence inherent in fairytales and the concept for *Pan's Labyrinth* bears this out. His two adaptations (2204, 2008) of Mike Mignola's comic *Hellboy* capture the warm humour that cuts through the horror and fantasy intensity. His films celebrate what geeks celebrate: the power of a compelling story to reframe reality.

His newly released, and hugely successful, animated series *Trollhunters* (2016–present) offers his trademark take on monsters, but allies it with a warmhearted set of human stories.

Online, del Toro's Twitter feed has become a treasure trove of suggestions for further reading and viewing and speaks to the wealth of references that he draws on to fashion his material. He can render an all-out kaiju-inspired spectacle in *Pacific Rim* (2013) or the intense fairytale/horror/romance of *Crimson Peak* (2015). Del Toro's long-gestating adaptation of Lovecraft's *At the Mountains of Madness* (1936) seems a perfect fit, but is currently not edging any closer to production. As of this writing, del Toro is directing a romantic fantasy, *The Shape of Water*.

CORNERSTONES OF GUILLERMO DEL TORO'S WORK

SYMPATHETIC MONSTERS AND EVIL HUMANS

10
OCTOBER

THE NOVEL *A PRINCESS OF MARS* WAS PUBLISHED IN FULL IN 1917

Fantasy writers often try plenty of others jobs before finding the work at which they excel: dreaming stuff up. Edgar Rice Burroughs was such a person. *A Princess of Mars* would prove the genesis for an essential American space adventure hero: John Carter of Mars and formerly of the American Civil War. Carter would provide the template for Flash Gordon, Luke Skywalker, Jake Sully et al.

Burroughs was partly inspired by the writing of Jules Verne, and he was lucky to be writing when films were increasing in popularity.

He initially kept his writing ambitions to himself: 'It seemed a foolish thing for a grown man to be doing.' He planned a pseudonym, 'Normal Bean', but changed it to Norman Bean.

In 1912, a second iconic hero sprang from Burroughs' imagination: Tarzan of the Apes. He proved hugely popular and twenty-three Tarzan novels followed, plus a wealth of merchandising.

Burroughs' work is defined by wilderness, civilisation and an atavistic inclination, and he stands as the precursor to Alex Raymond and George Lucas.

11
OCTOBER

IN 1987 *CAPTAIN POWER AND THE SOLDIERS OF THE FUTURE* AIRED ITS EPISODE 'PARIAH'

A Canadian-American series that ran from 1987–88, *Captain Power* told the story of how the human race rose up against robotic entities in the aftermath of the Metal Wars.'Pariah' was the fourth episode in the series. *Captain Power* was to prove low on fuel and it was cancelled after only one series, yet it has something of a cult following.

THE HITCHIKER'S GUIDE TO THE GALAXY
WAS PUBLISHED IN 1979

The Hitchiker's Guide to the Galaxy is Douglas Adams's witty celebration of time travel and a whole bunch of sci-fi tropes, all anchored around a very unassuming British man named Arthur Dent.

THE USES FOR A TOWEL

- Giving warmth to figure in a desolate landscape
- Lying on it on a beautiful white beach
- As a blanket while sleeping in the desert
- A sail on a raft on a river
- As a weapon if used when wet
- Wrapped around the head
- Waved as distress signal
- Bargaining chip used to persuade people to let you borrow other items like a toothbrush, flannel, soap, biscuits, flask, compass, map, string, bug spray, wet weather clothes, space suit.
- To dry yourself

IN 2016 *THE FILM DOCTOR STRANGE*
PREMIERED IN HONG KONG

Doctor Strange was created by Steve Ditko and Stan Lee and was a character onto which Marvel Comics were able to graft more overt fantasy to their superhero output. The character tapped into a 1960s pop culture interest in all things Asian.

14
OCTOBER

MARGARET ATWOOD WROTE ABOUT SPECULATIVE FICTION IN 2011

The writer Margaret Atwood wrote a critical piece in 2011 for the *Guardian* newspaper in the UK in which she resisted labelling her novels such as *The Handmaid's Tale* (1985) as sci-fi, preferring instead to call them speculative fiction. This was to prove a controversial viewpoint.

15
OCTOBER

IN 1944 HAIM SABAN WAS BORN

Israeli media tycoon Haim Saban founded Saban Entertainment which produced and distributed *Power Rangers* in the US. First shown in 1993, the success of the teen heroes continues unabated.

16
OCTOBER

IN 1968 THE BLACK POWER FIST OF DEFIANCE WAS RAISED AT THE OLYMPICS

The Black Power salute was a gesture of protest that resounded across global media and it made superheroes of those athletes making the gesture: Tommie Smith and John Carlos. Smith and Carlos would go on to be recognised for their contribution to America's Civil Rights movement.

There are numerous black characters in comics, but this has not been without controversy. Black characters are more likely to be stereotypical or take the role of sidekicks and assistants. The very first African-American comic book star was Lobo, but this only ran for two issues in 1965.

By the 1970s a number of black heroes were introduced to the world of comics. Bumblebee, who first appeared in *Teen Titans* No. 45 in 1976, was DC Comics' first African-American female hero. Black Panther (aka T'Challa) first appeared in 1966 in issue 52 of the *Fantastic Four*. Luke Cage, another Marvel Comics hero, first appeared in print in 1972 in *Luke Cage: Hero for Hire* issue 1. Also known as Power Man, Cage has skin that can't be broken and super strength.

Then, too, there's Sam Wilson (Falcon) from the *Captain America* comics; Storm in the *X-Men* comics; and Cyborg, best known as a Teen Titan.

More recently, there's Michonne from *The Walking Dead* comic series (which predates the TV series), the vampire hunter Blade and Miles Morales from Spider-Man.

The black superhero is a key part of geek culture and in 2016 American writer Ta-Nehisi Paul Coates wrote a new Black Panther story for Marvel comics, illustrated by Brian Stelfreeze. Of this version of the character Coates explained, in an article in *The Atlantic*: 'The questions are what motivate the action. The questions, ultimately, are more necessary than the answers.'

JERRY SIEGEL WAS BORN IN 1914

Jerry Siegel, co-creator of Superman, saw in his creation an opportunity to find a way to express his feelings about his father, who died as a result of a robbery.

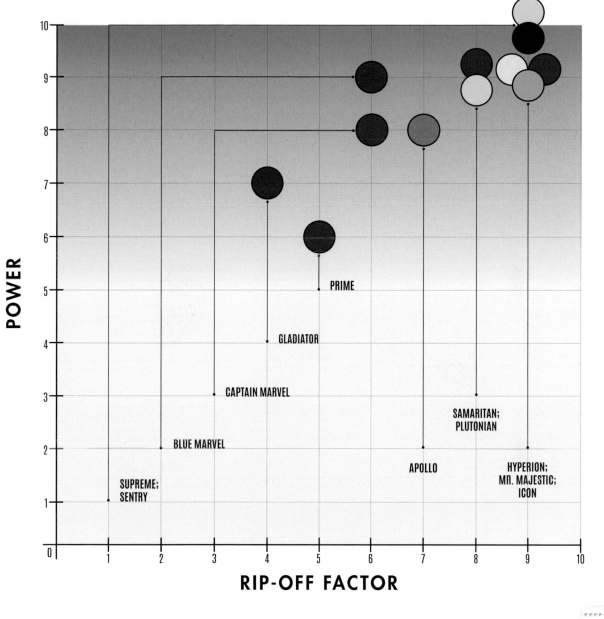

POWER

RIP-OFF FACTOR

PRIME

GLADIATOR

CAPTAIN MARVEL

SAMARITAN;
PLUTONIAN

BLUE MARVEL

APOLLO

HYPERION;
MΠ. MAJESTIC;
ICON

SUPREME;
SENTRY

ISABEL BRIGGS MYERS WAS BORN IN 1897

Along with her mother, Katharine Cook Briggs, American author and theorist Myers developed the Myers–Briggs Type Indicator (MBTI) – a test to assess personality type.

19
OCTOBER

PHILIP PULLMAN WAS BORN IN 1946

Philip Pullman's *His Dark Materials* trilogy of novels (1995–2000) is replete with the sheer delight of imaginative invention: it uses the classic devices of a quest, talking animals, magic, sheer villainy and a sense of the real world sitting right alongside any number of other realities.

The world of the trilogy depicts conflicts between the powerful and the powerless and between ideas: knowledge versus faith; self-determination versus grace; innocence versus experience.

In the trilogy, a number of characters posses a daemon, the animal spirit that embodies and represents their essential being.

20
OCTOBER

JAPANESE WRITER TAKU MAYUMURA WAS BORN IN 1934

His novel *EXPO '87* was published in 1968 and was set in the near-future. He followed this with a series of sci-fi novels set in the much further future.

URSULA K. LE GUIN WAS BORN IN 1929

Still a seemingly very male-dominated world, the terrain of comics and novels shines brightly with the work of Ursula K. Le Guin. Her novels *The Left Hand of Darkness* (1969) and The *Disposssed* (1974) were both, like so much of her work, exploring the drama inherent in clashes of culture and gender. *The Lathe of Heaven* (1971) focuses on dreams and the power they can exert on our waking lives.

Le Guin has the remarkable distinction of having won the Hugo Award, the Nebula Award, the Locus Award and the World Fantasy Award each more than once.

For young readers, her *Earthsea* novels (1964– 2014) might well have been the stories that captivated imaginations and introduced them to the wonders of fantasy. They focus on a boy named Ged, who lives in a world of magic and dragons and learns how to use his powers.

TORCHWOOD PREMIERED IN 2006 ON BBC TV

Created by Russell T. Davis, *Torchwood* was a spin-off from *Doctor Who* and the show's title referred to a clandestine agency charged with investigating unusual phenomena.

TORCHWOOD INSTITUTE FOUNDED BY QUEEN VICTORIA IN 1879

TORCHWOOD 1 LONDON

YVONNE HARTMAN (DIRECTOR), DR RAJESH SINGH (SCIENTIST), MICKEY SMITH (SCIENTIST), LISA HALLETT, ADEOLA SMITH (SCIENTIST), IANTO JONES (RESEARCHER)

TORCHWOOD 2 GLASGOW

ARCHIE

TORCHWOOD 3 CARDIFF

CAPTAIN JACK HARKNESS (LEADER), GWEN COOPER (POLICE LIAISON), DR OWEN HARPER (MEDICAL OFFICE), TOSHIKO (COMPUTER EXPERT), IANTO JONES (ADMINISTRATOR), SUZIE COSTELLO (WEAPONS SPECIALIST), DR MARTHA JONES (UNIT LIAISON, MEDIC)

TORCHWOOD 4 UNKNOWN LOCAL

MISSING TORCHWOOD DELHI, INDIA: ELEANOR, DUCHESS OF MELROSE (LEADER), MR DAZ (SECRETARY), GEORGE GISSING (STRATEGIST), MAHAJAN (SUPPORT STAFF)

183

MICHAEL CRICHTON WAS BORN IN 1942

Michael Crichton's name was everywhere, it seemed, in the early 1990s. His novel *Jurassic Park* was published in 1990 and the film adaptation of it released in 1993. In fact, this was just the latest in a run of science-fiction novels and films created by Crichton.

His credits include the books *The Andromeda Strain* (1969) and *Sphere* (1987) and the film *Westworld* (1973). Key to Crichton's work was the research he undertook in order to make the fantasy as believable as possible.

FOX MULDER IN *THE X-FILES*, JOINED THE FBI IN 1984

Played by David Duchovny, Fox Mulder investigated mysterious and paranormal cases that the mainstream FBI couldn't solve. He adamantly believed in a government conspiracy to hide the truth about UFO's and is facinated by the possibilities of otherworldly and supernatural encounters and phenomena.

VINCENT PRICE DIED IN 1993

Vincent Price's voice was hugely recognisable as it rolled elegantly and playfully across the words he spoke. It is showcased in Michael Jackson's hit song 'Thriller' (1982), and Tim Burton's short film *Vincent* (1982). The feature film *Edward Scissorhands* (1991) put Price front and centre in their own particular ways.

Price had become synonymous with a number of horror films adapted from Edgar Allan Poe stories and directed by Roger Corman: *House of Usher* (1960), *Pit and the Pendulum* (1961) and *The Raven* (1963).

IN 1985 MARTY MCFLY GOES BACK TO 1955

26
OCTOBER

Back to the Future is probably the most well known time travel movie in history and in the story Marty McFly and Dr Emmett Brownl bounce around time across the 1980s, 1950s, 1880s and the early 21st century. Along the way, Marty learns the lesson that the future isn't written.

| 1885 | 1955 | 1985 | 2015 |

TIMELINE 1

TIMELINE 2

TIMELINE 3

TIMELINE 4

TIMELINE 5

TIMELINE 6

TIMELINE 7

TIMELINE 8

MARTY   DOC   BIFF   JENNIFER   BACK IN TIME   FORWRD IN TIME

DYLAN THOMAS WAS BORN IN 1914

A Welsh poet and a popular Italian comic book hero is an unlikely cultural collision but, sure enough, Dylan Thomas (the first 'rock and roll poet') inspired the name of Italian comic book hero Dylan Dog.

Dylan Dog, created by Tiziano Sclavi was first published in 1986. Focused on a London investigator, it is part of a strong Italian comic book legacy. In 1908 *Il Corriere dei Piccoli* (*The Children's Courier*) was published. This was the first mainstream Italian publication that focused on comics. The first issue featured a strip drawn by Attilio Mussino about a boy named Bilbolbul. He is considered to be the first Italian comic book character. *Il Corriere dei Piccoli* also showcased a number of American comics, such as *Happy Hooligans* and *Felix the Cat*.

Under Facism, comics were utilised for propagana aimed at young Italians and by 1 January 1939 all foreign comics were banned. the only exception was Topolino, as Mickey Mouse was known in Italian. Allegedly this exception was granted because of the affection Mussolini's children had for the Disney star.

The end of the Second World War saw a welcome return of many comics that had to cease production during the conflict. These would eventually prove more popular than the imported American comics, with one of the most successful being *Tex Willer*, created by Gian Luigi Bonelli and illustrated by Aurelio Galleppini. An important series published in the 1960s is about master thief Diabolik. First published in 1962,this was the first Italian comic with a villain at its centre, and was created by sisters Angela and Luciana Giussani.

By the 1960s, homegrown Italian material was coming in to its own. Guido Crepax, Milo Manaa and Hugo Pratt are just three artists who played an important in the evolution of Italian comics.

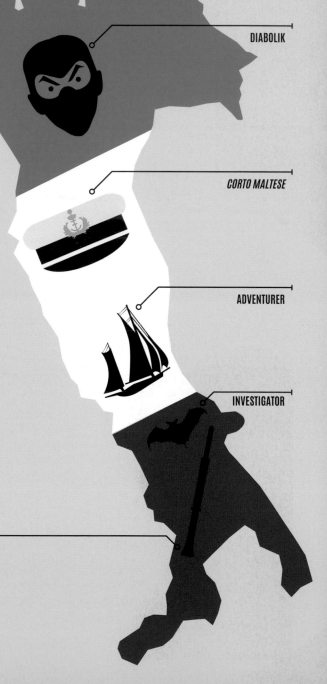

MASTER THIEF

DIABOLIK

CORTO MALTESE

ADVENTURER

INVESTIGATOR

DYLAN DOG

IN THE 1993 FILM, THIS IS THE FINAL DAY OF *MATINEE*

Joe Dante's much-loved films include *The Howling* (1981), *Gremlins* (1984), *Innerspace* (1987) and *Small Soldiers* (1998). A filmmaker with respect for the less prestigious genres, Dante makes films that are satirical, political and suffused with that essential geek question: 'What if?'

DANTE'S BOX OFFICE

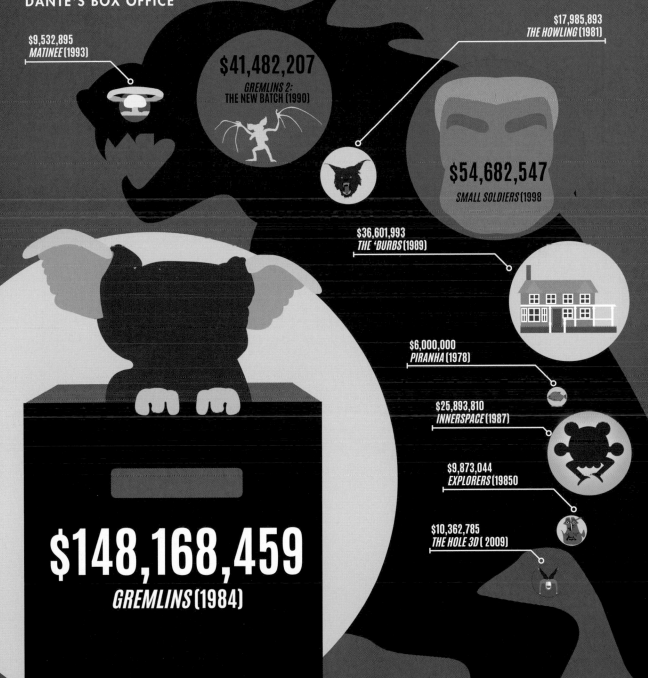

$9,532,895
MATINEE (1993)

$41,482,207
GREMLINS 2: THE NEW BATCH (1990)

$17,985,893
THE HOWLING (1981)

$54,682,547
SMALL SOLDIERS (1998

$36,601,993
THE 'BURBS (1909)

$6,000,000
PIRANHA (1978)

$25,893,810
INNERSPACE (1987)

$9,873,044
EXPLORERS (19850

$10,362,785
THE HOLE 3D (2009)

$148,168,459
GREMLINS (1984)

29 OCTOBER

IN 1993 STOP-MOTION FILM *THE NIGHTMARE BEFORE CHRISTMAS* WAS RELEASED AT CINEMAS IN AMERICA

The Nightmare Before Christmas is now a landmark Christmas and Halloween perennial. A stop-motion feature from a concept by Tim Burton, it's the story of Jack Skellington who leaves Halloweentown and discovers a place called Christmastown.

30 OCTOBER

IN 1938 ORSON WELLES' VERSION OF *THE WAR OF THE WORLDS* WAS BROADCAST ON AMERICAN RADIO

Orson Welles' radio broadcast may not have quite been the grand hoax of popular myth, but it still remains a key moment. Adolf Hitler even referenced the broadcast in a speech later that year.

31 OCTOBER

ET SET OUT FOR HOME IN THE FILM *ET: THE EXTRA TERRESTRIAL*

After a fast, furious and ultimately jubilant escape from the authority of adults, Elliot and his BMX-riding buddies bring E.T. to safety in the moonlit forest, whereupon they say a tearful farewell – faith in friendship and the outsider shining as brightly as E.T.'s heart.

HELLO KITTY WAS 'BORN' IN LONDON IN 1974

Kitty White, better known as Hello Kitty, has become a massively successful geek character appearing in an animated series and in comics. Kitty is an anthropomorphic cat and her image appears on clothing, jewellery and stationery. Her 'origin' in London is on account of the popularity of many things British in Japan in the early 1970s.

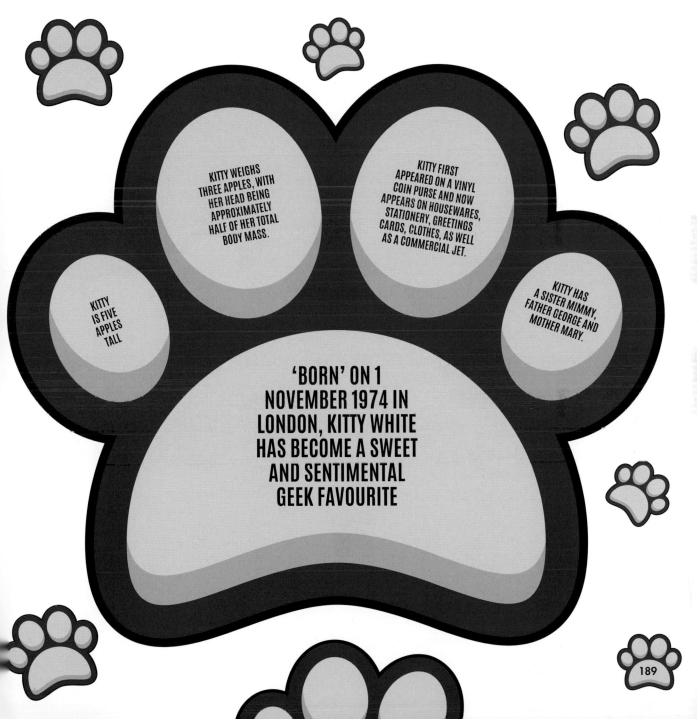

KITTY WEIGHS THREE APPLES, WITH HER HEAD BEING APPROXIMATELY HALF OF HER TOTAL BODY MASS.

KITTY FIRST APPEARED ON A VINYL COIN PURSE AND NOW APPEARS ON HOUSEWARES, STATIONERY, GREETINGS CARDS, CLOTHES, AS WELL AS A COMMERCIAL JET.

KITTY IS FIVE APPLES TALL

KITTY HAS A SISTER MIMMY, FATHER GEORGE AND MOTHER MARY.

'BORN' ON 1 NOVEMBER 1974 IN LONDON, KITTY WHITE HAS BECOME A SWEET AND SENTIMENTAL GEEK FAVOURITE

THRILLER RELEASED AS A SINGLE WORLDWIDE IN 1983

Picture the moment: America's pop music enjoys a new shot of creative marketing in the form of music videos, and onto this new platform stepped Michael Jackson.

A self-described fan of Walt Disney and fantasy, Jackson saw the potential of the music-video format. He always described his music videos as short films and his music videos celebrated the geek pleasures of science fiction, fantasy and master monster movies.

1983 was a seismic shift, thanks to the hugely hyped American TV premiere of the music promo for his song 'Thriller'. Directed by John Landis (who had directed *An American Werewolf in London*, 1981), the video was a loving pastiche of the zombie genre as well as the teen werewolf movie subgenre of the 1950s. Creepy, comic and massively catchy, 'Thriller' famously featured the voice of Vincent Price.

Disney soon called on Jackson and developed a science fiction adventure short film project entitled *Captain EO* (1986). A celebration of music and dance, it was directed by Francis Coppola and produced by George Lucas, the Lucas influence clear to see in almost every shot.

Jackson's subsequent feature length film *Moonwalker* (1988) pulled together a number of his music promos from the album *Bad*. His later short film *Ghosts* (1996), directed by Stan Winston, was inspired by Edgar Allan Poe.

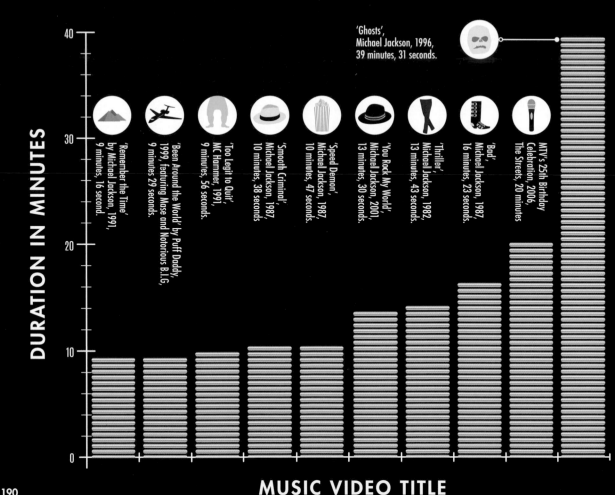

'Ghosts', Michael Jackson, 1996, 39 minutes, 31 seconds.

DURATION IN MINUTES

40 — 30 — 20 — 10 — 0

'Remember the Time' by Michael Jackson, 1991, 9 minutes, 16 second.

'Been Around the World' by Puff Daddy, 1999, featuring Mase and Notorious B.I.G., 9 minutes 29 seconds.

'Too Legit to Quit', MC Hammer, 1991, 9 minutes, 56 seconds.

'Smooth Criminal', Michael Jackson, 1987, 10 minutes, 38 seconds.

'Speed Demon', Michael Jackson, 1987, 10 minutes, 47 seconds.

'You Rock My World', Michael Jackson, 2001, 13 minutes, 30 seconds.

'Thriller', Michael Jackson, 1982, 13 minutes, 43 seconds.

'Bad', Michael Jackson, 1987, 16 minutes, 23 seconds.

MTV's 25th Birthday Celebration, 2006, The Streets, 20 minutes.

MUSIC VIDEO TITLE

GOJIRA (*GODZILLA*) WAS RELEASED IN 1954

Is there a more famous monster? A symbol of Japan's anxieties about science, technology and its effect on nature, Gojira rises up from deep beneath the ocean's surface to wreak havoc. An iconic example of tokusatsu (the Japanese term for 'special filming', meaning visual effects), Gojira films embrace the stomping, chomping and unfettered natural power that does indeed make humanity look pretty puny.

The *kaiju eiga* (monster movie) subgenre was a highlight of Japanese film production during the 1950s and 1960s. It's worth noting, too, that Gojira was not Japan's first science fiction film; that distinction goes to *Invisible Man* (Tomei Ningen Arawaru, 1949).

Gojira represents abused atomic power: it was the radioactive contamination of a fishing boat following a US hydrogen bomb test on Bikini Atoll that spawned the beast. Check out too *The Mysterians* (1957), in which an alien race – the Mysterians – come to earth following the nuclear war on their own planet.

THE FOURTH SEASON OF *BABYLON 5* TV SERIES PREMIERED IN 1996

Babylon 5 followed in the tradition of *Star Trek* and, like that landmark series, sought to identify recognizably human dramas and dilemmas that could play out against an interstellar setting.

IN 1605 GUY FAWKES ATTEMPTED TO DESTROY THE HOUSES OF PARLIAMENT IN ENGLAND WITH HIS GUNPOWDER PLOT

The comic *V For Vendetta* focuses on an anarchist in rebellion against a totalitarian government. The comic's story is informed by the writing of George Orwell, Aldous Huxley and Harlan Ellison's short story '"Repent, Harlequin!" Said the Ticktockman.'

IN 1983 THE STORY THAT IS TOLD IN THE SERIES *STRANGER THINGS BEGINS*

Stranger Things (2016) powerfully returned some, and introduced others, to the 1980s milieu of fantasy, science fiction and horror. The first series captured the small-town ordinariness against which extraordinary and menacing events unfold.

GEARS OF WAR WAS RELEASED IN 2006

A pioneering shooter game in which humans on the planet of Sera battle
The Locust Horde. To date, there are four *Gears of War* games.

WEAPONS
- Hammerburst II
- Scorcher flamethrower
- Bolo grenade
- Smoke grenade
- Mulcher
- Mark II Lancer assault rifle
- Boom shield
- Longshot sniper rifle

CHARACTERS
- Marcus Fenix
- Adam Fenix
- Dominic 'Dom' Santiago
- Myrrah
- Samantha Byrne
- Damon Baird
- Anya Stroud
- Augustus Cole

Coalition of Ordered Governments (COG) values
- Order
- Loyalty
- Diligence
- Honor
- Faith
- Labor
- Humanity
- Purity

IN 1961 *THE FANTASTIC FOUR* DEBUTED IN MARVEL COMICS

The Fantastic Four, Marvel's first superhero team, burst on to the comic book scene,
with a quartet of heroes: Reed Richards (Mr Fantastic), Ben Grimm (The Thing),
Johnny Storm (The Human Torch) and Susan Storm (The Invisible Woman).

IN 1967 *VALÉRIAN AND LAURELINE* PUBLISHED

Valérian and Laureline is a French comic book phenomenon by illustrator Jean-Claude Mézières and writer Pierre Christin. French geek culture is replete with comics and this one is essential.

Its premise is that Valérian, a pilot in the twenty-eighth century, teams up with a time-travelling young woman named Laureline. Together they undertake missions for Galaxity, serving as border guards in outer space, across which humanity has made settlements. Where Valérian tends to go by the book, Laureline operates in a somewhat more maverick way.

This is space opera in the tradition of E. E. 'Doc' Smith and Alex Raymond and, like plenty of other science fiction, weaves real-world ideas into the intergalactic fantasy. The stories, first published in *Pilote* magazine, ran from 1967 until 2010, and a film adaptation was released in 2017.

VALÉRIAN AND LAURELINE
STORIES OF 67-84

1967 BAD DREAMS
1968 THE CITY OF SHIFTING WATERS
1970 THE EMPIRE OF A THOUSAND PLANETS
1971 WORLD WITHOUT STARS
1972 WELCOME TO ALFOLOL
1973 BIRDS OF THE MASTER
1975 AMBASSADOR OF THE SHADOWS
1977 ON THE FALSE EARTHS
1978 THE HEROES OF THE EQUINOX
1980 METRO CHATELET, DIRECTION CASSIOPEE
1981 BROOKLYN STATION, TERMINUS COSMOS
1984 THE GHOSTS OF INVERLOCH

NEIL GAIMAN WAS BORN IN 1960

Neil Gaiman's fantasy writing includes the series *The Sandman* (from 1989), *Coraline* (2002) and the epic novel *American Gods* (2001).

THE BOOK *FAERIES* WAS REPUBLISHED IN 2002

The names of Brian Froud and Alan Lee immediately speak volumes to those enthusiasts of high fantasy and the world of fairies and elves.

Together, these two British artists collaborated on a bestselling book entitled *Faeries*, that was first published in 1978.

Where Lee's images skew slightly more towards a sense of realism, Froud's style is slightly more heightened and his fairy faces are immediately identifiable.

Both Froud and Lee's have parlayed their talents into films. Froud collaborated with Jim Henson to visualise the worlds and characters of *The Dark Crystal* (1982) and *Labyrinth* (1986). Lee has worked with Peter Jackson to visualise *The Lord of the Rings* trilogy (2001–03) and *The Hobbit* (2012–14).

IN 1990, TIM BERNERS-LEE PUBLISHED A PROPOSAL FOR A TECHNOLOGY KNOWN AS WWW

The Internet has proved to be a powerful force in uniting geek interests and cultivating discussion.

ASSASSIN'S CREED WAS RELEASED IN 2007

This bestselling computer game focuses on a conflict between the Assassins and the Knights Templar. Both of these societies have a connection to an ancient, pre-human species. Descended from the Assassins is an 'ordinary' man, Desmond Miles, who finds himself embroiled in a project to reconnect with his ancestral memories as a way to bring the fractured human race together. The series of games take place across a range of time periods. In 2016, a lavish film adaptation was released.

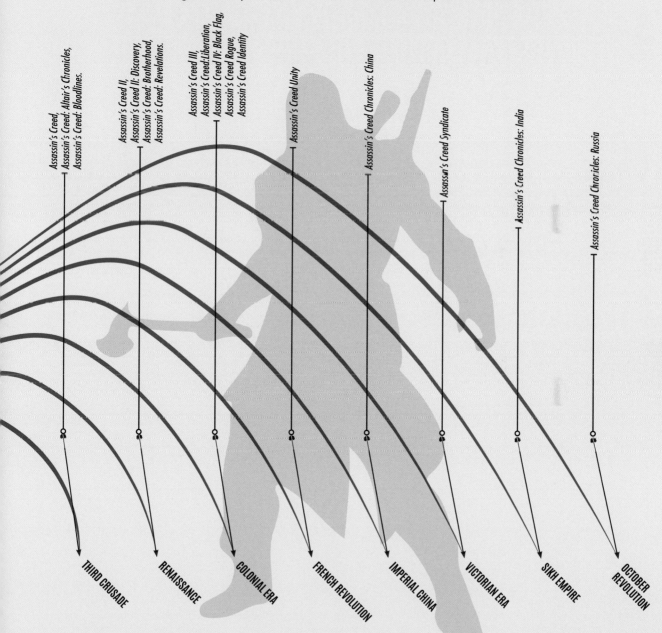

Assassin's Creed,
Assassin's Creed: Altaïr's Chronicles,
Assassin's Creed: Bloodlines.

Assassin's Creed II,
Assassin's Creed II: Discovery,
Assassin's Creed: Brotherhood,
Assassin's Creed: Revelations.

Assassin's Creed III,
Assassin's Creed:Liberation,
Assassin's Creed IV: Black Flag,
Assassin's Creed Rogue,
Assassin's Creed Identity

Assassin's Creed Unity

Assassin's Creed Chronicles: China

Assassin's Creed Syndicate

Assassin's Creed Chronicles: India

Assassin's Creed Chronicles: Russia

THIRD CRUSADE

RENAISSANCE

COLONIAL ERA

FRENCH REVOLUTION

IMPERIAL CHINA

VICTORIAN ERA

SIKH EMPIRE

OCTOBER REVOLUTION

AMERICAN TV PRODUCER GLEN A. LARSON DIED IN 2014

His name was a staple of so much genre programming in the 1970s and 1980s. Larson not only produced *Battlestar Galactica* (2004–2009), but also the series *Buck Rogers in the 25th Century* (1979–1981), *Knight Rider* (1982–1986), *Manimal* (1983) and *Automan* (1983–1984).

IN 2001, THE COMPUTER GAME *HALO* WAS FIRST RELEASED ON THE SONY XBOX CONSOLE

Halo began as a third person shooter and traded, rather brilliantly, in a familiar and always compelling scenario: a human combat against an alien force.

First released in 2001, with the title *Halo: Combat Evolved*, part of the game's appea is the integrity of its world building. The game's landmark status is also attributable to being the signature game of the Xbox during the time it was taking on the Sony PlayStation2. The UK's *Guardian* newspaper described *Halo* as having 'turned the whole concept of the console shooter into a distinct and credible art form.'

In May of 2013, Steven Spielberg announced the development of a TV series based on the game: a sure sign of a property's pop culture standing. Whilst that project has yet to materialise the game continues to be hugely popular. Indeed, predating Spielberg's connection to the *Halo* property, filmmaker Neil Blomkamp of *District 9* (2009), *Elysium* (2013) and *Chappie* (2015) had endeavoured to launch a feature film adaptation of the game back in 2005.

CLOSE ENCOUNTERS OF THE THIRD KIND WAS RELEASED IN AMERICAN CINEMAS IN 1977

Close Encounters of the Third Kind remains the cinema distillation
of so much of Steven Spielberg's filmmaking sensibility.

CLOSE ENCOUNTERS OF THE FIRST KIND

A SIGHTING OF A UFO (UNIDENTIFIED FLYING OBJECT) THAT APPEARS TO BE LESS THAN 500 FEET AWAY FROM THE PERSON SIGHTING IT

CLOSE ENCOUNTERS OF THE SECOND KIND

A UFO INTERFERES WITH HUMAN TECHNOLOGY, ANIMALS REACT, THE ENVIRONMENT IS IMPACTED BY THE UFO

CLOSE ENCOUNTERS OF THE THIRD KIND

A HUMAN MEETS AN ALIEN CREATURE WHO APPEARS TO OCCUPY THE UFO

CLOSE ENCOUNTERS OF THE FOURTH KIND

ABDUCTION OF A HUMAN BY AN ALIEN

IN *STAR TREK: THE NEXT GENERATION* WESLEY CRUSHER UNDERTOOK HIS FINAL MISSION

Portrayed by Will Wheaton, Wesley Crusher was a major character in *Star Trek: The Next Generation* (1987–1994), the son of a man killed while under the command of Captain Picard.

ALAN MOORE WAS BORN IN 1953

Alan Moore's recently published novel *Jerusalem* (2016) vividly reimagines his hometown of Northampton, and it's typical of his creative vibe to have fused the everyday so powerfully with his more fanciful musings. His work for the comic book medium is a major contribution: *Watchmen* (1986–87), *The League of Extraordinary Gentlemen* (1999–present), *From Hell* (1999), *V For Vendetta* (1988–89) and more recently Nemo: Heart of Ice (2013).

JACK DORSEY WAS BORN IN 1976

Twitter (created by Dorsey, Noah Glass, Biz Stone and Evan Williams) has become a source of much geek-friendly opportunity for conversation, debate and discussion.

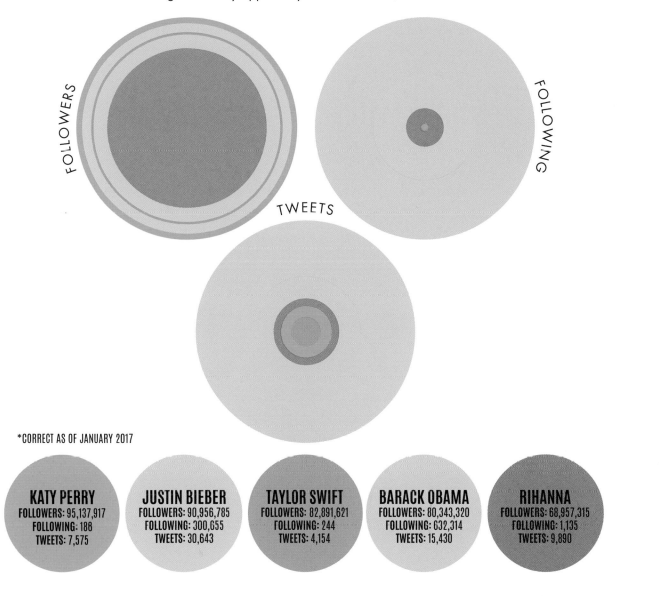

FOLLOWERS

FOLLOWING

TWEETS

*CORRECT AS OF JANUARY 2017

KATY PERRY
FOLLOWERS: 95,137,917
FOLLOWING: 188
TWEETS: 7,575

JUSTIN BIEBER
FOLLOWERS: 90,956,785
FOLLOWING: 300,655
TWEETS: 30,643

TAYLOR SWIFT
FOLLOWERS: 82,091,621
FOLLOWING: 244
TWEETS: 4,154

BARACK OBAMA
FOLLOWERS: 80,343,320
FOLLOWING: 632,314
TWEETS: 15,430

RIHANNA
FOLLOWERS: 68,957,315
FOLLOWING: 1,135
TWEETS: 9,890

IN 2007 *MASS EFFECT* WAS FIRST RELEASED

Mass Effect is a science-fiction computer game set in 2183, which trades on a number of essential types of science-fiction elements: a portal allows an advanced race of starships to threaten human life, and players must stop it from being opened.

RETURN OF HOWARD THE DUCK ANNOUNCED IN 2014

At the end of the movie *Guardians of the Galaxy*, 1970s comic book anti-hero Howard the Duck (created by Steve Gerber and published by Marvel) is glimpsed. A popular cameo, Howard then returned to comics in 2015. Howard was trapped in a world he never made, having been blasted from his Duckworld planet to Cleveland Ohio. Howard sees the absurdities of the human condition. In 1986 a now-cult movie was released.

22

NOVEMBER

ARTHUR MATHER WAS BORN IN 1925

When we think of comics, we tend to think of America and Japan in particular,
but it would be remiss to overlook the Australian comic-book tradition.-

Shining brightly in the antipodean comic book firmament is Arthur Mather, creator of Captain Atom. Atom first appeared in January 1948, just a short time after the A Bomb was exploded at Bikini Atoll in the Pacific Ocean. In Australia, *Captain Atom* comics outsold Superman comics. The first issue alone sold more than 100,000 copies. A glow-in-the-dark Captain Atom ring was a popular piece of merchandise. The series ended in 1954, after 64 issues.

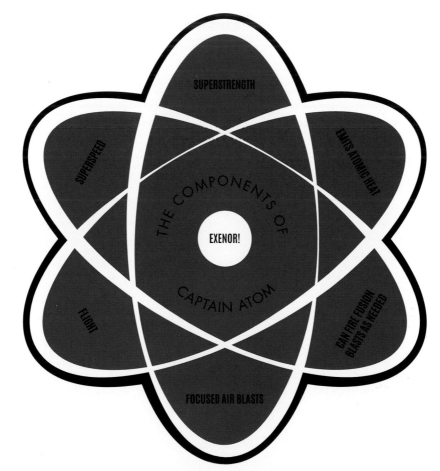

DOCTOR WHO APPEARS FOR THE FIRST TIME IN 1963

Who wouldn't want at least a second chance to start again? Well, every few years *Doctor Who* has that chance, thanks to the process of regeneration: a biological feature of the Time Lords of Gallifrey.

To date, the Doctor has manifested thirteen regenerative identities, and whilst his appearance changes, his name always remains the same.

However, the big question that looms over the compelling regeneration process is this: what really is the regeneration limit for the Doctor, given that in the episode 'The Deadly Assassin' (1976), the rule of the regeneration game was laid down: a limit of thirteen. However, there appears to be some intergalactic wriggle room here as the High Council of Gallifrey can sanction further regenerations when the times are desperate enough to warrant them. In fact, it might well be that 507 regenerations are available.

Understandably, the Doctor's regeneration makes for a dramatic highpoint. When the first Doctor regenerated the screen simply whited out. By the time of the eleventh and twelfth regenerations, blasts of golden light surged spectacularly from the Doctor.

But surely wouldn't the most dramatic regeneration be for the Doctor to renew as a woman?

THE COLOUR OF MAGIC WAS FIRST PUBLISHED IN 1983

Pratchett's novels are set in Discworld, which is a flat disc that rests on the backs of four elephants standing atop the shell of a giant turtle. The Discworld stories have a richness of invention and sense of humour that has travelled far and wide. But, amidst all of the invention and fantasy, the novels have found opportunities to explore our real world concerns.

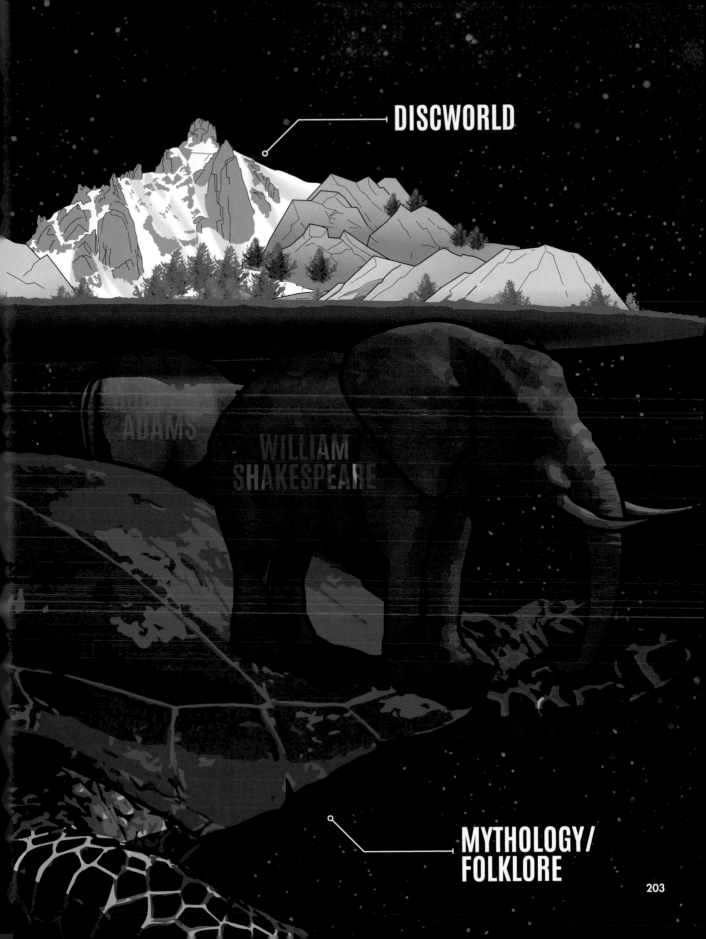

DISCWORLD

ADAMS

WILLIAM SHAKESPEARE

MYTHOLOGY/ FOLKLORE

25 NOVEMBER

THE ANIME *PAPRIKA* WAS RELEASED IN 2006 IN JAPAN

Satoshi Kon's anime visions are key to anime culture and have done much to broaden the interest for the form beyond Japan. He was one of the great Japanese filmmakers, and his work as an anime director came to an end all too soon with his death at the age of 46.

As a child he had loved anime, watching series including *Astro Boy* (1952–68), *Mobile Suit Gundam* (1979–80) and *Space Battleship Yamato* (1974–75). The first anime that Kon worked on was *Roujin Z* (1991): it's about geriatric hackers and machines at war, and he painted the backgrounds.

He would go on to direct four feature films and a TV mini series, determined always to take anime beyond the familiar situations and character types. Kon typically set his films in contemporary Tokyo, threading fantastical situations through them.

Kon's other films were the horror *Perfect Blue* (1997), the fantasy *Millennium Actress* (2001) and the Christmas-themed film *Tokyo Godfathers* (2003). When Kon died, he was in process with his next film, *Dreaming Machine* about futureworld robots.

26 NOVEMBER

ALICE IN WONDERLAND WAS FIRST PUBLISHED IN 1865

Lewis Carroll's *Alice's Adventures in Wonderland* – to give it its proper title – is a playful fantasy that pits the logic of a child against the seeming illogic of adults.

Carroll's book has been adapted for film on many occasions: Walt Disney produced an animated version (1951) and animator Jan Svankmajer has directed a surreal nightmare version (1988). Tim Burton's lavish rendition (2010) stays true to a number of core ideas in the novel. Perhaps one of the most fascinating versions of Carroll's book, though, is *Dreamchild* (1985), which alternates between reality and a fantasy world enlivened by a number of creatures performed by Jim Henson's troupe of puppeteers.

FILM DIRECTOR KATHRYN BIGELOW
WAS BORN IN 1951

Kathryn Bigelow has a rather special distinction: she has directed a number of films in genres more typically associated with male directors. Her directing debut was *Near Dark* (1987, in which a family of vampires encounter a young man in a small town in the American Midwest. *Near Dark*, was one of several vampire films released at around the same time, notably *Fright Night* (1985) and *The Lost Boys* (1987).

Near Dark though, was the least popular. It does, however, enjoy a cult reputation today.

Bigelow would go on to direct the science-fiction film *Strange Days* (1995), which explores virtual reality and the increasing ways in which human beings are becoming one with technology.

FILM DIRECTOR ALFONSO CUARÓN
WAS BORN IN 1961

Harry Potter and the Prisoner of Azkaban (2004), directed by Alfonso Cuarón, is widely considered the most involving of the film adaptations of the Potter novels. It moves confidently between whimsy, menace and mythic grandeur.

C.S. LEWIS WAS BORN 1898

29
NOVEMBER

C.S. Lewis's *The Chronicles of Narnia* (1950–56) are classics of geek literature, showcasing just how much can be achieved in fantasy and allegory. Lewis's world of Narnia owes a debt to classical Greece and medieval myth and, in turn, his books have influenced generations of writers since.

The most famous title in the series is *The Lion, The Witch and the Wardrobe* (1950), faithfully adapted into a lavish Disney film in 2005.

Importantly Lewis was a friend and colleague of J.R.R. Tolkien and they read and commented on each others' work.

Lewis wrote an essay 'On Three Ways of Writing for Children' in which he argued that children's literature should indeed be judged as literature and not regarded as something lesser.

30
NOVEMBER

FILM DIRECTOR RIDLEY SCOTT WAS BORN IN 1937

Alien. Blade Runner. Legend. Ridley Scott's significant contribution to science fiction and fantasy displays a commitment to serious spectacle.

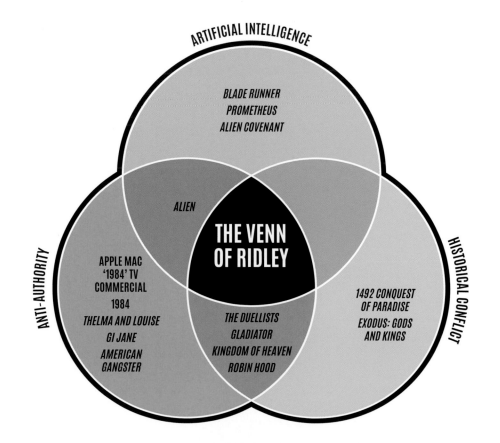

ALEISTER CROWLEY DIED IN 1947

Playwright, poet, scholar, self-declared Magus and keen mountaineer, Aleister Crowley professed to be a genuine believer in magic, which he chose to spell as Magick to distinguish it from stage conjuring.

During his life he wrote voraciously, writing scores of magical texts, plays and poetry espousing his personal beliefs, as well as investigating, refining and then performing occult ceremonies with the help, and sometimes opposition, of other figures in British and international magical communities.

He was a member of various mystical groups such as The Hermetic Order of the Golden Dawn, the *Ordo Templi Orientis* (O.T.O.) and most significantly his own religion, Thelema. Scientology founder and science fiction author L Ron Hubbard dabbled in Thelema in the 1940s, along with rocket scientist Jack Parsons.

Though he was seen as extremely charismatic and persuasive, Crowley loved to provoke and outrage normal moral sensibilities and it was sometimes difficult to tell his actual beliefs from ones designed to upset. His personal motto was 'Do What Thou Wilt' and his shameless behaviour earned him the title 'the Wickedest Man in the World' by the British press, something he revelled in.

He travelled the world and moved in and out of poverty, sometimes trapped in obscurity and sometimes associating with famous figures, like Ian Fleming, Dennis Wheatley and Roald Dahl when they worked for British Intelligence. Wheatley's novel *The Devil Rides Out* (1934) features a villain who may have been based on Crowley, and it's suggested that he may have also been the basis of Le Chiffre in Fleming's *Casino Royale* (1953).

Crowley's influence on science fiction extends from the exploration and incorporation of his beliefs into various magic systems used in fiction, to his appearance as an actual character in *Masks of The Illuminati* (1981) by Robert Anton Wilson, the short story 'Angel Down, Sussex' (1999) by Kim Newman, and the comics series *Promethea* (1999–2005) by writer and magical practitioner Alan Moore, along with J.H. Williams III and Mick Gray.

JOHN WYNDHAM'S NOVEL *THE DAY OF THE TRIFFIDS* WAS PUBLISHED IN 1951

Wyndham describes the impact of a meteor shower on Britain, which renders people blind. The Triffids, aggressive, carnivorous plants, are now able to take over, wreaking revenge on the human race. The novel captures a sense of British unease during the 1950s.

KILLER PLANTS

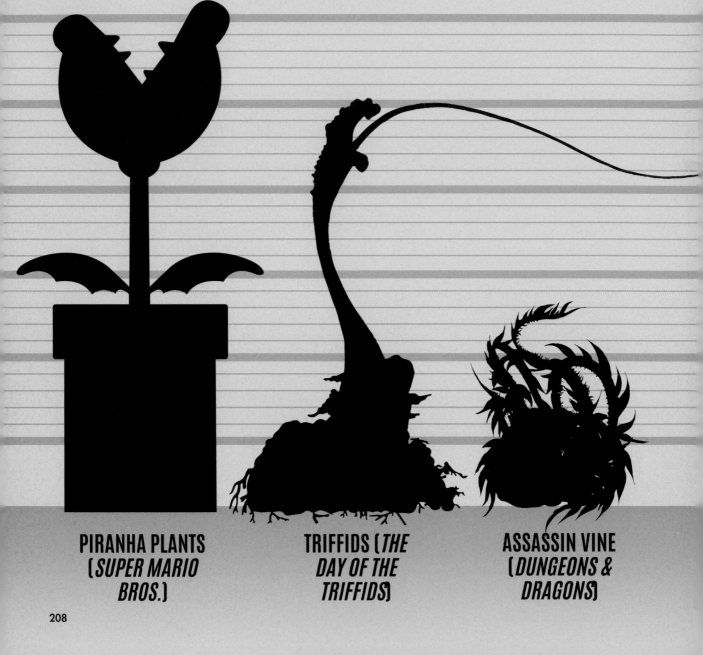

PIRANHA PLANTS (*SUPER MARIO BROS.*)

TRIFFIDS (*THE DAY OF THE TRIFFIDS*)

ASSASSIN VINE (*DUNGEONS & DRAGONS*)

THE MOVIE *MONSTERS* WAS RELEASED IN 2010

Across Christmas 2016 and New Year 2017, *Rogue One: A Star Wars Story* hit the bullseye (or womp rat, if you know the lingo), becoming massively popular. The film was directed by Gareth Edwards, who began his filmmaking career as a visual effects artist. He then parlayed this know-how into his debut feature, a low-budget piece entitled *Monsters* (2010).

Emphasizing the 'Wars' part of its larger story, *Rogue One* was carried by a sense of kinetic immediacy and showcased a new female hero, Jyn Erso, who certainly continued the tradition of Leia, Padme and Rey.

Edward was then springboarded into the mainstream by another monster movie, *Godzilla* (2014), which boldly set much of its action at night and captured a real sense of terror and the menace of the unseeable.

FORREST J. ACKERMAN DIED IN 2008

Forrest J. Ackerman published a magazine entitled *Famous Monsters of Filmland* between 1958 and 1983. A hardcore enthusiast of what we now call geek, Ackerman was so well known in the science-fiction and horror community that he even cameos in the music video 'Thriller'.

FLASH GORDON WAS RELEASED IN 1980

Mike Hodge's adaptation of Alex Raymond's iconic comic strip character tells the 'origin' story of Flash Gordon as intergalactic hero. With its vivid bursts of colour, notably its candyfloss pink skies across which The Hawkmen fly, the film was given additional energy by its now so-well-known soundtrack by Queen.

POD (*INVASION OF THE BODY SNATCHERS*)

KILLER TOMATOE (*ATTACK OF THE KILLER TOMATOES*)

AUDREY II (*LITTLE SHOP OF HORRORS*)

IN THE ANIME *AKIRA* A TRAUMATIC EVENT OCCURS IN 1988

Akira (1982–1990) is a landmark, one of several releases that introduced American and European audiences to anime. The film presents the urban sprawl as being a dangerous space that harbours violence and secrecy. Its closing image shows a ravaged NeoTokyo, – but this is also the first time real sunbeams have shone through, suggesting better times ahead. The sunlight striking the city echoes the helicopter searchlights that swept the city earlier in the film.

There is a powerful sense of rebirth, and certainly the metaphor of akira ('life energy') is key to the meaning. Energy is one thing; harnessing it appropriately is another – a classic science-fiction motif that reaches back at least to Mary Shelley's novel *Frankenstein* (1818). The more compelling aspect of the film is the idea of an almost genetic memory in all of humanity, relating to the idea of a life force.

The film has a dark fairy-tale quality that is most powerfully unleashed in the nightmarish visions of the toys come to life. In this film, even childhood is not innocent.

The teenage Tetsuo is besieged and attacked by nightmarish dreams of oversized toys, and then ventures into the toy room. The moving toys there recall the robo toys of *Blade Runner*, especially when he imagines miniature versions of them marching across his pillow towards him.

The other standout stylistic device is the multiplane imagemaking of the city as the camera tracks between the shifting perspectives of the skyscrapers and roadways. This approach immerses the audience in the environment, until they become more than observers and ever closer to the characters.

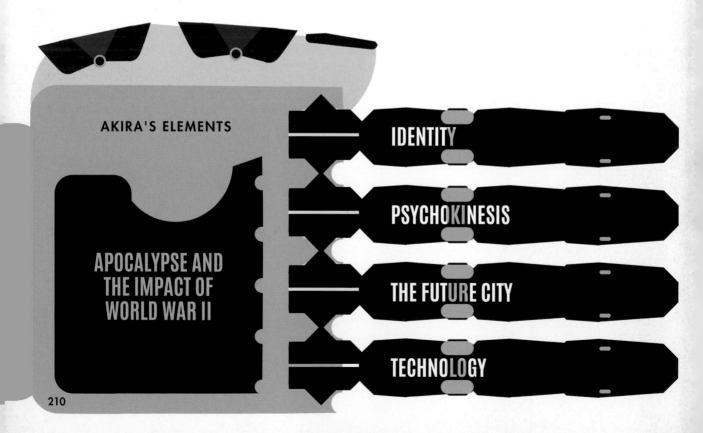

AKIRA'S ELEMENTS

APOCALYPSE AND THE IMPACT OF WORLD WAR II

IDENTITY

PSYCHOKINESIS

THE FUTURE CITY

TECHNOLOGY

A major moment in *Star Trek*'s life as a pop culture phenomenon, the film focused on the original *Enterprise* team reuniting to save Earth from an approacing and dangerous alien cloud.

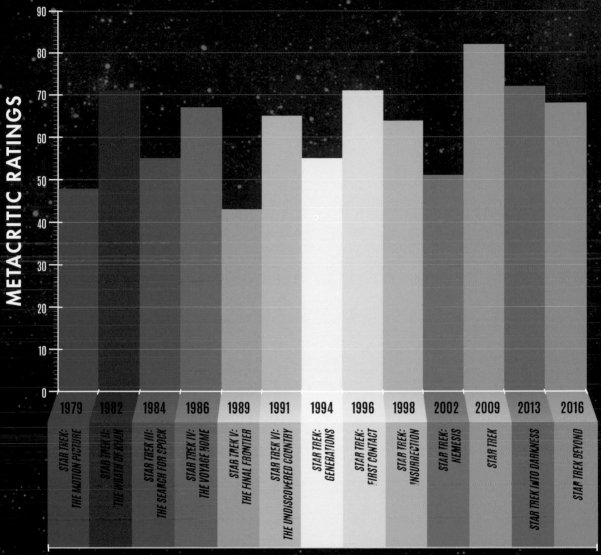

STAR TREK MOVIE AND YEAR

One of the pleasures of sci-fi and fantasy is the chance to encounter some wonderful character designs. Rick Baker has defined monster design and make-up for over 30 years, applying a sophisticated air-pumped kit to the process of applying prosthetics. Key projects include 'Thriller' and *Men in Black*,

SCIENCE FICTION FANS BEGIN MEETING WEEKLY IN LONDON IN 1937

These gatherings of the Science Fiction Association fuelled the British fanbase for tales of wonder and imagination, including the development of *Interzone*, Britain's longest running science-fiction and fantasy magazine. Established in 1982, the magazine helped to develop the careers of a number of high-profile science-fiction writers. The very first issue of the magazine included content written by Angela Carter and Michael Moorcock.

DOOM WAS LAUNCHED IN 1993

When *Doom* was released, it ushered in a new era of kinetic intensity for computer games. The game allowed players to fight an oncoming army of demons. Doom's hellish scenario set something of a template for subsequent computer games. A sequel game *Doom II: Hell on Earth* was released in 1994 and in 2005 a feature film based on the game was released.

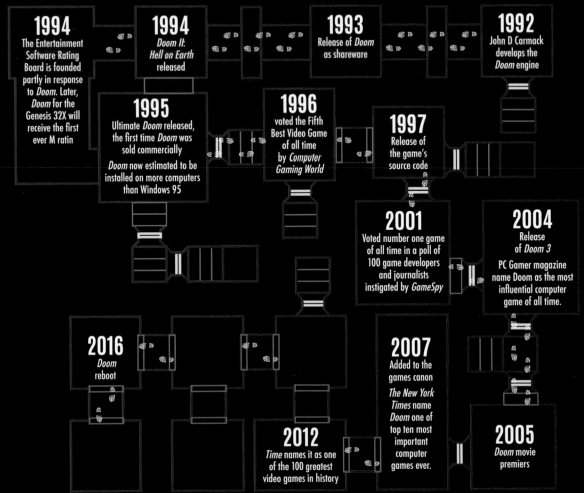

1994
The Entertainment Software Rating Board is founded partly in response to *Doom*. Later, *Doom* for the Genesis 32X will receive the first ever M ratin

1994
Doom II: Hell on Earth released

1993
Release of *Doom* as shareware

1992
John D Carmack develops the *Doom* engine

1995
Ultimate *Doom* released, the first time *Doom* was sold commercially

Doom now estimated to be installed on more computers than Windows 95

1996
voted the Fifth Best Video Game of all time by *Computer Gaming World*

1997
Release of the game's source code

2001
Voted number one game of all time in a poll of 100 game developers and journalists instigated by *GameSpy*

2004
Release of *Doom 3*

PC Gamer magazine name Doom as the most influential computer game of all time.

2016
Doom reboot

2007
Added to the games canon

The New York Times name *Doom* one of top ten most important computer games ever.

2012
Time names it as one of the 100 greatest video games in history

2005
Doom movie premiers

DICK TUFELD WAS BORN IN 1926

Visuals may come to mind initially with much science fiction TV programming, but don't forget what you hear. It's Dick Tufeld's voice that brought to life the robot in the TV series *Lost in Space* (1965–68) and provided voices and vocalizations for *The Time Tunnel* (1966–67).

JENNIFER CONNELLY WAS BORN IN 1970

Connelly's appearances in a number of high-profile, science-fiction and fantasy films over the past thirty years have led to her becoming somewhat synonymous with these genres. She has starred in *Labyrinth* (1986), *The Rocketeer* (1991), *Dark City* (1998), *The Hulk* (2003) and *The Day The Earth Stood Still* (2008), lending the fantasy and unreality unfolding a real sense of human emotional scale.

ULTRAMARINE WAS RELEASED IN 2010

Ultramarines, A Warhammer 4,0000 Movie is a hugely popular miniature war game game, typically played by two players. Released by Games Workshop in 1987, the game's vivid world-building focuses on a dystopian future and warring factions. The animated film adaptation centred on a group of Ultramarines who embarked on a mission to answer a distress call from the planet of Mithron and was faithful to the dense world-building of the game.

EDWARD SCISSORHANDS WAS RELEASED IN 1990

It's not too inaccurate to say that part of geek life is being regarded as a little bit of an outsider, a little bit different. Edward Scissorhands is a paean to that feeling and so, perhaps, it's no surprise that the film rings so true for so many.

Based on a concept by the film's director, Tim Burton, *Edward Scissorhands* tells what happens when a creation is left unfinished when its inventor dies. Venturing into a nearby suburban cul-de-sac, Edward finds both acceptance and rejection – and true love.

Enriched by Danny Elfman's much mimicked score, the film is a melancholy one and its production design merrily twists reality just that little bit. Edward Scissorhands recalls Heinrich Hoffmann's creation, *Der Struwwelpeter* (1845).

SIMON MARIUS OBSERVES THE ANDROMEDA GALAXY WITH A TELESCOPEIN 1612

In 1957 the Russian novel *Andromeda: A Space-Age Tale*, written by Ivan Yefremov, was published, imagining a future in which a communist utopia thrives.

PHILIP K. DICK WAS BORN IN 1928

Dick's name and work have become known to many, perhaps more on account of the typically engaging film adaptations of his work than the source material itself. Hence, B*lade Runner* (1982), *Total Recall* (1990, 2012), *Screamers* (1995), *Minority Report* (2002), *A Scanner Darkly* (2006) and *The Adjustment Bureau* (2011). In 2015, *The Man in the High Castle* (1962) was adapted for TV.

Dick's work is characterised by a sharp awareness of how power can be abused and by a potent sense of how there are many sides to reality. His first story was published in 1951 and this approach runs through all his work. In 1974,

Dick had a mystical experience that affected him for the final years of his life. He died in March 1982 just months before the release of the film *Blade Runner* – after initial reservations, a work-in-progress cut of the film won him over.

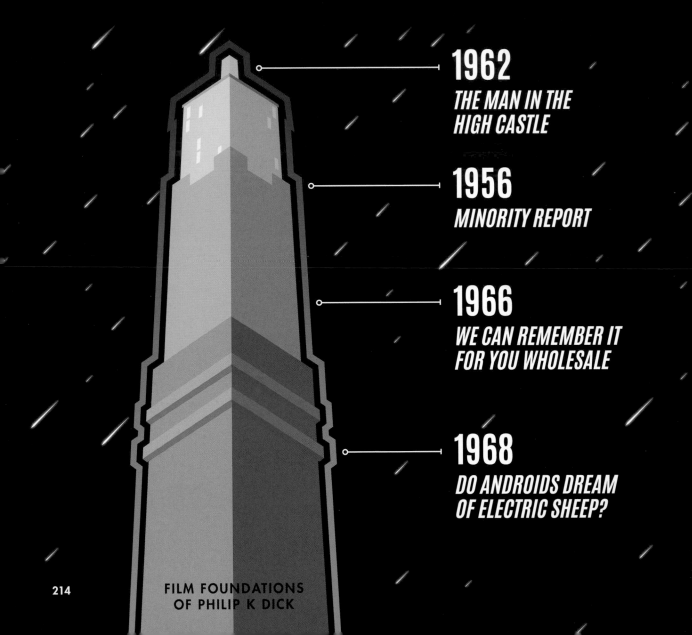

1962
THE MAN IN THE HIGH CASTLE

1956
MINORITY REPORT

1966
WE CAN REMEMBER IT FOR YOU WHOLESALE

1968
DO ANDROIDS DREAM OF ELECTRIC SHEEP?

FILM FOUNDATIONS OF PHILIP K DICK

AVATAR WAS RELEASED IN 2009

Avatar synthesized a number of geek touchstones: not only in terms of visual effects and animation, but also in terms of invoking the spirit of Edgar Rice Burroughs and Alex Raymond.

Cameron's film stays true to his moviemaking interest in humans and tech coming together to form something super-powerful.

Filmed using mo-cap and digitally realised environments,

Avatar represented the apogee of this kind of digital filmmaking. Cameron is due to return to the world of Pandora and reopen otherworldly, atavistic adventures there. There are four confirmed sequels planned.

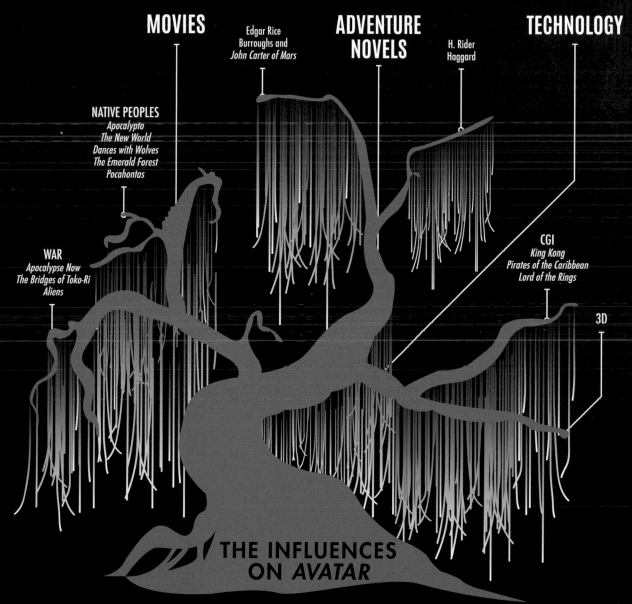

MOVIES

Edgar Rice Burroughs and *John Carter of Mars*

ADVENTURE NOVELS

H. Rider Haggard

TECHNOLOGY

NATIVE PEOPLES
Apocalypto
The New World
Dances with Wolves
The Emerald Forest
Pocahontas

CGI
King Kong
Pirates of the Caribbean
Lord of the Rings

WAR
Apocalypse Now
The Bridges of Toko-Ri
Aliens

3D

THE INFLUENCES ON *AVATAR*

18 DECEMBER

STEVEN SPIELBERG WAS BORN IN 1946

It could be a light in the darkness, or an immense life form making all human life look just plain puny. It could be a spectacle of sound, image and music or a quiet moment of contact between life on earth and life from far away.

Steven Spielberg's imprint on geek culture since the mid-1970s is almost impossible to ignore. And there's something for everyone.

From directing *Close Encounters of the Third Kind* to executive producing Transformers, from writing many storylines for his shortlived fantasy TV series *Amazing Stories* to directing a terrifying adaptation of *War of the*

Worlds and a suitably whimsical adaptation of *The BFG*, Steven Spielberg has delighted us all.

No surprise, then, to be anticipating Spielberg's adaptation of instant classic geek novel *Ready Player One*, due in 2018. If Spielberg does what he's so highly regarded for, he'll find a way to vividly tease out the book's adventure of both heart and mind.

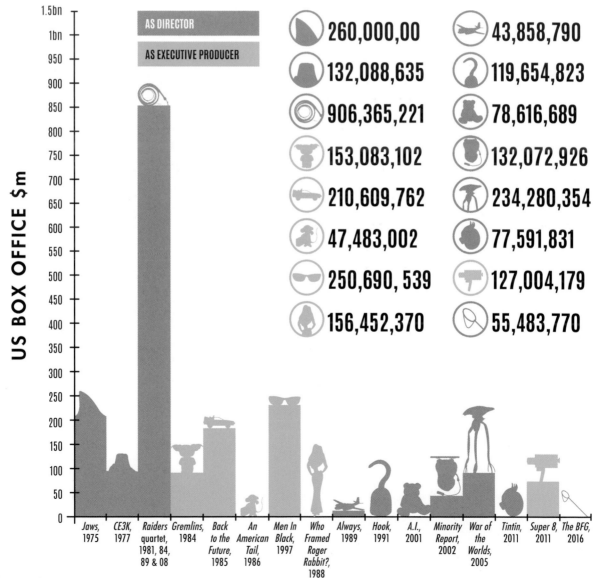

US BOX OFFICE $m

1.5bn / 1bn / 950 / 900 / 850 / 800 / 750 / 700 / 650 / 600 / 550 / 500 / 450 / 400 / 350 / 300 / 250 / 200 / 150 / 100 / 50 / 0

AS DIRECTOR

AS EXECUTIVE PRODUCER

260,000,00
132,088,635
906,365,221
153,083,102
210,609,762
47,483,002
250,690,539
156,452,370

43,858,790
119,654,823
78,616,689
132,072,926
234,280,354
77,591,831
127,004,179
55,483,770

Jaws, 1975 / *CE3K,* 1977 / *Raiders quartet,* 1981, 84, 89 & 08 / *Gremlins,* 1984 / *Back to the Future,* 1985 / *An American Tail,* 1986 / *Men In Black,* 1997 / *Who Framed Roger Rabbit?,* 1988 / *Always,* 1989 / *Hook,* 1991 / *A.I.,* 2001 / *Minority Report,* 2002 / *War of the Worlds,* 2005 / *Tintin,* 2011 / *Super 8,* 2011 / *The BFG,* 2016

THE LORD OF THE RINGS: THE FELLOWSHIP OF THE RING WAS RELEASED IN UK IN 2001

Beginning a massively successful trilogy of adaptations of J.R.R. Tolkien's novels, these were directed by Peter Jackson, and their gorier parts linked him to his horror movie beginnings.

Jackson had previously directed the dazzling *Heavenly Creatures* (1994) and the very energetic *The Frighteners* (1996), which featured a brilliant star turn by actor Michael J. Fox.

Jackson's mobile camera, swooping and sometimes gently drifting through the action, energises every frame – whether it's a Middle Earth escapade or a trek through a lost world in his adaptation of *King Kong* (2005). *The Lovely Bones* (2009) adapted Alice Sebold's novel, creating a vividly fanciful afterlife and capturing the evil that can be lurking right next door.

His subsequent adaptation (2012–14) of Tolkien's *The Hobbit* (1937) captured the novel's affection for landscape and nature, and both Jackson and screenwriter Phillippa Boyens embellished Tolkien's source material inventively.

Jackson's films celebrate fantasy, horror and science fiction (he also produced *District 9*, 2009) and amidst all of the visual spectacle he's adept at holding onto the human relationships and feelings. A telling glance or unspoken reaction often communicates more than a line of dialogue ever could.

Jackson's standing as a filmmaking hero to geekdom is assured and the news, at the time of writing, that Jackson is producing an adaptation of the novel *Mortal Engines* (2001) seems like a perfect fit.

SGT. KIRK IS PUBLISHED FOR THE LAST TIME IN ARGENTINIIAN COMIC MISTERIX IN 1957

Hugo Pratt's *Corto Maltese* is an iconic Italian comics series that was also published in *Misterix*. The Italian academic Umberto Eco tellingly once commented that when he wanted something serious to read, he'd settle down with a *Corto Maltese* story.

Maltese's adventures first appeared in print in 1967 and he fits that decade's ideal of a globetrotting hero perfectly. So important is the character to the terrain of comic-book culture that American comic artist Frank Miller named an island for Maltese in *The Dark Knight Returns*.

Hugo Pratt's conception for *Corto Maltese* was influenced by American comics, notably Milton Caniff's Terry and the Pirates. *Corto Maltese* is Pratt's most celebrated creation and it represented the apotheosis of his work in comics that had begun with his *Sgt .Kirk* material for *Misterix*.

In the stories, Corto Maltese's death is never described, so he lives on.

THE ADVENTURES OF TINTIN WAS RELEASED IN 2011

Tintin is the globetrotting hero of Georges Remi (writing under the pen name Hergé, reversing his initials GR to RG). A reporter, Tintin embarks on various international adventures, aided by his faithful dog Snowy and his reckless friend Captain Haddock.

In 1981, when his film *Raiders of the Lost Ark* was released, director Steven Spielberg first became aware of Tintin via mentions from European reviewers. Intrigued and allured, Spielberg secured the rights to a film adaptation, initially developing a screenplay for a live action film scripted by Melissa Matheson. It wouldn't be until 2011, however, that Spielberg's version, adapting *The Secret of the Unicorn*, would reach cinemas and it

was a beautifully rendered take on the story.

The Tintin adventures number twenty-four titles, the first of which was *Tintin in the Land of the Soviets*, published in 1929. Notable for its dynamic clear line visual style, panel for panel, Hergé's art is elegant, whimsical and lively. Tintin embodies a sense of youthful adventure and delights in history and the pursuit of knowledge.

Belgium	21	Czech Republic	1
France	6	Austria	1
UK	4	Netherlands	1
Germany	2	Yugoslavia	1
Switzerland	1	Monaco	1
Iceland	1	Democratic	
Malta	1	Republic	
Gibralta	1	of Congo	1
Soviet Union	1	Egypt	3
Spain	1	Morocco	1
Poland	1	Alegeria	1
Italy	2	Tunisia	1
Portugal	2	Libya	1

TINTIN'S TRAVELS

United States	1	Singapore	1
Jamaica	1	Nepal	1
Dominican		China	1
Republic	1	Sri Lanka	2
Barbados	1	Yemen	1
Peru	1	Lebanon	1
Columbia	1	Israel	1
Venezuela	1	Indonesia	1
Ecuador	1	Japan	2
Saudi Arabia	1	Iran	1
India	1	Australia	1
Pakistan	1	Antarctic	1

THE FIRST FILM TITLED *THE MUMMY* RELEASED IN 1932

Along with Frankenstein, Dracula and Wolfman stands The Mummy.

A holdover from that moment in archaeological history when mummified corpses were unearthed in Egypt, a mummy, wrapped in cloth, took on a terrifying quality quite easily.

In 1999 came a new film version, replete with visual effects to reanimate *The Mummy*, and in 2017 Tom Cruise starred in a new iteration.

Outer Space	1
The Moon	1

FICTIONAL

Syldavia	1
Borduria	1
Bagghar	1
San Theodoros	1
Nuevo Rico	1
Sao Rico	1
Abudin	1
Khemed	2
Sondonesia	1
El Chapo	1
Pilchardania	1
Poldavia	1
Gaipajama	1

IN 2008 THE ERA OF VHS VIDEOTAPES ENDED WITH WIDE REPORTING OF THE FINAL CONSIGNMENT OF TAPES

VHS cassettes are a now fondly remembered, long gone symbol of home entertainment in the 1980s. The format benefited a seemingly infinite number of science-fiction films – some prestigious, others less so – bringing them to the attention of viewers worldwide.

VHS tapes became a staple of film viewing, and it's a sure sign of their impact that today's film fans have started rendering contemporary film posters in the format of VHS covers.

Without VHS a whole range of films might not have enjoyed a second life after their theatrical releases had proved unpopular. Certainly, Quentin Tarantino provides a clear example of the power of the VHS video store to provide an astonishing depth and breadth of film knowledge. VHS tapes, then, now feel like tangible artefacts from a lost age in geek history.

24 DECEMBER

ON THIS NIGHT IN 1843, EBENEZER SCROOGE GOES TIME TRAVELLING.

Probably Charles Dickens's most famous book, *A Christmas Carol* was first published in 1843. A mash-up of time-travel, ghost story and Christmas fantasy, it reminds us of the power conjured when fantasy intervenes to sharpen our sense of reality.

25 DECEMBER

CHRISTMAS DAY - THE HIGHLIGHT OF THE SEASON IN WHICH *THE BOX OF DELIGHTS* UNFOLDS

Herefordshire is a rural county forming part of the border between Wales and England. Of course, it's often on the borders that the most interesting stories are told. British fantasy literature has its healthy share of titles, but *The Box of Delights* (1935) by John Masefield is perhaps a little lesser known. Masefield, born in Ledbury, Herefordshire, certainly drew on aspects of his home county's rich folklore to craft his fantasy story.

Masefield's fantasy adventure novel was made into a TV series adaptation in 1984, which enjoys a healthy, cult following even now.

The Box of Delights tells the story of schoolboy Kay Harker, back home from school at Christmas, who becomes embroiled in a back and forth tussle for ownership of the titular box. First shown to Kay in a pub by a roaring fire , the box conjures visions and transports Kay from the known world to other realms: for example, he witnesses a phoenix leaping from the flames of a fireplace.

A Christmas classic, *The Box of Delights* is in fact the second Kay Harker adventure, following *The Midnight Folk* (1927).

BRITISH TV PRODUCER GERRY ANDERSON DIED IN 2012

Pioneering Gerry Anderson elevated TV fantasy and science fiction by maximising the sophistication of puppetry to bring his worlds to life.

Across his series *Thunderbirds* (1965–66), *Captain Scarlet and the Mysterons* (1967–68), *Stingray* (1964–65), *Fireball XL5* (1962–3), *Joe 90* (1968–69) and *Terrahawks* (1983–84, 1986), Anderson refined a technique he named Supermarionation. The technique was about using technology to create increasingly believable puppet performances.

Many of Anderson's visual effects team went on to work on the big budget American films shot in the UK during the 1970s and 1980s.

1. GENUINE PROSTHETIC EYES MADE AT ONE-THIRD SCALE.

2. ROLLING ROAD TECHNIQUE: A SEEMINGLY ENDLESS STRIP OF ROAD THAT IS MOUNTED ON ROLLERS. MODEL VEHICLES, OR EVEN PUPPETS, ARE STATIONARY ON THE MOVING ROLL OF ROAD.

3. REALISTICALLY SCALED PUPPET HEADS.

4. PRERECORDED DIALOGUE WAS SYNCHED WITH THE MOUTH MOVEMENT OF THE PUPPETS FOR INCREASED BELIEVABILITY.

JOHANNES KEPLER WAS BORN IN 1571

Kepler developed laws of planetary motion and he is the subject of John Banville's book *Kepler: A Novel*.

STAN LEE WAS BORN IN 1922

Lee's name is to comic history what Shakespeare's is to drama and his career has been as epic as any one of the numerous superhero story arcs that he has written.

His writing first appeared in *Captain America Comics* No. 3 and by the 1950s he was edging towards the material with which he is now synonymous. Collaborating with Jack Kirby and Steve Ditko, Lee wrote *Journey Into* *Mystery* and *Amazing Fantasy* (1962–630. In 1961 Lee created the Fantastic Four – and the possibilities were boundless.

TWELVE MONKEYS HAD A LIMITED RELEASED IN THE US IN 1995

Terry Gilliam's films have been vital geek favourites for forty years now. *Twelve Monkeys* (1995), from a screenplay by David Peoples (co-writer of *Blade Runner*), is like much of Gilliam's work in that it celebrates the need for fantasy as a way of reconciling ourselves to reality.

50%	AIR-BRUSHED DRAWINGS	
20%	COPYRIGHT FREE ENGRAVINGS	
15%	CLASSICAL PAINTINGS	
5%	PHOTOS OF SELF	
20%	VICTORIAN PORNOGRAPHY	

EDWIN HUBBLE ANNOUNCED THE EXISTENCE OF OTHER GALACTIC SYSTEMS IN 1924

No wonder, then, that science fiction flourished from that point onwards. The intergalactic as subject and setting has become part of the DNA of geek culture.

NEW YEAR'S EVE – THE DATE ON WHICH THE SCIENCE FICTION FILM *STRANGE DAYS* REACHES ITS CLIMAX

Strange Days (1995) was directed by Kathryn Bigelow from a screenplay by James Cameron and Jay Cocks. Cameron had written a 'scriptment', a fusion of script and prose treatment document, and from this Jay Cocks wrote the actual screenplay.

Jay Cocks had once been a film critic and had long been close with the group comprising the American New Wave of filmmakers that emerged in the late 1960s and early 1970s: George Lucas, Steven Spielberg, Francis Coppola and Martin Scorsese.

Issues of gender and race are powerfully dramatized and visualized in *Strange Days*; it's 'proper' science fiction, rich with ideas. Cameron explained of the genesis for *Strange Days* that: 'I was fascinated by the dramatic and thematic potential of the millennium, and the idea of doomsday as a backdrop for the redemption of one individual.'

INFOGRAPHIC CREDITS

1 January: Tesseract: Robert Webb's Stella software, http://www.software3d.com/Stella.php. 10 January: http://metropolis1927.com/#home Steve Hills / Eureka Entertainment. 13 January: Jackson, Kevin. "Real Horrorshow: A Short Lexicon Of Nadsat". *Sight and Sound* (9): 24–27, 1999. 3 February: http://www.the-numbers.com/movies/production-company/Pixar © 1997-2017 Nash Information Services, LLC. 20 February: http://www.the-numbers.com/movies/franchise/Planet-of-the-Apes#tab=summary (?) © 1997-2017 Nash Information Services, LLC; http://www.boxofficemojo.com/franchises/chart/?id=planetoftheapes.htm © IMDb.com, Inc. 23 February: The Bulletin of the Atomic Scientists, http://thebulletin.org/timeline, © 2017 Bulletin of the Atomic Scientists. All Rights Reserved. 2 March: http://www.the-numbers.com/movies/franchise/King-Kong#tab=summary © 1997-2017 Nash Information Services, LLC. 12 March Wyndham Estate: https://southwarknotes.files.wordpress.com/2013/06/heygate-1975-jdh11.jpg, Southwark Notes; Nakatomi Plaza: http://www.skyscrapercenter.com/building/fox-plaza/4047, © 2017 Council on Tall Buildings and Urban Habitat. 18 March: https://en.wikipedia.org/wiki/The_Fifth_Element; Besson, Luc (1997). *The Story of the Fifth Element: The Adventure and Discovery of a Film*. London: Titan Books. 21 March: https://en.wikipedia.org/wiki/San_Diego_Comic-Con; 'Comic-Con: Where 'nerd has become normal', by Scott Bowles (July 29, 2007), *USA Today*, a division of Gannett Co. Inc.; 'Comic-Con Seeks Bids from Hotels', by Lori Weisberg, (May 25, 2010), *The San Diego Union-Tribune*; 'Comic-Con Registration Crashes for Second Time', by Lori Weisberg, (November 22, 2010), *The San Diego Union-Tribune*; 'Fourth and final day for Comic-Con and over 126,000 attendees', KFMB-TV, (July 24, 2011), Midwest Television Inc, CBS; 'Comic-Con attendees reflect on the convention's changing atmosphere', by Sarah Parvini (July 14, 2012), *The San Diego Union-Tribune*; 'Comic-Con wraps after 4 days of pop-art indulgence', by Sandy Cohen (July 16, 2012), Associated Press; 'About Comic-Con International', *Comic-Con International: San Diego*, © 2017 SAN DIEGO COMIC CONVENTION; 'San Diego Comic-Con: By The Numbers', by Kyle Hill (July 21, 2014), *Nerdist*, 'How the security team at Comic-Con worls to keep fans safe', by Beatriz Valenzuela (July 16, 2016), *Los Angeles Daily News*, © *LA Daily News*; 'Comic-Con badges sell out in record time' by Lori Weisberg (February 21, 2015), *San Diego Union Tribune*. 26 March: *Bodies in Heroic Motion: The Cinema of James Cameron* by James Clarke, Wallflower Press / Columbia University Press, 201. 30 March: Will Brooker, *Batman Unmasked: Analyzing A Cultural Icon*, Continuum, New York and London, 2005, p.23. 31 March: http://www.boxofficemojo.com/movies/?id=matrix.htm © IMDb.com, Inc.; http://www.boxofficemojo.com/movies/?id=matrixreloaded.htm, © IMDb.com, Inc.; The Matrix DVD, press release, © Warner Bros., Inc. All Rights Reserved; http://www.filmscouts.com/scripts/matinee.cfm?Film=matrix&File=bul-tim 'The Matrix: Capturing the Action: Bullet-Time Photography', *Film Scouts*, 1994–2008 Film Scouts LLC; https://en.wikipedia.org/wiki/List_of_accolades_received_by_the_Matrix_film_series. 15 April: http://www.the-numbers.com/movies/franchise/Teenage-Mutant-Ninja-Turtles#tab=summary © 1997-2017 Nash Information Services, LLC. 22 April: *A Brief History of Manga*, by Helen McCarthy, 16 June 2014, Ilex Press; http://tezukainenglish.com/wp/?page_id=734 © 2017 Tezuka In English; http://www.mangauk.com/tezukas-gamble/ MangaUK © 2017 Manga Entertainment Ltd. S; http://dragonball.wikia.com/wiki/Dragon_Ball_(anime) Clements, Jonathan and McCarthy, Helen, *The Anime Encyclopedia: Third Edition*, Muramasa Industries, 2015; http://www.pokemon.com/uk/ © 2017 Pokémon/Nintendo; http://www.cartoonbrew.com/feature-film/summer-wars-by-mamoru-hosoda-31311.html © 2004-2017 Cartoon Brew, LLC. 5 May: 'Minecraft has smashed 120m copies milestone', by Tom Phillips (27 February 2017), *Eurogamer*, © CBS Interactive Inc.; OCCC Calendar of Events – July 2013 Through December 2013, Orange County Convention Center; Mojang; *Guinness World Records 2016*, by Guinness World Records, 2015; 'Minecraft is Now Part of Microsoft, and It Only Cost $2.5 Billion', Matt Peckham (September 15, 2014), *Time*, © Times Inc, 2017; http://fotisi.com/extra/convention/minecon/what-is-minecon.php; 'Geodatastyrelsen giver de unge hele Danmark i 3D' (The Geodata Agency gives the youth whole Denmark in 3D), press release, The Danish Geodata Agency, 24 April 2014; 'Minecraft passes 100 million registered users, 14.3 million sales on PC', by Eddie Makuch (February 26, 2014), *GameSpot*, © CBS Interactive Inc. 13 May: Hughes, David, *The Greatest Sci-Fi Movies Never Made*, Titan Books, 2008. 14 May: http://www.the-numbers.com/person/88340401-George-Lucas#tab=summary; © 1997-2017 Nash Information Services, LLC; Clarke, James, *The Pocket Essentials: George Lucas*, Oldcastle Books, 2002. 15 May: Baum, L.Frank, *The Annotated The Wizard of Oz*, edited by Michael Patrick Hearn, W.W.Norton & Company, 2000; http://oz.wikia.com/wiki/The_Wizard_of_Oz_Wiki. 18 May: http://steampunkscholar.blogspot.co.uk/2009/06/steampunk-pastiche-elements.html. 20 May: © 1990-2017 IMDb.com, Inc. 22 May: http://www.thocp.net/software/games/golden_age.htm. 25 May: Barr, Patricia, Bray, Adam, Wallace , Daniel and Windham, Ryder, *Ultimate Star Wars*, Dorling Kindersley, 2015. 27 May: https://en.wikipedia.org/wiki/Space_Mountain_(Magic_Kingdom); IFI CLAIMS Patent Services; 'The Space Mountain Homepage (unofficial)', by Kevin Yee (August 10, 2008), *Ultimate Orlando*, www.ultimateorlando.com; https://rcdb.com/267.htm © 1996-2017 Duane Marden. 30 May: https://en.wikipedia.org/wiki/Big_Trak; 'BigTrak: A History'; http://www.bigtrak2010.co.uk:80/history.html, November 25, 2010. 1 June: 'Space Invaders vs Star Wars,' *Executive*, Volume 24, Southam Business Publications, 1982, University of Michigan; 'Making millions, 25 cents at a time', *The Fifth Estate*, Canadian Broadcasting Corporation, November 23, 1982, ©2017 CBC/Radio-Canada. All rights reserved; 'CanAsterioids Conquer Space Invaders?', *Electronic Games*, issue 31, Winter 1981, © 1981 Reese Publishing Company, Inc. All rights reserved; 'Video arcades rival Broadway theatre and girle shows in NY', *InfoWorld*, volume 4, number 14, April 12, 1982. © 1982 Popular Computing, Inc.; *Asia Pacific Perspectives, Japan* by Jiji Gaho Sha, Inc., 2003, University of Virgina; 'The video game boom has yet to come', by Stephen Hutcheon, *The Age*, (June 7, 1982). 7 June: 'Dracula and Beyond: Christopher Lee's Greatest Roles,' by Tim Robbey, (June 12, 2015), the *Telegraph*, © Copyright of Telegraph Media Group Limited 2015. 20 June: http://www.the-numbers.com/movie/Jaws#tab=summary, © 1997-2017 Nash Information Services, LLC. 26 June: 'How Magic the Gathering Became a Pop Culture Hit – and Where it Goes Next', by Owen Duffy, (July 10, 2015), the *Guardian*, © 2017 Guardian News and Media Limited; http://gatherer.wizards.com/Pages/Default.aspx, © 1995 - 2017 Wizards of the Coast LLC, a subsidiary of Hasbro, Inc. 27 June: 'New series gives Hawaii 3 TV shows in production', by Tim Ryan, *Honolulu Star-Bulletin*, (May 17, 2004), © 2004 Honolulu Star-Bulletin; 'Season Program Rankings from 09/20/04 through 05/19/05', ABC Medianet, (June 21, 2005), © 2014 American Broadcasting Companies, Inc.; 'Season Program Rankings from 09/15/05 through 05/31/06', ABC Medianet, (May 31, 2006), © 2014 American Broadcasting Companies, Inc. 1July: http://indianajones.wikia.com/wiki/Jones_family. 16 July: http://www.boxofficemojo.com/movies/?id=monsterhunt.htm, © IMDb.com, Inc. 25 July: Barnes, Alan, *Sherlock Holmes On Screen*, Titan Books, 2011. 31 July: *Harry Potter and the Philosopher's Stone*, J. K. Rowling, Bloomsbury Childrens, June 26, 1997; *Harry Potter and the Chamber of Secrets*, J. K. Rowling, Bloomsbury Childrens, July 2, 1998; *Harry Potter and the Prisoner of Azkaban*, J. K. Rowling, Bloomsbury Childrens, July 8, 1999; *Harry Potter and the Goblet of Fire*, J. K. Rowling, Bloomsbury Childrens, July 8, 2000; *Harry Potter and the Order of the Phoenix*, J. K. Rowling, Bloomsbury Childrens, June 21, 2003; *Harry Potter and the Half-Blood Prince*, J. K. Rowling, Bloomsbury Childrens, July 16, 2005; *Harry Potter and the Deathly Hallows*, J. K. Rowling, Bloomsbury Childrens, July 21, 2007; all film run times from the British Board of Film Classification, http://bbfc.co.uk/. 10 August: http://marvel.wikia.com/wiki/Spider-Man_Villains; http://hero.wikia.com/wiki/Spider-Man . 25 August: 'LEGO Fun Facts', http://www.brickrecycler.com/, Copyright © 2017 BrickRecycler | All rights reserved; Wiencek, Henry (1987). *The World of LEGO Toys*. New York: Harry N. Abrams, Inc., Publishers; 'Child's Play' by Frances Corbet, *Develop 3D*. X3DMedia: 25–27, September 2008, ©2008-2017 X3DMedia; https://www.lego.com/en-us/stores/stores, ©2017 The LEGO Group; 'Everything You Always Wanted to Know About Lego', By Jesus Diaz, June 26, 2008, Gizmodo, http://gizmodo.com/5019797/everything-you-always-wanted-to-know-about-lego, ©2017 Gizmodo Media Group, 'How Lego Bricks Work', by Tracy V. Wilson, How Stuff Works, http://entertainment.howstuffworks.com/lego.htm, © 2017 HowStuffWorks,a division of InfoSpace Holdings LLC; 'Now Open: Legoland Dubai', by Paul Crompton, October 31, 2016, *Gulf News*, © Al Nisr Publishing LLC 2017. All rights reserved; 'Space Shuttle Endeavour Launches Tomorrow With a Special Payload' by Dave Banks, April 28, 2011, Wired News, © Condé Nast UK 2017, 'Desgining General Grievous', by George Meno, June 7, 2008, www.brickjournal.com, 006-2011 BrickJournal Media, LLC. BrickJournal Media, LLC; "Matematik-professoren leger med lego-klodser", by Ali Roshanzamir, December 10, 2013, University of Copenhagen Faculty of Science; http://www.wisegeek.com/how-many-lego-bricks-would-it-take-to-reach-the-moon.htm, © 2003 - 2017Conjecture Corporation; 'How tall can a Lego tower get?', Ruth Alexander, December 3, 2012, BBC News, © 2017 BBC; 'The Making of … a LEGO' by Joseph Pisani, November 29, 2006, Bloomberg Businessweek, ©2010 BLOOMBERG L.P. ALL RIGHTS RESERVED; 'Lego in Numbers', August 30, 2011, the Telegraph, © Copyright of Telegraph Media Group Limited 2017; https://kidskonnect.com/fun/lego/. 28 August: '15 Most Powerful Pokémon of All Time', by Andrew Lewis, *Screen Rant*, August 7m 2016, http://screenrant.com/most-powerful-Pokémon-all-time/, © 2017 Screen Rant. All rights reserved. 6 September: 'Beauties and the Beast', by David Hochman, December 5, 1997, *Entertainment Weekly*, © 2017 Time Inc, 'When is Alien: Covenant set and how does it link to Prometheus? The Alien Story so far', by Rebecca Hawkes, May 14, 2017, the *Telegraph*, © Copyright of Telegraph Media Group Limited 2017. 13 September: 'How Super Mario became a global cultural icon', December 24, 2016, *The Economist*, © The Economist Newspaper Limited 2017. All rights reserved; http://www.gamesradar.com/26-jobs-mario-inexplicably-qualified/ by David Houghton, March 1, 2013, GamesRadar, © Future Publishing Limited . 23 September: '8 Far-Out "Jetsons" Contraptions That Actually Exist Today,' by Nina Zipkin, April 17, 2015, *The Entrepreneur*, © 2017 Entrepreneur Media, Inc. All rights reserved. 25 September: http://www.boxofficemojo.com/franchises/chart/?id=ghibli.htm, © IMDb.com, Inc. 6 October: 'TV Legends Revealed: "Big Bang Theory"'s Sheldon Originally Had a Sex Drive', by Brian Cronin, November 20, 2013, *TV News*, Copyright © 2017 CBR; *The Big Bang Theory* episode lisitng in *TV Guide*, © 2017 CBS Interactive Inc. All rights reserved; Listings: The Big Bang Theory, http://www.thefutoncritic.com/listings.aspx?id=20090220cbs03, the Futon Critic; http://bigbangtheory.wikia.com/wiki/The_Opening_Night_Excitation..17 October: '15 Comic Book Characters that Are Blatant Superman Rip-Offs', by Perdi Thomas, June 6, 2017, *The Richest*, Copyright © 2017 TheRichest.com. 28 October: http://www.the-numbers.com/movies/franchise/Gremlins#tab=summary, © 1997-2017 Nash Information Services, LLC. 1 November: 'Hello Kitty Hooks Generations on Cute, Kitsch', by Mandalit Del Barco, December 3, 2010, Morning Edition, npr, © 2017 npr; https://www.sanrio.com. 2 November: 'Michael Jackson's 20 Greatest Videos: The Stories Behind the Vision,' June 24, 2014, *Rolling Stone*, Wenner Media LLC. 16 November: Allen J. Hynek defined the stages of an encounter, Close Encounters of the Third Kind Official Collector's Edition magazine, 1977. 19 November: Twitter. 7 December: http://www.metacritic.com/pictures/star-trek-movies-ranked-worst-to-best, © 2017 CBS Interactive Inc. All rights reserved. 10 December: 'The History of Doom', January 27, 2009, NowGamer.com, https://www.nowgamer.com/the-history-of-doom/, Imagine Publishing; 'The Age of Doom', byLev Grossman/Mesquite, August 2, 2004, *Time* magazine, © 2016 Time Inc. All rights reserved; 'This classic '90s video game is the reason games like "Halo" and "Call of Duty" exist today', by Corey Protin and Ben Gilbert, June 29, 2015, *Business Insider*, © 2017 Business Insider Inc; https://en.wikipedia.org/wiki/Doom_(series). 18 December: http://www.boxofficemojo.com/people/chart/?id=stevenspielberg.htm, © IMDb.com, Inc. 21 December: https://en.wikipedia.org/wiki/List_of_The_Adventures_of_Tintin_locations. 26 December: 'Filmed in Supermarionation', by Paul Mount, *Starburst* magazine; http://gerryanderson.wikia.com/wiki/Supermarionation